COLLECTED PLAYS

COLLECTED
PLAYS

RONALD DUNCAN

Rupert Hart-Davis London

Granada Publishing Limited

First published 1971 by
Rupert Hart-Davis Ltd
3 Upper James Street
London W1R 4BP

ISBN 0 246 64004 9

Printed in Great Britain by
Cox & Wyman Limited, London,
Fakenham and Reading

Contents

Introduction	vii
THIS WAY TO THE TOMB	1
ST SPIV	91
OUR LADY'S TUMBLER	151
THE REHEARSAL	193
THE SEVEN DEADLY VIRTUES	261
O—B—A—F—G	333
THE GIFT	347

Introduction

Any dramatist finds that his plays fall into two categories: those for which he had some hopes but which went wrong either in the writing or in the production; and those for which he had none, and surprised him by achieving public approval. *This Way to the Tomb* fell into the latter category.

The initial stimulus for writing a Masque was given me by Lord Portsmouth when he showed me the ruins of a Priory in the park at Hurstbourne in 1941, and remarked that he thought the site might be suitable for some kind of entertainment. I had been reading the masques of Ben Jonson, as I was interested in dramatic forms which had music integrated within them; it occurred to me to write a modern masque for this setting. The war prevented this plan, but the idea of a masque came to my mind again when I was running a farm on community lines. I had been asked to write something which the members could perform in the open without any scenery. But I lacked a subject. This was given to me accidentally a few months later, when T. S. Eliot suggested to me that I should call on Michel St Denis. In his flat I idly picked up a book of reproductions of Hieronymus Bosch and was arrested by his St Antony meditating with an old sow at his feet. The apparent incongruity of the Saint's companion revived two images in my mind. The first was the story of the Reverend Stephen Hawker, who used to walk over the cliffs from Morwenstowe to Welcombe with a lop-eared black sow at his heels. When asked why he did so, he replied that 'being a priest he liked to have a real Christian as a companion to talk to'. The second association was more immediate: a few years previously I had spent some time living with Gandhi at Segoan, his Ashram near Wardha, and had been fascinated by the various facets of the Mahatma. He was venerated as a saint during his lifetime. Motoring with him, we were frequently held up by people struggling to touch his clothes. 'I am not a saint', he kept telling me, 'but very much a man with all a man's weaknesses.' On another occasion he told me why his wife was still unable to read or write. 'I married her in her early teens,' he said, 'and as a young man I made her go to bed with me rather than let her study.' This picture of the sensual man within the saint fascinated me. I felt intuitively that spiritual awareness was inseparable from physical vitality. This aspect of 'wholeness' interested me particularly because I felt that dramatisations of such people had often been weakened by concentrating on their spirituality and playing down their carnality. I thought this criticism applied to Thomas à Becket in Eliot's *Murder in the Cathedral*, and regretted that Eliot had not allowed Becket to look back over his shoulder at the young man he had been, even if those temptations were all behind him. When I decided to use the Temptation of St Antony as the subject for a masque, I was not, of course, unaware that I was treading closely on Eliot's heels. I told him of my plans and he did not discourage me.

In order to dramatise the incongruous parts which make up a whole man, I decided to personify the saint's physical appetite, sensual tastes, and intellectual pride, as three separate characters. These projections of Antony's personality could then be used to externalise his own temptations.

In the 1940s it was, as it still is to a very large extent, a theatrical assumption that a character in a play should be a consistent type. I reacted strongly against this simplification. I knew of nobody who was consistent, including myself.

The other theatrical convention I was reacting against was the frivolity of the social and the topical, and the triviality of the political theme, devoid of any universal application. I wanted to help break down the convention of naturalism in the theatre with all its clutter of box sets and papier mache props; naturalism which pretended to be realism but which, to my mind, was so far from reality as to be fantasy or pantomime. I maintain that all of us live at various levels at one and the same time. Although we may exchange inanities over the coffee-cups or sherry glasses, it is not the dramatists job to reproduce life naturalistically, but to give it depth. And for a time in the 1940s, with the so-called revival of verse drama at the Mercury, it did seem that we had the theatre of 'realism' on the run. But the victory was brief. Within a few years naturalism became the fashion again. The only change was that the convention of Shaftesbury Avenue duchesses fiddling with flower vases was replaced by Jimmy Porters picking their noses in public.

Whatever theories a dramatist may have, he has only words as tools. I decided to use verse, not to see whether I could write a poetic drama—a phrase which I have always disliked, because it puts the poetry before the drama—but because I wanted the language to carry the maximum charge. What is poetry but language at its most intense? Since a play only lasts a couple of hours and the dramatist has to convey the maximum in that time, it is unreasonable to restrict him to the language of conversation. At the same time no dramatist wants to write poetic language which removes his characters from life and sets them in literature. Eliot had tackled the problem, I thought, admirably in *Sweeny*. It was my ambition to forge a flexible verse which would contain the run and rhythm of everyday language and yet move on the muscles of thought. I wanted to write poetry which would carry the intensity I aimed at, but which would not be labelled poetic.

At the same time I was nauseated with the flood of so-called 'free verse'. As I have admitted elsewhere, it was an incident in my garden which solved this technical problem for me. I was watering the vegetable garden. I observed that the intensity of the jet of water was governed by restricting the outlet. Though obvious,to me this was a revelation; I realised that intensity in language can only be achieved by running it against a defined form, otherwise you get a dribble and not a jet. I therefore decided in writing this masque to use various verse forms with strict limitations. A year or so previously Ezra Pound had read to me his translation of Guido Cavalcanti's *Canzone, Donna me Pregha*. I chose this form for St Antony's Meditations because of its complicated structure, its division into five strophes, each subdivided into three stanzas with sixteen internal rhymes. My hope was that I could contain the form without it sticking through the fabric like the bones of a corset.

Writing these speeches I found that the form did not inhibit what I wanted to say. On the contrary, it drove me to a concision and an intensity which I certainly would not have achieved otherwise.

In place of self-expression I was trying to achieve self-suppression: in place of freedom of expression I was interested in writing within defined limits. Perhaps freedom for people and artists lies in the limitations they accept? Art without form is a contradiction in terms.

My other preoccupation was to find opportunities for music and song, as I was at this time collaborating closely with Benjamin Britten. The basic form of the Ben Jonson Masque is: a Masque in which a theme is treated seriously, followed by an Anti-Masque which parodies the theme. I adapted this form, adding a final scene to complete the circle.

As I say, the play was originally intended for one performance in a field on my farm. That, instead it ran for 18 months in the West End of London proves, I suppose, that a dramatist seldom knows what he is doing.

But in spite of the success of *This Way to the Tomb*, if success is measured by the number of performances, I came quickly to regard the play as a failure. Eliot thought of *Murder in the Cathedral* in a similar way. We both saw that by writing plays about saints in a remote period we had evaded the essential challenge, which was to find a flexible verse form to express the age we lived in, on the stage. I tried to console Eliot by pointing out that, to my mind, his play carried more philosophical meat than *King Lear* or *Hamlet*. But he would have none of this, and we applied ourselves, he to *The Cocktail Party*, I to *Stratton*. Though I do not think I got near to finding a solution to the problem of language in the contemporary situation until I came to write *The Catalyst* many years later.

When *St Spiv* was produced by Kenneth Tynan at the Watergate Theatre in 1950, the title of the play was changed to *Nothing Up my Sleeve*. I made this change because Eliot persuaded me to do so!

It was a play I enjoyed writing, because in it I was able to draw on the Cockney characters which I had known as a child. I lived in South London until I was sixteen, and before I was ten I had persuaded my mother to allow me to go to Covent Garden Market at 6 a.m. with a florist; to sit on a high, two-wheeled butcher's cart on his round; to serve behind a bar at the Union Arms; to spend many evenings selling newspapers at a news-agents, and even to take the pennies at a salad stall in Brixton Market.

From this background I knew that the raciness of the Cockney's language had lost nothing since Elizabethan days, and in this comedy I tried to reproduce some of it. I had Ben Jonson in mind again, particularly *Volpone* and *The Alchemist*, and sought to integrate a vein of contemporary satire and topical allusion within the framework of the comedy.

Horace, the hero, or rather the anti-hero, of the play derives also from my childhood, from Charlie Chaplin. *City Lights* influenced me particularly, because it contained the character of a down-and-out who was taken up by a millionaire whenever he was drunk, and then thrown out whenever he was sober. The situation struck me as having universal application, and in Horace I tried to depict the human condition of ridiculous optimism perpetually frustrated.

Another aspect of Horace is comparable to the character of Brother Andrew in the play *Our Lady's Tumbler*, which I wrote for the Festival of Britain. I suppose they are both dramatic parables about humility.

The character of Penny, in *St Spiv*, is another attack on con-ventional ideas of virtue. She is a ragamuffin, an urchin who does not fit into society and refuses to conform to it. She has nothing but herself, and this she gives away. It is the only thing she has to offer and she does not value it. In her I tried to depict an unworldly heroine of the streets who is moved by Horace because he is '*like a sparrow with a broken wing*'.

The Spiv's activities in Harley Street, with the cash register that plays a hymn, is an extension of the Astral Group in the Anti-Masque of *This Way to the Tomb*. This is known as an irreligious age, but that is not an accurate description. It is not that we have no religion, but too many: not that we have no god, but strange ones. In the cocktail party scene I tried the experiment of using the inanities that are utteèred at a cocktail party and formalising them into a verbal pattern. It seemed to me that the frivolity and vacuity of such occasions could be heightened by this method.

I wrote *The Seven Deadly Virtues* in 1961. My purpose was to dramatise my belief that we cannot judge an act as either good or evil unless we know the circumstances and the person's intention. I therefore wrote two playlets in which the seven virtues are shown as vices and the seven vices as virtues. My intention was not to ridicule ethics, but perhaps to make people think again about what constitutes morality; and as in *St Spiv* and other plays, I inclined to the view that there is often more virtue in the woman of easy virtue than there is in the chaste prig.

Producers often ask me how this play should be directed. Their difficulty is to relate the frivolous and sardonic tone of Satan and the Angel with the serious predicament of Christopher and Melanie. The answer is that consistency should not be attempted. What I have tried to do is to give a sardonic framework to the two playlets which must be played straight. Flexibility in direction is necessary, since there is nothing consistent in life.

In 1960 Dame Peggy Ashcroft asked me if I would write a play for her. *The Rehearsal (Still Life)* was the result of this invitation. I had written several plays with a man as the principal character, and I was glad of the opportunity to write a big role for a woman. Eliot had used a Greek play in *Family Reunion*. I followed his example, using the central situation of *Phaedra*, and tried to find the contemporary equivalent. I took the central theme of a middle-aged woman falling in love with a young man (in this case her son-in-law) from the Greek play, but in addition I was concerned with the problem that people are not only strangers to themselves, but to one another, however intimate their lives may superficially appear to be. In this play none of the four characters are aware of their own motives. I saw it as a play not of four characters, but eight: as each is both the character he thinks himself to be, and the character he really is. This dichotomy fascinated me, and I think it has more universal application than the consistency of character which is forced on drama. The two couples are intimately involved with each other, but not yet introduced to one another. It is a picture of matrimony in which complete strangers stand in an intimate embrace. If we do not know ourselves, it is not strange that others should not know us at all.

The other theme running behind the play is one which I touched on in *Stratton*, and has to do with the way the young generation find their feet fitting into the previous generation's footsteps. It is about the tyranny of inherited limitations: the pattern repeats, and our only freedom resides in the acceptance of these limitations. In emphasising the power of inherited influences, I was making an unpopular comment in an age which believes that environment is the only factor. As a pig breeder I have never found that true.

The central scene of the play, and the one I most enjoyed writing, is the one where the woman, who had indulged her fantasy of a love scene with the young man, now forces him to take up the precise positions and say the exact words she had given him in her fantasy. To my mind fantasy is one of the dimensions of our reality: people live more in the world of their daydreams than anywhere else.

When I had completed *The Rehearsal (Still Life)*, the actress did not wish to play in the part I had written for her. The play was finally produced on television.

O—B—A—F—G was commissioned by the Devon County Council, who wanted a play without characters or scenery, using stereophonic sound. *The Gift* was commissioned by the same body.

This Way to the Tomb

A MASQUE AND ANTI-MASQUE

Dedicated to
the Rt Hon Gerard Vernon Wallop
Ninth Earl of Portsmouth

B

The Masque

CHARACTERS

AN ANNOUNCER

FATHER ANTONY, ABBOT OF ST FERRARA

Three Novitiates

MARCUS, A PEASANT   JULIAN, A POET

BERNARD, A SCHOLAR

GLUTTONY

LECHERY

SIGHT

A WOMAN

THE VOICE

The Masque is so written that it can be performed by a cast of 5 men and 2 women.

The Sets are: Back stage Right a rock representing the place of the Saint's meditation. Front stage L. a form or bench, representing the cell. Sets lit alternately, according to the action.

NEL
MEZZIO DEL CAMMIN
DI NOSTRA VITA
MI RITROVAI
PER UNA SELVA OSCURA
CHE LA DIRITTA VIA
ERA SMARRITA

The Masque

CHOIR A CAPELLA

*Deus in adjutorium meum intende: Domine, ad adjuvandum me
   festina.*
Confundantur et revereantur qui quaerunt animum meum:
Avertantur retrorsum, et erubescant, qui volunt mihi mala:
Avertantur statim, erubescentes, qui dicunt mihi, Euge, Euge.
Exsultent et laetentur in te omnes qui quaerunt te, et dicant semper:
Magnificetur Dominus: qui diligunt salutare tuum.
Ego vero egenus et pauper sum: Deus adjuva me.
Ajutor meus et liberator meus es tu: Domine ne moreris.
*Gloria patri, et filio, et spiritui sancto Sicut erat in principio, et
   nunc, et semper, et in saecula saeculorum. Amen.*

ANNOUNCER

Tonight we present 'This Way to the Tomb'.
It is a Masque with Anti-Masque.
The former focuses on the past,
The latter looks at the mere present
And what the whole reflects is as permanent
As loose words are, fitted to the hoof of time,
Telling in precise design a half-forgotten vision
And finding in form the liberty of our tradition.
The poet dedicates this Masque
To Benjamin Jonson—and the Director of Television.
The Time: the fourteenth century; and the Place:
The Island of Zante, which is near to Thrace.
Here St Antony
   *Curtain rises. A rock back stage centre; a bench front
   right.*
                    recent Abbot of Santa Ferrata
Lived as a hermit
With three young novices...

MARCUS

...on bread and wine and honey;

Not much wine, and little honey.
Sometimes there's goat's milk,
If I can catch the goat.
Always it's Marcus who must catch the goat.
For Julian is writing, and Bernard is reading,
And, after all, they say:

JULIAN

        ...you are the youngest

BERNARD

...and the son of a farmer!

MARCUS

There, that's what they always say.
And what I say, is:

JULIAN

If I must catch the goat

BERNARD

How shall I ever learn to read or to write?

MARCUS

Or have time to listen to Julian's Song
Or Bernard's opinion on St Thomas's heresy.
If it weren't for Father Antony
I would get you nothing to eat
But braised metaphors for breakfast
And just words and words for meat.

JULIAN

There's the goat going up the hill.

MARCUS

Quick, pass me the milk jug.

Exit MARCUS

BERNARD Has he caught her?

JULIAN I can just see the nannie climbing the hill and Marcus is
scrambling up behind her. He's cut her off!

BERNARD When Marcus first came to St Ferrata, he told me
proudly that goats were never kept on his father's farm because
they had horns and were the cattle of Satan.

JULIAN I remember Marcus's face when Father Antony accepted
the nannie as a present from old Riggio. But Marcus is so

devoted to Father Antony he would do anything for him, from chasing Mephistopheles with a milk jug to grinding flour with his fist and fetching and carrying as he has done for three years.

BERNARD Is it three years?

JULIAN There have been three fiestas at Santa Ferrata whilst we have been here on Zante.

BERNARD That had not occurred to me. But I suppose I must have been about a year on my Treatise on Astronomy, and eighteen months on my Life of Giromo...And how long have I been reading Occam?

JULIAN What a man, he measures his days by paragraphs; and the seasons by folios. Well, let us say we have been here three volumes.

BERNARD I believe you are homesick for the monastery.

JULIAN Sometimes I do not know what I am or where I belong. I was never happy at St Ferrata. It was a beautiful place, and I enjoyed the singing. There was order and leisure there. When I first saw the monastery with the smooth lawns and the cloister —do you remember the cloister surrounded with fan-trained peach trees—I thought I had found the place where I belonged; and I hoped that I would never leave it. And here it is mostly menial work, endless; day after day—and no lawns, choir or fan-trained trees—just a rock in the sun and austerity.

BERNARD Why did you come here?

JULIAN Father Antony came, I am lost without him. Sometimes I feel I have no choice, and am nothing but his shadow.

Enter MARCUS

MARCUS Look, a quart at least; and there would be more if she hadn't stepped in it. Is Father Antony coming? It must be time for Compline. Do go and see if he is coming Julian, whilst I get the supper—it will be extra special tonight for look what I found on the cliff!

BERNARD What are they?

MARCUS Gulls eggs, and early too. I have never known them so early. Go on, Julian, do go and see if Father Antony is coming down the hill.

JULIAN All right! Mind how you cook the eggs. I like mine well done.

MARCUS There are only two and I shall make Father Antony an omelette.

JULIAN—which he will divide into three pieces for us, pretending he has indigestion.

MARCUS If he does, swear you won't take any, Julian. Will you swear, Bernard?

BERNARD Readily.

JULIAN We both swear, Marcus. Poor Marcus, don't worry. I'll go up the hill and see if he is coming.

Exit JULIAN

MARCUS It's a long time since I made an omelette.

BERNARD We haven't had an omelette on Zante. And that's three years.

MARCUS Bernard, how long do you think we will be here?

BERNARD Are you homesick, too? Why don't you and Julian return? I can look after Father Antony.

MARCUS Oh no! I don't want to leave here. And besides, how could you look after him? He needs more than arguments which you give him, he needs food which I prepare; and songs and poems which Julian sings and recites. I don't want to leave here. I was only frightened that Father Antony might be returning soon.

BERNARD Why, what makes you think that?

MARCUS The way Father Antony stays up on the hill under that dead tree and sits for hours and hours; and looks at everything as if he were saying goodbye to it and will never see it again. He used to take an interest in the garden and talked of making a terrace for vines, but he doesn't do that now. Do you know, yesterday he stopped by the stream and looked at it as if he had never seen it before and would never see it again. I am sure he must be thinking of going back to be the great Abbot of St Ferrata again, with the endless procession of coaches and important portfolios.

BERNARD No! he will not do that: he has more pride than to give in, you needn't worry, he'll not return.

MARCUS I am glad of that, for if he were to return, it would not do him good. Too many banquets, too much worry, endless worry. And I'd see little of him then, he in the study, I in the kitchen.

BERNARD He won't return. Leave that to me.

MARCUS Yes, he listens to you. It is strange, he'll listen to you and nobody else. But I can't understand how a man can spend his life reaching such a proud position, the most influential abbot in the whole state and such luxury, and leave it all to become the hermit of Zante. He was used to a busy life, a grand life. Now he sits on an old board under a dead tree and doesn't even read. I cannot understand it.

BERNARD Can't you? Why, the whole Church is talking about his renunciation, his sacrifice, and already calling him a saint.

MARCUS But what does he do up there for ever, sitting, not even reading or writing, just staring at something I cannot see.

BERNARD He is meditating, thinking.

MARCUS But if it does not make him happy, why does he do it?

BERNARD You must ask him that at supper. Shall I light the candles?

MARCUS No, not till Father Antony comes. We are short of them. I wonder what has happened to him and where's Julian?

BERNARD He's coming now, alone.

Enter JULIAN

JULIAN Oh it's cold out. I can't find him.

MARCUS Have you been down to the beach?

JULIAN I have been everywhere, to all the usual places, and called and called but there's no answer.

MARCUS I think I know where he might be: up on the hill by the waterfall. For the other day, yesterday, when we were walking back, he stopped there a long time just looking into the water. I asked him what he could see. And he said he could see a proud old man full of fear and full of desire. That's where he'll be. Let's go and see if he's there for it's getting dark and cold; and he may have fallen asleep or is sick. He's had nothing to eat since breakfast. Throw a log on the fire, Julian, so that the cell is warm when we come in again.

Exeunt omnes. They walk across the darkening stage

BERNARD You lead the way, Marcus.

JULIAN Is it far?

MARCUS No, just up by the waterfall. Listen!

BERNARD I can't hear anything.

JULIAN Nor I.

MARCUS Listen.

JULIAN Well, what do you hear?

MARCUS A voice. Father Antony's voice. Let's hurry: perhaps
there is something wrong. I'll call. Father Antony!

They go off back stage calling

Light picks out FATHER ANTONY *seated on rock back
stage centre*

VOICE Father Antony.

ANTONY Yes, I am coming.
Agnus Dei,
   qui tollis
      peccata mundi:
miserere nobis. Yes, yes, yes.
Lord, pity me, for with imperfect faith
I am full of fear.
I have gleaned the dry stubble of sixty years,
And have gathered up my faith like a hungry widow;
And stored each grain of Thy Love in repeated prayer;
Yet I have nothing, but myself talking to myself
And the fear.
Dear Christ, how fear's hurricane threshes my heart hollow
And winnows my faith till it is lost with the waste
The grain swept away with the straws of doubt.
And now they are coming to call me to supper.
And the sun drops like a coin
Into the hands of those who have begged another day,
  another tomorrow.
For me, another night nearer. Nearer?
Thy Love to enfold me, as closely as the finch's wings
Fit the finch's body as it alights;
Or nearer the greedy earth's slow digestion?

Yes, I am coming.
Coming from birth going to death.
My mind wandering and my breath
Failing, as the leaves fall, are falling, have fallen.
Oh God, why did you wake opaque nothingness
   to restlessness?
And take a handful of dust, and make
Me only to leave me
Alone, cursed with the flesh and damned with the bone.
Joy is forgetting the knowledge.
Hope is ignoring the knowledge,
Love is in spite of the knowledge,
And the knowledge is the certainty
And the certainty is death.
This is the point to which my mind is tethered.
I see death wherever I see life.
I see his unalterable pair of eyes
Staring through successive generations:
From father to son, from son to grandson,
The same eyes, they are death's eyes, this is the certainty
To which I am coming.
Agnus Dei,
       qui tollis
           peccata mundi:

                    Enter MARCUS

Miserere nobis.

MARCUS Father Antony!

ANTONY Yes, my son.

MARCUS It's time for supper, and it's getting dark. You will get a cold sitting here by the water. Is there nobody with you?

ANTONY No.

MARCUS We thought we heard voices and so we called to you. Here's Bernard, and Julian. We all thought something might be wrong.

ANTONY
No, nobody was here

It was I you heard talking.
I speak my thoughts aloud.
For I find that in silent meditation
The agile mind conjures an awkward conclusion
Into a comfortable cushion
On which the soul sits like a lap dog
And dreams. Dreams the frantic hare is caught
Then barks and wakes to disappointment.
As a poet, Julian, you'll have found that pleasant dreams
Often make unpleasant poetry.
And Bernard will agree, too,
That though dreams and prophecy
Contribute to theology,
Their drunken logic will not mix
With strict philosophy.
And who'd drive a straight furrow, Marcus,
With one eye on his fame and the other on his glory?
Dreams mirror our self-esteem,
　　behind the glass—is another story.
MARCUS Father, the sun has set.
ANTONY Let us pray.

They kneel

'Almighty and most merciful God, listen we beseech thee, to our prayers, and so free our hearts from temptation to evil thoughts that they may deserve to be accounted worthy dwelling places of the Holy Ghost. Through Jesus Christ, Our Lord. Amen.'

'Their habit is coarse, their girdle harsh, feet are unshod, food is scanty, purse and goods are cast aside: for Francis disdains earthly riches, poverty is all he craves for.'

'He seeks a place of tears, where in bitterness of heart he weeps over all the precious time lost in the world. In the loneliness of a mountain cave he weeps prostrate on the earth; till at length he is comforted.'

They rise and chant Gregorian

Agnus Dei,
                    qui tollis
                              peccata mundi:
miserere nobis.
MARCUS Father.
ANTONY [*to himself*]
'Quaerit loca lacrymarum,
Promit voces cor amarum,
Gemit moestus tempus carum,
Perditum in saeculo.'
MARCUS Father Antony.
ANTONY
'Montis antro sequestratus,
Plorat orat humi stratus,
Tandem mente serenatus
Latitat ergastulo.'
MARCUS Father, you must be cold, and supper is ready.
JULIAN The dew has fallen. This grass is wet.
ANTONY [*as if in a trance*]
'Tandem mente serenatus
Latita ergastulo.'
Which is what I have sought,
It is what we all seek;
Each according to his own perception
Seeks his idea of God.
I, in my cloister; my brother, in uniform;
Some seek it in power
Some seek it in prayer
Some think it is plenty
Some think it is poverty.
If it were in power,
                    I should have found it,
For an Abbot is powerful,
                              but I did not find it:
For me it was not in power.
If it were in plenty
                    I should have found it

For I was rich
            but I did not find it:
For me it was not in riches.
If it were in poverty
            I should have found it
For I have nothing
            but I have not found it:
For me, it is not in poverty.
In power there is the desire to be more powerful
And the fear of being disobeyed.
In wealth there is the desire to be more wealthy
And the fear of being cheated.
And in poverty there is the pride of poverty
And in prayer the pride of prayer.
Only he who has found God
Can believe in God.
Only he who has belief can find.
Perhaps He is not in power or plenty
Neither in poverty nor in prayer.
Perhaps God has no permanent reality
But exists as and when we create Him,
Through the labour of humility
He is born in the death of pride.
Marcus, you look sad. I did not mean to make you miserable.
And even our lively Julian is half asleep. So get along, the three
of you, and have a hot supper.

MARCUS But Father you must not stay up here any longer. You
have not eaten since this morning. And it is damp here by the
water and you are sure to catch a cold.

ANTONY No, I am not cold. I am too old to catch a cold.

MARCUS Father, please come back to the cell now for supper. I
have prepared a special surprise for you. Something that was
even a delicacy at Santa Ferrata.

ANTONY Thank you my son, but I must stay here.

MARCUS Then I will go and bring your food here, Father. And
I'll bring an axe and the three of us will cut some olive wood
and make a fire to keep you warm.

JULIAN That's a good idea Marcus. Let's make a huge bonfire, a
crackling blaze of olive and thorn. You love to see the sparks
and the smell of it, don't you, Father?

BERNARD No, Julian. It is better for you and Marcus to return,
for you are cold and hungry. I will stay with Father Antony.

MARCUS Father, may I bring you some bread and honey? Please,
let me, Father.

ANTONY
No, Marcus, I shall eat no more.
I will stay alone, here by the water
Till death relieves me
Or Christ receives me;
This my soul's resolved upon.
    Oh my sons, how can I tell you
What I have known forever
And yet not known before;
Known in my heart and known in my bone
As an indissoluble certainty:
But to my mind, that was not fact enough.
Age makes us slow-witted, and this is an advantage;
For then, our heart's sure beat can compete
With the mind's argument
And give the soul back its first dumb certainty.
    I remember as a child running to my widowed Mother
And saying: 'Are you looking for God, Mother?'
And the bereaved woman fingered her crucifix and nodded;
And I said: 'Don't worry, Mother, I am God: I am God.'
My Mother fell on her knees to redeem my blasphemy.
    Then I grew up to the endless worries of a small estate,
Forgetting my certainties in making ends meet.
And then the slow ascent up the corkscrew stair
Which leads nowhere,
And the higher you go, the lower you go:
    Stepping up from knowledge to get a view of doubt;
    Rise from desire, see, cloud banks of sorrow;
    Climbing, forgetting, descending, remembering,
    Up from ambition to ambition,

Till pride's pinnacle is just in view,
And on the last step success stands
                    With a bell, a box and a sprig of yew.
You see, Marcus, as old men we face death
With our souls in pawn to our business
And none of our business accomplished.
For living is an endless chain of interlocking actions,
Distractions disguised as important actions.
I will do this, when I have done that.
I will do that, when I have done this.
And so on and so on and so on.
The Abbot's wealth was the Abbot's distraction.
The Hermit's poverty is the Hermit's distraction.
For here on Zante, our poverty and simplicity
Can be made a distraction also.
You know how it is, Julian,
When the garden is dug and the seed sown,
Then, then we shall have time
And then, when the seed is sown,
The garden needs another digging,
And the time is never given.
Nothing is given. Opportunity is time taken.
Taken from this self-spun web of distraction,
In which the bewildered mind becomes enmeshed
And cannot unravel, can only break through;
And this, Bernard, this I do: to find my first certainty and
    final faith.
By fasting with no attachment to life,
I pray I may lose my fear of death.
By contemplating the object of my dreams
I hope to shed my desire.
By meditating on my intentions
I hope to achieve my object
    Which is the comfort of His Compassion
And the simple peace within the tumult of the mystery.
It may well be that it is a sin to seek so high.
That may well be: Yes, certainly.

But I do not think either the love of woman or the love of God
Come to a man like an unexpected letter.
Love must be dredged out of our own souls
By our own effort:
And this is the only love we know
Though it may not be the only love we receive.
And I believe Christ lies in my heart like a green leaf in an
old book
Revealed, if only I could find my heart, open it and look.

MARCUS Father, do you mean you will never eat again?

ANTONY Yes, Marcus, I have vowed to fast and meditate.

MARCUS But Father, if you fast what will become of me,
what shall I do? For I can only cook for you. There is nothing
else I can do. That is why I am here. I cannot sing to you
as Julian does, or talk like Bernard can. What can I do for
you?

ANTONY Nothing now, my son. Go back to the cell and say a
prayer for me.

MARCUS A prayer? That won't feed you. Besides, I can't make
prayers by myself. What use are prayers now? It's hot soup you
need.

ANTONY You are tired, my son.

MARCUS Yes, I am tired. I am sorry. Good night, Father.

ANTONY Good night, Marcus.

Exit MARCUS

Bernard, follow him, he is distraught. And Bernard, remember
to water the vine cuttings for me. And Bernard, when the old
farmer, Riggio, comes to the cell in the morning to have his leg
dressed, remember to wash out the foul ointment which he puts
on it; and tell him to keep it clean with salt water.

BERNARD Yes, I will do that. Don't worry, Father.

Exit BERNARD

JULIAN And can't we have a fire here, after all?

ANTONY No Julian. But you may sing a song for me. I have
gone without my supper but let me have a song.

JULIAN What shall I sing, Father?

ANTONY Sing of the evening, Julian.

c

JULIAN [*sings*]
> The red fox, the sun,
> tears the throat of the evening;
> makes the light of the day
> bleed into the ocean.
>
> The laced grace of gulls
> lift up from the corn fields;
> fly across the sunset,
> scarlet their silhouette.
>
> The old owl, the moon,
> drifts from its loose thatch of clouds,
> throws an ivory glance
> on an enamelled sea.
>
> Eyes of mice, the stars,
> from their privacy of light
> peep into the darkness
> with the temerity of night.

ANTONY You poets are strange; you know more than you learn. Music is a short cut. It is a way I cannot follow but it reveals the destination. Good-night, Julian. You must make me a song for another night.

JULIAN Tomorrow night, Father?

ANTONY No Julian, not for another week. I wish to be left entirely alone for a week and then you may all come up and see me. Now, good night my son, you are cold.

JULIAN Good night, Father.

He goes off back stage calling

Bernard! Bernard! Wait for me. Oh there you are. Where's Marcus?

They enter stage

BERNARD I expect he's home now.

JULIAN A whole week, Bernard, what will become of him? For Father Antony says we are not even to visit him for a week. Poor Marcus, and the very day he found some gull's eggs! How can Marcus understand? I find it difficult. Do you understand, Bernard?

BERNARD Yes, I understand; Father Antony has made the decision.

JULIAN What was that? I thought I heard something.

BERNARD It's Marcus, look over there. He's climbing across the hill. I do believe he's trying to avoid us, and what's that he's carrying? Marcus! He pretends he can't hear. After him.

They exit and re-enter following MARCUS

JULIAN Marcus, let's go home.

BERNARD What's that you're carrying? Oh how thoughtful of you Marcus. Look Julian, Marcus has brought us up some hot soup.

MARCUS No Bernard, give it back to me, please Bernard.

BERNARD But it's lovely soup and it was so thoughtful of you to bring it up here for me.

MARCUS It's not for you, Bernard.

BERNARD Then who is it for?

MARCUS Oh you can drink it. I was taking it to Father Antony. But I suppose it's no use.

BERNARD No, it's no use. Father Antony has made a vow. You wouldn't tempt him to break it, would you?

MARCUS Yes, you don't understand. He will die like a calf on the hill if he fasts in this damp coldness. Oh why did he have to fast? We were so happy. It is we who will suffer for it, not he. Bernard, you could dissuade him, couldn't you?

BERNARD Possibly. But I am glad; for now he is a saint. There is nothing we can do. Let us return and pray, and leave him to meditate.

MARCUS I can hear his voice now.

BERNARD Come, Marcus.

MARCUS I'm coming. But I can hear his voice. The night carries the sound.

The three move front stage R. and kneel. The light moves from them to the rock on which ANTONY *is sitting.*

ANTONY

It is winter. Again, winter.
The blind mouth of the earth sucks a dry udder.
Only leaves, falling over and over disturb the year's slumber.
 And my mind clings to the past,
 Like a velvet train dragged on wet grass.

Once it was spring. The almond broke
Out with a mad frail enthusiasm from its tight bark;
And the cherry and peach stood within my reach.
 My glad eyes grazed on the glory of it.
 And my heart held part of the power of it.

It was summer. The sun shining.
A slow wind walked the cornfields combing
Wheat into waves, which followed one after another till the
           whole was flowing.
 Then my soul crowed like a cock loud
 And trod the future like a lot of hens, proud.

Autumn's a woman. A woman's a vine.
Carrying the soil's lust into the pressed wine:
Both blood and the grape, incarnadine.
 I heaped a girl's lap with lemons
 Oh! who could not sing of such a season.

But it is winter. Again winter.
And I am an old man with a fixed future;
To which the sand in the glass dribbles as I sit by the water
 Dreaming, resisting contemplation
 On the precise point of meditation,

Which is my fear. What are my fears?
Of all my fears, it is loneliness which wears
The worst mask, with lips bitten and bleeding, and its eyes red
              with tears.

Loneliness is the soul's wilderness and I
Am alone, Jesu, unless in Thy Company,

Which I have known—when you had left me,
For when you were with me, I was not lonely;
But then I, full of the strength of you, denied I needed you;
and I,

Blind fool and prig and called a saint
Am lonely now, and cry of this complaint.
SOPRANO SOLO [*sings off stage*]
Oh proud heart take pity on that part of me
Which lies in you as your own lost heart.
Now I must sing the oldest song
That was ever sung in this or any other tongue.
It is the song of her short sweep of beauty, and what it did
become

And always will, as if as punishment
To those who love, their love keeps time's appointment.

How I fear Time: which is all change.
Oh, where is there a fair face found to challenge
Advancing age, with his full equipage and cortege, and not
surrender?

I have pressed my lips upon
Helen's mouth and kissed a skeleton.

And who owns the eyes which do not show
The faint lines like a bird's feet in the snow
Which deepen perceptibly, as time leads and we follow?
An old crone cutting the heads off a pail of fish
Stands on the feet that were my mistress's.

I've lost the past and feared the present,
And in the future have foreseen this moment
Of decision, which I have delayed by prompt postponement.
A farmer avoids his corn in a bad season.
And I have put off this moment for a similar reason,

The same reason, as you might say,
Just as a man who takes a holiday
And then, recalls his dog's at home chained and unfed, and
                                    hopes it frees itself whilst he's away,
And returning, fears to look in case starvation
Killed the dog; so I've put off this introspection

On my lean soul, which I have fed
Worse than a dog, fattened it on flattery instead
Of starving it, thrown it whole joints of vanity, and taken it to
                                    bed,

    And suckled it on the cream of self-deception
    —Which for any soul or dog spells indigestion.

What is my soul? It is that part
Of me which is no more my head than it is my heart;
And if my mind or blood directs me, it is my soul that suffers
                                    hurt.

    It is the crumb of Christ within me, which description
    Is neither blasphemy—nor definition.

And what is fear? It is conceit:
Knowing sufficient of the future to dislike it.
And insufficient to ignore it, it is self-love implicit.
    It is a strutting sort of clumsy confidence
    Which, arresting Destiny, gaols Fate—then loses half the
                                    evidence.

I have described myself and fears
Because the one is made up of the other;
And because, clarity towards one's conscience is a kind of
                                    prayer.

    But eloquence and verbal gymnastics
    Only persuade, against the run of logic,

And leave one where one was before:
The same old man in the same cold year;

Only water, flowing incessantly, insanely, quietens my fear.
May this ocean of night wash over me
A wave of sleep to comfort and silence me.

ALTO SOLO [*off stage*]
Quaerit loca lacrymarum
Promit voces cor amarum
Gemit moestus tempus carum
Perditum in saeculo.

[*The light leaves* ANTONY *and, after a few seconds,
shines on the three novitiates. They are kneeling. They
rise and sing in Gregorian chant.*]

OMNES

Agnus Dei,
            qui tollis
                      peccata mundi;
miserere nobis.
                 Donna nobis pacem.
*With stylised movement, they go F. stage centre and take
up statuesque positions*

MARCUS

Today is Monday. Yesterday was Sunday. Today is Monday.
Everyday treads on the toes of yesterday
And today on the heels of tomorrow
Which will come, but comes slowly,
Slowly to those who worry.
Monday means firewood; today we cut firewood
All day today we have been cutting firewood;
Olive burns well, but it is tough on the saw and hard on the
    axe,
And both are hard on the shoulder.
I am used to work but not to worry.
It is already a week since Antony has eaten.
He fails, like a calf that won't suck; you can watch him failing.
I swing the axe hard to fell this tree worry;
Never have I cut so much timber
As today, my axe blunt, I, weak, only worry drives me.
            They again move and take up new positions

SOPRANO SOLO [*off stage*]
Montis antro sequestratus
Plorat orat humi stratus
Tandem mente serenatus
Latitat ergastulo.

JULIAN

Marcus thinks I am callous,
Cold, indifferent to Antony's suffering
Because I do not show my feeling
At the time of feeling.
And because on Tuesday, yesterday, I wrote a song
Which contained no reference to fasting
Or to our present anxiety.
As if I wrote with my heart as an ink pot
And could not compose a line till I had wept a little
Besides, I have seen all this before.
It is not for nothing I have lived a thousand years.
The age of a poet
Is the age of poetry.
Not from my skin can you gauge my suffering.
I know more of death than a doctor or a grave digger.
I know more of birth than a woman or a matron.
For after one has been born a dozen times
One has a prescience to experience.
I do not fast with Father Antony,
Yet I shall die with Father Antony.
But death cannot disturb my continuity.

They take up new positions

TENOR SOLO [*off stage*]
Ibi vacat rupe tectus
Ad divina sursum vectus
Spernit ima judex rectus
Eligit coelestia.

MARCUS

Thursday, the sun is cold with indifference.
Surely he will moisten his lips with water.
My mouth is dry with his thirst.

When he sleeps, I will moisten his lips with water.
What is the body's sin but frailty?
Frailty is no sin—it is a state of nature.
Thirst is the meaning of the word water.
All day we have been pruning the vines
Without any heart in the work,
And with no hope in the future.
What is the time, Bernard?

BERNARD I don't know.

MARCUS What is the time, Julian?

JULIAN
The time must be late
Or the birds must be early;
For the gulls are flying back to the sea.
And there's Riggio coming to fetch his cattle.
It must be time to go back to the cell.
Let's stop now and go home for supper.

They move right and take up new positions

BASS SOLO [*off stage*]

Carnem frenat sub censura
Transformatam in figura
Cibum capit de scriptura
Abigit terrestria.

MARCUS
Friday.
Time does not march.
Time must be pushed like a barrow.
And it is uphill and it is all heavy.
It is eleven days since Father Antony has eaten.
When the others sleep, I climb the hill
And take him food which is never eaten.
He does not notice me. His eyes are open
But he does not see, he stares into the water.
Oh Bernard, do go up and see him.
He will not mind if you go up and see him:
He will listen to you, only you can dissuade him.

BERNARD No, Marcus, it will soon be Sunday and then we can
   go up. He said we were not to disturb him.

JULIAN I am tired.

MARCUS I, too.

BERNARD There ends another day.
   The light is taken off the three who kneel stage right. The
   light shines on the rock.

*   *   *

                                                        (Canzone)

ANTONY
   How still the valley
                       this is the dead end of the year,
   And the cut back vines
                       show no signs
                                   of life, leaf;
   Even the olives have felt the grief
                       of the cold Mistral.
   The pruned trunks stand ugly
                       sometimes they appear
   To shake as a fist; Thine
                       Hand Divine?
                                   Raised in wrath?
   Then held for a brief
                       moment which was merciful.

   Not even the nettles lolling up against the wall
   Have strength to fall.
                       Only the wind, now shepherding
   The shaggy clouds going
                       over the hill for the night
   Has any energy, as it flees from itself in flight.

But it is not deadness, nor is it tranquil.
It is all
        appetite, the blind roots seeking
Twisting and desiring;
                        sensualism out of sight
Like a saint who fasts when hunger's his perverse delight.

                        *

Age is deceptive;
                often its continence
Is not chastity,
                but merely
                                restraint
Imposed upon the ill-clad saint
                        by lack of appetite.
Here I sit pensive
                and look like innocence.
An old crow perched by me,
                        pities me;
                                age, my complaint;
It is not self-restraint
                till she again teases my sight,
                SOPRANO [*off stage*]
                Oh proud heart take pity on that part of me
                Which lies in you as your own lost heart.

And tempts the torrent of my blood to flood the desert of her
                                                eyes
Then, when I rise
                from such a wilderness
With no wantonness
                quenched, drenched and no fire
Burning my brain away, then can I say I'm chaste with no
                                                desire.

Till then, till time returns and smooths the skin of her disguise,
Age makes me wise
                              and temperate without excess
Of anything but sadness.
                              Years made the youth a Prior
Not his own effort, but the falling off of his desire.

                                    *

But all this is nothing:
                              the flesh is moderate;
Well, by comparison.
                              It's ambition,
                                          the spirit
Which bids and bids without a limit
                                          whatever its resources;
With vanity nagging,
                              conceit nudging,
                                          the rate
Of bids races the auction,
                              and discretion
                                          makes pursuit
And then is pawned for the deposit
                                          —all the sale produces.

No sooner have we found than we begin to search,
Then to reach
                              for what we threw away
Last Saturday.
                              The soul knows gluttony,
And drinks its own cheap wine in its own debauchery;

Indulging in its self-esteem it drinks its way to church
Kneels, lurches
                              from smugness to pride and prays

For its sins, itself and says:
                          'Lord, give me Mercy
—My right!'—Then confesses with a modest brevity.

                              *

I fast, my mind feasts,
                          my skin hangs like a sack;
There, protrudes the bone,
                          the skeleton,
                                    which will come
In handy to beat the drum
                          made from my cured skin's agony;
Drum to frighten the beasts,
                          the fears, that were at my back;
Fear of being alone,
                    fear of my own
                              fear, and the tomb
—So much like a womb,
                    that birth and death have fixed affinity.

The flesh assists in its own mortification.
Starvation
            (Same thing for poor or holy
Eventually)
                    underlines our nature
Dust, and slowly unveils our final figure.

But the obstinate mind still plans perfection.
Privation
            adds to its supply
Of dreams and only
                    removes the body's anchor,
The mind released, feasts—a self-contained epicure.

                              *

Desire is the beginning
                    and the end is sleep;
And in sleep
            dreams are,
                    and in dreams, desire;
This keeps us forever in the wilderness
                              within the pendulum
Of being and non-being,
                    walking in each other's sleep
Within God's nightmare.
                    It is there,
                            and in this
Our inert franticness
                    our staid delirium.

And desire for no desire is a desire also.
This I know.
              You cannot get away from it.
We are caught in it,
                    like a mouse within a wheel
Or a snake devouring its own endless tail.

It is plain that where you are there you cannot go.
Is it so?
          I, of God's heart a grain of it?
How then to enter it
                    and escape from this ordeal
Of being the part outside the whole?
    To lose that part is to reveal that whole!

                    *   *   *

The light is taken off the rock and the three figures are lit
JULIAN Marcus, wake up Marcus. It's Sunday today. The week's
past. We can go and see Father Antony this morning.

MARCUS I cannot go.

JULIAN Why? Bernard and I are going.

MARCUS I am too weak to go.

JULIAN We'll carry you.

MARCUS No, Julian, you are not well enough.

JULIAN But Bernard can—there is nothing wrong with Bernard. He's strong enough. Bernard, help me to carry Marcus.

They move off to centre of stage, carrying MARCUS

BERNARD We should not take Marcus up to see Father Antony.

JULIAN Why, you know how he has looked forward to going and how he has worried. What do you mean?

BERNARD If Father Antony sees him so ill and weak he may feel obliged to break his fast on account of Marcus.

JULIAN And that might upset your plan of writing the Account of the Fast of St Antony. Is that it?

MARCUS No Julian; Bernard is right. It would be unfair to go. I will stay here. Put me down. I'll stay here in the shade.

They put him down

JULIAN Shall I stay with you?

MARCUS No, Father Antony is sure to ask you to sing to him. It is the body he punishes; but he will enjoy a song.

JULIAN I will come back here. Bernard wait for me, I am too weak to climb alone.

They go off stage and re-enter behind the rock

ANTONY Julian, why what is wrong with you?

JULIAN I am not well and the hill is steep.

ANTONY And where is Marcus?

JULIAN He is too ill to come.

ANTONY What is wrong with you both? You are not eating enough. It is I who fast, not you. Look at Bernard, here; he's fit and well. I have been looking forward to your singing to me. I have only heard the old crow since you last sang to me.

JULIAN Yes, I have made a song for you.

ANTONY Then sing

JULIAN [*sings*]
Morning is only
A heron rising

With great wings lifting
   day into the sky.

Morning is only
A scarlet stallion
Jumping the ocean.
   Its mane aflame on the sea.

Morning is only
The white plumes of smoke
As the velvet snake
   Night leaves the green valley.

Morning is only
Women bent at the well
Lifting their pails full
   Of their hearts, too heavy.

ANTONY How music runs like a torch through the body.

BERNARD Julian, you had better return to Marcus.

JULIAN Father, shall I go?

ANTONY If Marcus is unwell, Julian. You must be with him; for
you two were always close together.

Exit JULIAN

   It is strange that they are ill.

BERNARD They do not understand.

ANTONY Perhaps I should break my vow for their sake.

BERNARD Many seed are sown for one to germinate. It would be
a pity to turn back for their sake.

ANTONY Yes, it is even possible to use Mercy to hide our weakness. I am tired, how tired.

BERNARD Then I will leave you alone to sleep awhile.

*   *   *

(Canzone)

ANTONY

Sleep? No. When wise men dream

               their reason's rudderless;

Their wills by tempest tossed
and their course is lost;
a drunken crew
Climbs on board and few
obey the captain;
And my sleep is too heavy with dreams
for me to lift it, for to dream is
To ferry a heavy ghost
across and across
a flooded river. And who
Can carry the old over the new
and out of the past lift now again?

Only God himself stands outside of Time's circle
And schedule.
For time is where there is movement;
It is energy's measurement.
And since all life is in Him spent,
God stands outside of Time, alone in still contentment.

I am not alone. Only God can be alone, His Soul
The Sentinel
guarding the fragile tent
Of creation against the dark waves of chaos, which bent
with inarticulate power roll back spent,
Into a calm nothingness, smoothed by the stroke of
His last sacrament.

BERNARD
And yet you are alone;
for you have rinsed your heart
Of fear and of desire,
and therefore are
free of time;

D

For by desire and fear we're chained to time,
  and by time locked within each other's hearts.

You are as the stone
                     is to the water, within yet apart
From the endless river,
                  which flows for ever; For you, within Time
Perceive the continuity of Time;
         And in that, find tranquillity, climb to the bank, apart.

ANTONY
Tranquillity? I have not found tranquillity.
And I am weary.
               I have turned over my heart
Like a coin in my pocket.
                  I now know my nature.
But to know oneself is not to change one's nature.
CHOIR A CAPELLA
   Deus in adjutorium meum intende
   Domine ad adjuvandum me festina.

It is to discover extreme disparity,
And the dishonesty
            of a Prince's court
Where vanity's the fashion and flattery's an art.
              The soul's a state in miniature;
In each of us all: king, slave, both rich and poor.

All the diversity of a city street walks
And talks
        up the bazaar within my brain.
Some laugh, some beg, some crawl in pain.

Then how am I alone or free
Until I clear this rabble which live within me and consume me?

* * *

Enter a figure from back stage

Who are you?

GLUTTONY

I am gluttony, the grease on your surplice,
Success and excess
I'm sweat from a poultice,
Juice from an abscess.
Me and my daughter Lechery
Are off to an exquisite debauchery.
Amorous eels are to perform on coagulated catarrh.
Jaundiced bile our wassail
Belch and biliousness.

ANTONY This is disgusting!

GLUTTONY

And crude, too?
You find it easy to reject me?

ANTONY I do.

GLUTTONY

Tempting yourself with me
You get off easily!

ANTONY I do, be off with you.

GLUTTONY

We were good friends once
Let's part friends now
Here, take this for old times' sake.

ANTONY What is it?

GLUTTONY

It's a ripe fig
Picked with the dew on it.
Take it, taste it, try it—
Go on—I've plenty more:
Look, a basket full, all purple ripe,
Plump as the belly of a toad.

ANTONY Take them away.

GLUTTONY

You're hard to please.
What is your tongue for if not to press
These big Muscat grapes against the dry roof of your mouth?
If your tongue's for logic,
It reasons badly
If you find evil in this fruit of God.

ANTONY

I see Gluttony makes as good a barrister
As a barrister makes a glutton.

GLUTTONY

You will have your joke.
There, that reminds me more of the Abbot of Santa Ferrata.
What did they use to say?
'Often without his trousers never without his wit.'
I thought we'd reach an understanding
So I brought this luncheon basket
Just in case.

ANTONY What have you there?

GLUTTONY

Only the wine
And here's the bread.
If you will not eat
Then take the sacrament instead.

ANTONY Away! Away! Oh misery.

GLUTTONY

All right St Antony.
I'll go St Antony
And leave you Lechery.
She'll cure your prudery
And blast your humbuggery
With one debauchery
Adieu Saint Antony.

> *Exit* GLUTTONY: *he takes up a statuesque position in front of the stage*

CHOIR A CAPELLA
Confandantur et revereantur qui quaerunt animam meam.
                            [*Enter* LECHERY, *a woman*]

LECHERY Hello, dearie, how are you both?

ANTONY Both?

LECHERY

Yes the two of you.
All men are two.
When one rises
The other falls;
When one falls,
The other rises.

ANTONY I do not understand you.

LECHERY You do, you will.

ANTONY Go, Lechery, and learn more subtlety.

LECHERY

I will if this wound will let me.
They say you heal.

ANTONY I sometimes wash men's wounds.

LECHERY

To heal is charity
Charity is not lechery.

ANTONY What's wrong with you?

LECHERY

I have a wound that burns with pain
A pain only you can cure.

ANTONY I'll see what I can do. Where is the wound?

LECHERY On my leg here. Higher. Higher.

ANTONY Oh! away with you.

LECHERY

I'll go St Antony
But there is one to follow me
Who has your own subtlety.

She takes up statuesque position front stage near GLUTTONY
Enter MARCUS *from back stage*

CHOIR A CAPELLA
Avertantur retrorsum et erubescant qui volunt mihi mala.

ANTONY
  You, Marcus?
  Not my own Marcus.
MARCUS Yes, Father.
ANTONY
  Why, you were like a son
  from my own body.
MARCUS
  I am your own body.
  Pity me or what is left of me.
  And eat for my sake which is your sake.
ANTONY Would you, too, tempt me?
MARCUS
  Not to Gluttony, nor to Lechery.
  I speak for moderation, and balance, poise.
  Think of the life we knew:
    Milk from the goat,
    Our own made bread,
  What evil was there in your ascetic life?
  Was it not a modest sacrament?
  Now by fasting you feed your mind to gluttony;
  Eat this and revive me, your body's agony.
BERNARD [*who is still standing in the shadow*]
  Moderation is a word, Father:
  Compromise is its meaning.
MARCUS
  Unless you eat, I must die
  For I am your body, Antony.
ANTONY I will not eat.

                              MARCUS *lies down as dead.*
                              Enter a young woman, SIGHT

CHOIR A CAPELLA
  Avertantur statim erubescentes qui dicunt mihi, Euge, Euge.
SIGHT Antony.
ANTONY
  Who are you? I cannot see your face. Come closer.
  My eyes are failing with my strength.

SIGHT Can you see me now Antony?

ANTONY Yes, and you are beautiful. Who are you?

SIGHT
I am sight, your eyes' pleasure.
What has been my wickedness
That you now starve me to blindness
And destroy your eyes, my treasure?

ANTONY I have no quarrel with you.

SIGHT Look, Antony!

ANTONY Where?

SIGHT
There, where a bushel of starlings are flung under the wind.
Look, like feathered spray, they lift, fall, away, away.

ANTONY Yes, God moves gracefully.

SIGHT
And look, there by the brook
A hot-blooded mare
Has lost her leggy foal,
Watch how her head's thrust back,
On her neck's great muscles;
And the white panic of her eyes.
Her nostrils dilate, she calls, and the furious engine stamps the
        earth.

ANTONY Yes, I see God is grace.

SIGHT
Antony, you cannot look anywhere
And not see God's face, this grace.

ANTONY No, nowhere.

CHOIR A CAPELLA
Exsultent et laetentur in te omnes qui quaerunt te et dicant semper.

SIGHT Then save me, your sight.

ANTONY
No, there is more to see than
The eyes see.

SIGHT You will not save me?

ANTONY No.

                SIGHT *takes up position with the others*

Why do you falter and fall on your way?
SIGHT Because you are blind, St Antony.

                    *   *   *

                                    (Canzone)

ANTONY
   Blind? Yes, I am blind
                    and the world's shut fast in my face.
   A door locking me
                    into memory
                                    my soul's cupboard.
   This will be worse,
                    for once memory's stirred,
                                    the heart's lost,
   To sights within the mind;
                    which, in my own case,
   Means I may now see
                    too clearly
                                    in the blind eyes record
   What sight hid, till it was just a word,
                    her name, the word I repeated most.
                    A voice singing behind rock

   But I can hear! A sound now above the laugh of the water.
   Who's there?
                    Oh echo do not tease my blindness
   And mock it to madness.
                    Who's there? Who's there?
   For pity's sake speak so that I may know that I can hear.

                    Enter JULIAN *singing*
   Julian! It's you. Oh Julian, come near and sing to me
   Loudly,
                    louder, come closer now and sing.

JULIAN I am too weak to sing.

ANTONY What must I do for you to sing to me?

JULIAN It is too late. For you are deaf Saint Antony.

JULIAN *lies near* MARCUS

* * *

ANTONY

  Deaf? Now I shall hear

               hear my soul's unanswered question.

  And blind

        I shall see,

            see that part of me,

                   which is not mine:

     SOLO SOPRANO [*off stage*]

      Oh proud heart take pity on that part of me

      Which lies in you as your own lost heart.

  My heart, where only she reclines

              as a chrysalis

  Embalmed, in a career

          of action and distraction,

  Buried but never dead,

         starved yet fed.

                What mysterious design

  The heart holds! Come then, all's thine!

          Make your metamorphosis.

     Enter a beautiful young woman

  No stay! I cannot bear to see, your look destroys me.

WOMAN Antony! Antony!

ANTONY

  Oh, take my heart that was not given

  And break my heart that was not broken

         then Now it is I who am forsaken

  By all but thee. Listen, my love, at last my heart has spoken.

Now your turn. Answer me, I have not long to wait.
WOMAN
   It is too late, too late.
                            I have by time been taken,
   To cruel time tied and then forsaken;
   This time, it's time that's spoken.
      At this the woman removes her mask showing the face of
      an old crone. She moves off to the other figures
CHOIR A CAPELLA
Magnificant Dominus qui diligunt salutare tuum.

                    *   *   *

ANTONY
   Well, now all's said;
                         Our time's run out
   To the last grain, the last hour.
                              And who's power
                                          or strength
   Can add a second to a minute's length
                                    and fill this glass again?
   Even the sea's vanquished
                           by little waves leading the tide in and out,
   Over and over; the mower
                            every blade devours
                                          But with strength
   I would not add to my life's length
                                    for life's preface is all pain.

   The plot disappointment; the end, pity, self-pity.
   From that: free!
                     At last, I'm out of fear's tight halter
   And desire's short tether,
                            both are broken behind me,
   They cannot retie me, for by my own effort, I am free.

From the tangle of teasing distractions which blinded me
Hid Christ from me.
　　　　　　　　　　Now, my will is my protection
And Christ alone my Master
　　　　　　　　　　　to Whose sweet tyranny
I will submit, and can submit, for I am free!

* * *

The figure of BERNARD *comes from the shadows*

BERNARD

Except, Antony, from me.
From me, you are not free.

ANTONY

What horror now invades my hollow heart
And parades the vacant cities of my brain?

BERNARD

Antony, don't you recognise me?
I, Bernard your nearest, closest friend?
With whom you've shared the secrets of your soul
And to whom your mind's intricate circuit
Is as a garden maze to the gardener?
And, Antony, have I not always walked
Before you, beside you and behind you
As your retinue, your substantial shadow
For you to lean upon and lead you on?
Was it not Bernard who made you Abbot
And did I not lead you from there, to here?
And have I not stood by you in your fast?
Why, your whole life's a pilgrimage to me:
By way of meditation you approached me
And by privation you have fed me.
Marcus, the peasant, was your own body and your sight
And Julian, the poet, your sensual appetite.
They weakened as you starved, and died.
But look, Antony, I, Bernard, thrived.

And stand still, the shadow at your side,
For, Antony, I am your own Pride.

* * *

ANTONY
Must a man crawl to God?
BERNARD
Pride is self-respect
By your own effort
                        your own thought
                                    you have reached here, where
There is no fear and no desire
                        the whole earth floats upon your reason.
ANTONY
But where's the peace of God?
                                    It is all loneliness except
In Him whom I have sought
                        Within this loneliness of thought and by this fire
Which has burnt out my heart and my desire,
                                    —and left self-love and reason.

Now blind and deaf and weak to death, I cannot struggle more
And therefore
                        I am free, without liberty
Imprisoned in my sad soul's captivity:
                                    my own mind, a tomb for me;
My own pride the punctual jailer of my pride's own tyranny.

Dear Christ, who stands above me and beyond me, restore
My sight before
                        I die, that I may see your sweet humility
And know you love me
                        Dear Christ, I sink in my own misery.

For pity's sake lift me into your Mercy, Mercy!
>*At this word Mercy,* BERNARD *falls by* MARCUS *and*
> JULIAN

CHOIR A CAPELLA
Ego vero egenus et pauper sum
Deus adjuva me.
Adjutor meus et liberator meus es tu:
Domine ne moreris.

Agnus Dei
     qui tollis
        peccata mundi;
Miserere nobis.
Mercy, Jesu, for I die.

      *   *   *

VOICE
Come, Antony, you are weak and tired.
Put down your burden of pride.
Kneel humbly, rise gladly.
      ANTONY *kneels then stands*
ANTONY Father!
VOICE   My son.
ANTONY Father, I have found you.
VOICE   My son, I had not lost you.
ANTONY Is this death, Father?
VOICE There is no death, my son.
ANTONY
Nor is there fear in you
Nor is desire in you.
VOICE Soon you will be free in me.
ANTONY Soon Father?
VOICE
Soon as you have renounced all pride
And eaten of humility.
ANTONY That I will do gladly.

VOICE Then go back to your body and eat what your poor
  servants brought to you. Then follow me.

ANTONY

  Marcus, wake up, my son,

  Give me the food you brought me.

MARCUS Praise be to God, Father, we thought you were dead.

ANTONY

  There is no death my son.

> ANTONY *takes the cup, drinks, then stands*
>
> Jesu, I come

CHOIR A CAPELLA

  Gloria patri, et filio, et spiritui sancto.

  Sicut erat in principio, et nunc, et

  Semper, et in saecula saeculorum. Amen.

CURTAIN

The Anti-Masque

CHARACTERS

THE PROLOGUE AND CHORUS

A RADIO ANNOUNCER

FATHER OPINE

A POSTCARD SELLER

A MAN OF CULTURE

A WOMAN OF LEISURE

A MOTHER

A WIDOW

A MOBILE WORKER

MISS PHILIPPA FORM

A CRITIC

THE POSTCARD SELLER'S WIFE

MEMBERS OF THE ASTRAL GROUP

AN OLD MAN

The scene: The same as The Masque
Time: Present

The Anti-Masque

Before drop curtain which is unlit

You have already heard how Antony
Fasted, on the small island of Zante,
Alone, during the fourteenth century;
And how by meditating on his fears
And on desire he came to shed those fears
Till his own pride revealed, brought him to tears
And made him cry to Christ for Mercy,
Which was confession of humility
A new strength found in his own frailty;
And how with this last prayer and effort
He climbed from sin to Christ's own comfort:
A final gesture of humility
A final offer for tranquillity:
Tempted and tormented by himself, he
The man, became the Saint, Saint Antony.

That's how the legend goes. It may be true
Or false—that's for theologians to review—
Yet what History denies, my Art can shew.
At any rate, the point is not in fact
But in the meaning of the Saint's last act.

Now we must leave the fourteenth century
And make our Masque more contemporary,
And alter time—no change of scene is necessary.
Our Masque's no more a Miracle. It is no Play,
For Television's here, and here to stay
Making all Art, impromptu shall we say,
With neither limit for its Time, nor Place,
Needing no plot or script, it can replace
All pens and poets by an active populace,
Which running up and down the world and street

Is for the Televisor equal meat
Making all poets obsolete.
The people act. They are the audience
As well as their own chorus; and pretence
Is no more prevalent than commonsense.
Instead of Art and the unnatural
We've now the hideously actual.
The play's no more. Now all is visual,
The world's a stage; indeed all men are equal
Souls, actors, heroes, pimps as well;
Recording is their constant ritual
And applauding it, it is still trivial;
The mobile microphone makes poets of you all
And magnifies your eloquence—Yet still you are a Fool!

Enter a RADIO ANNOUNCER

ANNOUNCER Do you refer to me?

PROLOGUE   I do.

ANNOUNCER I'd have you know, Sir, that this is Clarence de la
Dell speaking. I am the premier announcer for the Oracle, and
this is an actuality relay from the sanctified studio reserved for
televising spiritual services and religious experiences. And who
are you? And how did you crawl in?

PROLOGUE   I am the Prologue.

ANNOUNCER The what?

PROLOGUE   I am the Prologue.

ANNOUNCER Poor chap. But never mind, just run along with
you.

PROLOGUE
To hell with you!
This was my play.

A light goes on

ANNOUNCER 'Ssh we're on the air.

PROLOGUE   To hell, I say!

ANNOUNCER Be quiet you fool!

PROLOGUE   I am a poet and a prologue too.
To hell with you!

ANNOUNCER [*whispering*]
'Ssh! Can't you see the light? We're on!
They hear us in the far Antipodes
You'll have to stay now
'Ssh! Be anything. Be dumb!

PROLOGUE [*shouting*]   A poet, dumb?

ANNOUNCER
'Ssh don't let it worry you.
Just join the crowd and do what I do,
Nobody will notice who or what you are.

PROLOGUE I'll join no crowd!

ANNOUNCER The Prologue's done, make up your mind; you
must either join the actors in the scene, or take your seat within
the audience.

PROLOGUE
A poet can do neither
Here's my place between the two.
I'll become the chorus, the modern commentator.

ANNOUNCER
Ladies and Gentlemen, this is Clarence de la Dell
Speaking and smiling. Good morning to you all.
This is the fifth program in the series:
'In search of Faith and religious experiences.'
Each week, as listeners and Viewers know
We follow the Astral Group, and shew
You what they see, and where they go
In search of faith.
For those who have not focused-in before,
I will repeat the outline of their tour.
First, the Group went to Canterbury
But finding no one there, flew on to Kiev
To interview the Dean on Christmas Eve
To a background of mounted Cassocks singing carols...

THE CHORUS [*still at proscenium arch*]
...Though dialectics is what they all believe!

ANNOUNCER
And the following week Dr Father Opine,

Who leads the Group, took us to Pimlico
Where in a well upholstered studio
Our dear ones who have passed beyond
Return...

CHORUS

...embroidered in cheap calico!

ANNOUNCER

And viewers will remember how the dead
Through 'Little Pansy' gave us messages
Concerning their good health, and better wages
For us within the circle; this séance proved,
There is no death...

CHORUS   ...For fools live in all ages!

ANNOUNCER

And the next week we joined the Gipsies' rites
In Hungary, then flew to India
In search of Faith and the great Yogi,
Whom as you know, we found at Manipur...

CHORUS

...sipping a gin and lime beneath a large umbrella!

ANNOUNCER

China has proved a happy hunting ground
For those in search of God: the soil's so poor
That nothing grows but faith and ancestors
Whose graves yield weeds for the tethered goat
From which it seems...

CHORUS

...that prayer goes with hand labour!

ANNOUNCER

The group has been to Mecca and Kabul
All religions have come within their scope
From Communism to the Band of Hope,
And from each creed they've culled a little Faith...

CHORUS

For us who've carried on with just a horoscope!

ANNOUNCER

And now today, Father Opine is here

To conduct the Astral Group to Zante
Where a christian ascetic, Antony,
Died exactly five hundred years ago.

CHORUS

And can you now record his exequies?

ANNOUNCER

Ladies and gentlemen. Let me introduce
Father Opine, our radio doctor
Eminent divine and commentator.

(Music alla marcia 1)

CHORUS   Where is this nomadic soul
Or is he stuck in some far orthodoxy?
A green light shines

ANNOUNCER

'Ssh. Over to Zante, over...

Exit ANNOUNCER. *The drop curtain lights up. It is a taunt muslin gauze with a black border and represents a television screen.* FATHER OPINE *stands behind the screen facing audience. The* CHORUS *remains at proscenium.*

FATHER OPINE

Friends, this is Father Opine speaking.
Mes amis ici Le père Opine encore.
Meine Freunde hier ist Vater Opine zu dichten
Good ones this is Father Thought to spoke...

CHORUS

...That last was basic English; you will note it rather flatters the
obese divine
—and what the devil did it do to his poor metre?

FATHER OPINE

Friends, here I am on the island of Zante
To record Antony's Anniversary
This program is by the great courtesy
Of Adriatic Hotels and company.
    The Astral Group now hovers into sight
One by one; the Adriatic sky's bright
With their heliotrope helicopters

As they circle the island sepulchre
Where we are to meet for this week's service.
   Enter several of group who sit in a circle round FATHER
   OPINE
Beside the Saint's ebony edifice
Which, over there, stands in strict austerity
A fitting tomb for the Saint Antony,
Who fasted unto death, for his soul's sake
But broke his fast, for pride was his mistake
Which hunger fed and dry thirst watered,
Till from his leathern skeleton appeared
The white and scarlet flower of secret lust
Which grows so well in all ascetic dust:
As rank and vicious weeds flourish from neglect
So hot desires grow in cold intellects
Until they melt the brain away, and age
Affects a buttonhole, taking courage
From desperation, makes a quick marriage
To a flirt—all impotency and rage,
That briefly explains the Saint's temptations
In terms of contemporary frustrations.
Saint Freud has more to say upon this subject
In his epistle to cause and to effect...

CHORUS
Observe:
This modern charlatan calls all in doubt
Science is his faith to Science he is devout
Cynicism is his psalm, fact his creed,
He follows reason where reason leads;
Though commonsense withdraws from the dull chase
He, riding reason, quickens the mad pace
In search of Faith, which he can never find,
For Faith is nothing but the state of mind
Of those who, knowing without the help of knowledge
See beyond and through the obscure image.

FATHER OPINE
I find nothing extraordinary

In these temptations of St Antony.
Desires like his may come to anyone,
The difference is: the Saint did not succumb.
But in the ecstasy of abstinence
Rose to perceive Christ's own sweet presence.
Was this a religious experience?
We do not know. Our terms of reference
Are inadequate for a conclusion
To be drawn: no doubt auto-suggestion
Will explain the case, or self-deception
Put it in its place of known phenomena
And alleviate our new dilemma
Of whether to believe in what we know
Or to believe in what we do not know.
That is called faith; or is it ignorance
Denying knowledge and experience
Their place in a rationalistic system
Which science and reason has accorded to them?
   Some viewers may have been here and will know
How picturesque this old myth is, and how
The Islanders of Zante still believe
That Antony comes back to them each eve
Of his anniversary, if they first
Put food for his fast and wine for his thirst
Beside his sepulchre, and there confess
Their fears, desires and wickedness.
And this they still do. In spite of their great poverty
Their best fruit or fowl is kept for their Saint Antony.
   Behind this speech: peasants place food at tomb, kneel and
   exit
   And now my Group alights to test this Myth
Before your eyes. We shall divide the truth
Strictly from the invented parable
Of traditional belief and fable;
So that members can base their faith on fact
If there is any here; and an exact
Record will be taken, any miracle weighed

Any levitation measured.
All resurrections accurately tested
And televised by disinterested
Observers of this Anniversary
Of St Antony's passion and Christ's mercy...
There! that zoom was our group leader's plane!
I know that pitch of her sports Hurricane
—a rocket firing model, emblazoned
With the doves of peace, and crowned
With the group's insignia: the double cross
The hammer, sickle, and the albatross.
Right now she's flown from Tokio
Where she's been lecturing to the Japanese
—they just come within her astral diocese.
And I daresay she stopped off at Mandalay
To see the golden shrine of Mrs Amie
Which she had put there
Replacing the old one of Buddha.
Here she comes now! Oh what a landing!
Viewers, excuse me. I'll just run and meet her.
Whilst I'm away—fill in the time with prayer.
                    Exit FATHER OPINE *back stage right*

CHORUS
Observe this priest of Science and Doctor of Divinity
With more caution than credulity
puffs out his puny chest with arrogance
To hide his heart's flat ignorance
Of God, to whom he kneels
    Only to count God's toes,
    To see whether the Divine conforms
    With homo sapiens and norms
    Laid down by anthropology,
    Modern hygiene and chiropody.
Give him his time, he will
Refurnish the bowels of hell
And with electric fans
Cool Satan's lust and make

Lazarus work an hydraulic ram
To raise up the last fall of man
From dust and hopelessness
To chromium progressiveness.
  Can no one stop this garrulous crusade
Before it converts us all to doubt,
And desecrates the Trinity,
Taking the square root of Faith
And hands us relativity?
Oh how the deserts of the heart contract
Watered by dryness and confounded fact!

(Alla marcia 2)

Re-enter FATHER OPINE, MISS PHILIPPA FORM *and
other members of group including* MAN OF CULTURE,
etc., etc.

FATHER OPINE
  Miss President, I have here a request
  From our group leader in the Philippines
  Which has joined the Oceanic League,
  And therefore is entitled to plug in
  To our wave band and hear our services,
  As we search for the international Faith
  Which will link men's hearts and souls together
  As closely as they're joined by telephone.
  The request is Miss Form that you should give
  A brief résumé of your spiritual crusade
  And tell the Filipinos how
  You came to found this astral group;
  Its aims, its charter and its privileges.
  Miss Form, why did you found the Astral Group?
MISS FORM [*approaching microphone*]
  Friends, that's a long story
ANNOUNCER [*poking head on to stage and whispering*]
                    Could you not make it shorter?
MISS FORM
  The red light to you!
                    Chants quasi blues

Well, my friends,
                    especially you Filipinos
I was born
                    Caesarian, in Minnesota
My mother was a baptist, my father was a jew
And I went to school in Tokio, to college in Peru.

And my friends,
                    I'm proud to be American,
Which makes me,
                    an international citizen
For as a child I saw a world split by religions
And divided by peculiar traditions.

But with the war,
                    the British joined with the Russians
And the Hindus
                    Yanks, chinks and the Mohamedans
Fought together for democracy
                    Which is the new form of Christian Orthodoxy.

Then with Peace,
                    I was appointed an official
To iron out
                    global differences, all spiritual
And make way for the era of co-operation
Which follows trade preceding all salvation.

Soon I saw
                    that regional culture was a heresy
Resisting
                    all new progress and efficiency.
I told my chief we must debunk all ancient deities
And found a faith on fact and sound bureaucracy.

The green light shone
                    'Philippa' he said 'O.K.' he said

And so I formed
                the Astral Group and went ahead
Testing myths
                and clearing out the Hindus' temples
And we took Mahomet from the Mohamedans.

And gave him
                for a while to the Tibetans
And we moved
                'That wise guy Kung' from the Confucians
And planted him amongst the Irish Catholics
All of which made everyone more eclectic.

And now friends
                here we are on this island Zante
To check up
                Saint Antony's centenary
And explode
                this medieval superstition
And open up the islanders' Horizon.

FATHER OPINE That Ladies and Gentlemen was the Founder,
Miss Philippa Form herself speaking and smiling to you from
Zante. Now everyone, let us join ourselves into the customary
circle round the microphone and then the new members will
appear and introduce themselves prior to their initiation.
    They begin to form circle, etc. FATHER OPINE *robes himself*
CHORUS
    At the grave risk of causing some offence
    To half the world and half my audience
    I must, as I'm a chorus, speak my mind
    Outright and tell you what I find
    Pertinent from this parade upon the stage
    And relevant to our dull dreary age.
    So at the risk of causing great offence
    To half the world and half this audience,
    I tell you that my nose does itch and that I smell
    Upon this stage the stench of some official.

And as you see, this one's a female
No woman! in officialese, a man's a male,
All buckets go as pails, and any bitch's a female.
— It saves some sorting at St Peter's Gate
And that old chap has strained his eyes of late
What with the Russians trying to get in
And Europe starved, too impotent to sin.
However, let us see this specimen
Who's neither hag, bitch, girl nor woman.
Note: that her bum is bigger than her head
And how her belly bulges with bureaucratic bread
White with the weight of all the alphabet
Of vitamins stuffed at last night's banquet
Given by a committee to a committee
To celebrate the birth of a committee.
And note how her little eyes are focused
To fit keyholes and how her lips are pursed
From sucking other people's privacy
And blabbing to divine bureaucracy.
See how she struts about the world.
Every state has bred its own disease, some
Have suffered from Republicans and some
From their own kings or ministers of state
Others by war or peace, and some from being great.
Each body distils its own foul poison
And dies too drunk to learn the lesson.
The Irish had their priests, the French were cursed
With Rousseau and Devonians depressed
by Wesley. And the Yanks by Henry Ford,
Spain by the Spaniards, Balkans by their discord
But no state or city sewer has bred so many Rats
As this great age with its small bureaucrats.

FATHER OPINE Now we are all ready, will the novices step
forward and share with us.

> *The* NOVICES *rise and one at a time approach micro-*
> *phone and sing a concerted number.*

> *(A Blues)*

GIRL

I'm a girl of Leisure
With nothing much to do
What other people go and see
I like to see it too.

I've seen all the releases
That have been on in Town
I've been all the places
And looked them up and down.

I've got an autogiro
And a television set
I've got a tiny studio
And I've taken on a bet

That I'll find a faith by Xmas
If I haven't got one yet
I've bought a Russian ikon
For what I just forget

But its quite queer and quaint
I'd like to buy a set
They'd go with my Picasso
Beside my novelettes.

My boy says I'm lacking
A sort of frigidaire,
Religion is exotic
And so I'm everywhere
    Searching for Faith and Love.

                              (A Boogie-woogie)

WOMAN

I'm a mobile worker
Without a fixed address
I follow Ernie Bevin
A caravan's my nest.

My husband's also mobile
We meet on New Year's Eve
At some quiet railway station
And then he takes his leave.

Last year he was a fitter
In the Southern Hemisphere
Whilst I was a truck driver
Going anywhere but there.

The worst of a mechanic
Is that they make love by phone:
My phone is not so phallic
To get children of its own.

I'm a mobile woman
And full of tenderness
My home's the post office
I've just a bank address

My days are quite legati
I wonder what I am at
My nights are Nagasaki
In other words just flat.
    Searching for Faith and Love.

MAN OF CULTURE
    I'm a man of culture
    With hands just like a fish
    I'm a sort of epicure
    Who'll eat from any dish

    So long as it's a rarity
    Cooked up by the minority
    With freedom and with haste
    I do not mind its taste.

I like my painting muddy
And all my verse obscure
My music without melody
You see I'm most mature.

Once when all religion
Did not fit into Marx
I debagged a curate
With comrades for a lark.

But fables myths and mysteries
Are quite the fashion now
And I'm a man of culture
Who's read his 'Golden Bough'.

I am a man of culture
I travel all alone
I've lost my destination
But I'm on the telephone
    Searching for Faith and Love.

CHORUS

The new illiterate is most well read
Quite half of Kant is carried in his head.
And he can write as well as any man
Free verse by yards or feet, his sonnets scan
And tell you more of culture, than they do of man.
Tea time conversation is his forte
He feeds in foyers at the ballet
Greets everyone who does not see him first,
For he never carries change but just a thirst
For culture, which only gin or sherry slakes;
Offer him another, if you pay, he takes;
If not, he leaves you with the bill and goes
Home, inspired with drink to be quite sick in prose;
Which if it reeks enough on quarto bond
Is called the novel of the week, second
Only to Mr...'s, but very near

In verbose reaching and diarrhœa.
The book is full of sexual intercourse
The Hero's normal; then the heroine's perverse.
No matter in chapter three they'll get together
And with more words than love seduce each other
Which shews they're cultured and intelligent
Characters
> *A Member of audience in stalls gets up and runs up main aisle*
        and like their author impotent.
A stall gets up and starts to sprint!
To Zwemmers?
Too late, Sir, the book is out of print!
> *The group encircle the Priest and partially disrobe*
> *(With accompaniment)*

FATHER OPINE
Now let our service
Start with our practice
Of five minutes' drill:
body relaxing,
deeply inhaling
one, two; one, two
there, that will do.
Now for a minute
Let's tone up our spirit
With your zippers undone
Let your thoughts have their run.
With our minds unrepressed
and our secrets undressed
let us reach for our goal
with a limbered up soul.
Now let us join hands and touch our feet
In a light fantastic beat
One two three and one
one two three and one
(A tune, someone)
one two three and one

that's well begun
we're in union.
Now that is done. We're in Union.
Will the novices approach the microphone.
                        They approach
Can you repeat the nine deadly sins.
                              (The following is intoned)
NOVICES Want is the first deadly sin.
FATHER OPINE   What is want?
NOVICES Want is the state of poverty.
FATHER OPINE   What is poverty?
NOVICES Poverty is the result of inefficiency.
FATHER OPINE   What is inefficiency?
NOVICES Inefficiency is the second deadly sin.
FATHER OPINE   And what is the third deadly sin?
NOVICES Peculiarity is the third deadly sin.
FATHER OPINE   What is peculiarity?
NOVICES Peculiarity is the state of the individual.
FATHER OPINE   What is the individual?
NOVICES The individual is abnormal.
FATHER OPINE   What is abnormal?
NOVICES Abnormal is the fourth deadly sin.
FATHER OPINE   And what is the fifth deadly sin?
NOVICES Tradition is the fifth deadly sin.
FATHER OPINE   What is tradition?
NOVICES Tradition is memory of the past.
FATHER OPINE   What is the past?
NOVICES The past is permanence.
FATHER OPINE   What is permanence?
NOVICES Permanence is the sixth deadly sin.
FATHER OPINE   And what is the seventh deadly sin?
NOVICES Disease is the seventh deadly sin.
FATHER OPINE   What is disease?
NOVICES Disease is the neglect of hygiene.
FATHER OPINE   - What is unhygienic?
NOVICES The unhygienic is the natural state.
FATHER OPINE   What is the natural state?

NOVICES The natural state is the eighth deadly sin.
FATHER OPINE   What is the ninth deadly sin?
NOVICES The love of the spirit is the ninth deadly sin.
FATHER OPINE   What is the spirit?
NOVICES The spirit is the unknown.
FATHER OPINE   What is the unknown?
NOVICES The unknown is where fear is.
FATHER OPINE   What is fear?
NOVICES Fear is the totality of sin.
FATHER OPINE Correct. You know your catechism. Can you
    repeat The Group's Motto?
NOVITIATES Eamus.
FATHER OPINE Which means?
A NOVICE Let's go!
FATHER OPINE Exactly. Do you promise to follow our leader?
A NOVICE We do.
FATHER OPINE
    And to pay your subscription regularly
    To fly the group's colours
    And make the group's sign?
NOVICES   We do.
FATHER OPINE
    And to each introduce a new member?
NOVICES   We do.
FATHER OPINE
    And to give freely of your libido to those within the group?
NOVICES   We do.
FATHER OPINE
    And to remain chaste and restrained with those outside the
    group?
NOVICES   We do.
FATHER OPINE
    And by these means introduce many a new member?
NOVICES   We do.
FATHER OPINE
    Disrobe, a little more please, stand unashamed.
    Do not be afraid: '*Per exhibionem inhibitiones purificamus*'

Now kneel and receive the group's insignia.

This entitles you to the Book of the Month each day of the week, free bed and breakfast at the group's hotel at Riga, Montevideo, Llasha, Chartres, Melbourne, Manipur and Yokohama. Also to a honeymoon chalet at Costa Rica, Dar-es-Salaam, Udaipur and Inverness. Now remain kneeling whilst the president performs the dance around you.

The group rise and dance around kneeling figures. They dance a Slow Waltz and freeze into statuesque positions within the dance when making their responses to FATHER OPINE *as follows:*

Do you believe in Man?

GROUP

Above man is thought
Below man is material
Man is the centre
We believe in Man
In his mind's effort
And his modest plan.

FATHER OPINE   Do you believe in Cause?

GROUP

Before Cause is effect
After cause is effect
Cause is the centre
We believe in cause
In known phenomena
And natural laws.

FATHER OPINE   Do you believe in Fact?

GROUP

Beyond fact is imagination
Behind fact is deception
Fact is the centre
We believe in fact
The recorded word
And the measured act.

FATHER OPINE   Do you believe in Reason?

GROUP
    Above reason is intuition
    Below reason is ignorance
    Reason is the centre
    We believe in Reason
    In strict deduction
    And comparison.

FATHER OPINE
    Let us sit down now and form a circle
    About the tomb and await the miracle.
                    The group seat themselves
    The time is eleven thirty-seven
    Precisely. At midnight the tomb opens
    And the Saint sheds his heavy sepulchre
    And blesses those who have confessed their fears
    here and knelt on knees that have knelt down for years
    wearing the stone away and washing it with tears,
    with bread in their hand for St Antony
    To eat and feed his hunger for humility.
    That is the myth. We shall see, and see all
    From here with eyes which are impartial
    And if by any chance a miracle
    Occurs, viewers will see it just as well
    As we will...

PHILIPPA FORM...Are the instruments in place?

FATHER OPINE They are.

PHILIPPA FORM Is the tomb adequately isolated?

FATHER OPINE
    Even the sepulchre is insulated
    No megacycle or spirit could intrude
    Into this circuit of investigation.
    Across the tomb photo-electric cells
    Direct their intersecting moon-like beams,
    Switch them on. You see they would deceive
    Any man or ghost by night. They are so sensitive
    A passing shadow will instantaneously break
    Their circuit and cause cameras to make

A record of any miracle or fake
And all this is automatically
Televised, instantaneously.

Enter an ISLANDER

ISLANDER
Postcards, postcards of the Tomb of St Antony.
One lira each.

FATHER OPINE Where are you from?

ISLANDER
From the village. Buy a postcard
Of the ebony tomb and help me to get some bread.

PHILIPPA FORM
We have our own cameras here,
Be quiet, sit down or go.

POSTCARD SELLER *sits on step of tomb*

FATHER OPINE Now who will volunteer to make a public confession of their fears?

PHILIPPA FORM That will be your honour, Father.

FATHER OPINE I did Miss President, just before you arrived.
Perhaps you will, as President?

PHILIPPA FORM Oh no, the privilege is for them who have just
joined us.

FATHER OPINE I agree. Will the novices then oblige and kneel
beside the tomb and confess their fears aloud and see if the Saint
appears. Everything is ready.

MOBILE WORKER. No, no. I can't do that.

THE GROUP Make her!

PHILIPPA FORM And why? Are you afraid?

MOBILE WORKER No, but I do not know what it is I fear.

THE GROUP Liar!

FATHER OPINE Then kneel, for they say, that in kneeling by this
tomb ourself is mirrored to ourself and our fears and faults
become as plain to us as are our neighbours' to us.

PHILIPPA FORM
It rises eleven forty.
Now then confess, and let

    Honesty produce its own lucidity
    And modesty persuade you into brevity.
THE GROUP Confess!
MOBILE WORKER [*kneeling*]
    I am afraid of remembering
    that which I have forgotten;
    I am afraid of forgetting
    that which I have remembered.
    For, all that I have is in dreams;
    Dreams which I remembered to forget
    and in dreams which I forgot to remember.
FATHER OPINE Now look into the tomb. Now.
MOBILE WORKER screams

    Do you see anything? Speak! Tell us what you see.
MOBILE WORKER I see a pair of eyes.
THE GROUP Whose eyes?
FATHER OPINE Are the cameras ready?
MOBILE WORKER
    I see who stares through my own eyes
    I see who lies behind my lies.
PHILIPPA FORM What lies behind the eyes?
MOBILE WORKER
    Nothing but nothing.
    All I can see is a pair of eyes
    There is nothing beyond
    And nothing behind
    but these eyes which are staring
    into these which are staring
THE GROUP. She's dreaming, she's dreaming, and wasting our
    time.
FATHER OPINE Nothing's recorded, quick, now your turn.
MAN OF CULTURE [*kneeling*]
    I fear all works of art
    I loathe its nudity
    and quick immediacy
    which disturbs the comfort of my mind
    and piercing the door to my upholstered soul

leaves me to plug the draught with argument,
theory and bits of critical detachment.
I fear all poetry
which takes me to the oasis
then leaves me in the desert of my soul's vacuity.

FATHER OPINE What do you see in the tomb? Does the Saint
appear?

MAN OF CULTURE I see a face.

THE GROUP First eyes and then face...

FATHER OPINE Whose face? Describe the face.

MAN OF CULTURE

I see a face
where neither character nor grace
disturbs the platitude of any feature;
indeed it's more a mask
portraying neither saint nor devil
with little virtue, much less evil.
The timid eyes with tiredness lean
against the mask and look
more indifferent than serene:
it is a neutral, normal look.

FATHER OPINE Still nothing is recorded. First eyes and then a
face. One more confession may bring the body, so kneel.

GIRL OF LEISURE [*kneels*]

I fear the time
when the phone is cut
When the tank runs dry
And the flick is shut.

I fear the time
When my book is read
When I've nothing to do
But say what's said.

I fear the time
When I'll wake up dead
And find death all dull
Like a day in bed.

FATHER OPINE Now look. Can you see anything?

GIRL Yes.

PHILIPPA FORM What?

GIRL A face.

FATHER OPINE Whose face? Whose face?

GIRL A woman's face.

FATHER OPINE A woman's? What is it like?

GIRL

I've seen this face somewhere before,
It's strange I can't quite place it
It must be someone whom I've met before
In the tube, or in a crowded shop's revolving door.
At anyrate, it doesn't matter,
She doesn't seem to know me either,
That's just as well, for I am sure
That we should never see
Eye to eye together.

FATHER OPINE Are you sure you see a woman?

GIRL Yes.

MEMBER OF GROUP The Saint was not a woman.

MEMBER OF GROUP Is anything recorded?

MEMBER OF GROUP Is the circuit broken?

MEMBER OF GROUP Nothing has passed the beams.

FATHER OPINE It is eleven-fifty. Miss Form, perhaps you will kneel and see what you can see.

PHILIPPA FORM No, after you.

FATHER OPINE [*goes to tomb*] Very well. How strange, I feel that I've stood beside this tomb before and that this tree's familiar. Which is impossible and only proves the complex mechanism of associated ideas, images and things.

PHILIPPA FORM And what do you fear, Father?

FATHER OPINE [*kneels*] This sudden voice within me.

PHILIPPA FORM What does it say?

FATHER OPINE

It says I fear Saint Antony
And hate him for his smug humility
And curse him for his bold simplicity

And that I fear his resurrection
More than the sea of doubt.

PHILIPPA FORM And do you see anything?

FATHER OPINE Yes.

GROUP

Oh hide us from the supernatural
This is enough, enough.

FATHER OPINE

I see a young man with an old book.
His lips in humble prayer, his eyes with a proud look
Look over my shoulder...
...Quick! A light here. There, there is nothing there.
Your vision of the saint was merely
Your own images reflected in the tomb's polished ebony.

PHILIPPA FORM And your vision, Father?

FATHER OPINE There's nothing here.

PHILIPPA FORM And your vision, Father?
Are you a young man with a proud look?

FATHER OPINE

It is difficult to judge the age of a face
When it is staring out of a tomb.
But there is nothing here,
Kneel for yourself Miss Form, and see there's nothing to fear.

PHILIPPA FORM

We've seen enough of nothing. Come on, let's go and eat.
[*Goes to microphone and puts hand over it*]
Is that mike dead? Well kill it!

Astral group go back stage and eat

CHORUS

As this Saint does not appear
It's plain that none of us need fear that time
When He who also died should rise again
And ask us what we have done with Him,
Whose Soul He said we are,
Whose Soul He said we wear
As borrowed clothes upon a borrowed back.

But Saint Antony does not appear
And we have proved that death is death;
And so; Rejoice! for Jesus cannot rise again
And mock our justice with his mercy
Puncturing our power with His meek piety
And damming up our passions with the cool austerity of love.
Rejoice! and welcome the new age of liberty
In which all men are free to die and doubt
And no one need kneel to faith's strict tyranny
For man is self-contained and there is no without.

CRITIC [*in audience*] And there I, for one, disagree with you. The Saint has not appeared for dramatic reasons. Not because this age lacks faith. One of the fundamentalweaknesses of this play is, to my mind, the author's shallow conception of the peoples' fears. The novitiates we have seen are mere clay pigeons for the point of cheap satire, quite unrepresentative of the public's inarticulate spiritual dilemma.

CHORUS That's true; is there anybody here who will volunteer to kneel by the Saint's tomb?

Two women approach CHORUS *from audience*

CRITIC
How can they when it is at Zante
and we are in the Ladbroke Grove?

CHORUS
We are where our thoughts are
Time was invented by clocks
And Place was discovered by Maps.
Allow me to accompany you
Chorus and two women step over black border of television screen into astral group scene.
                                   to where you are
And introduce you to Father Opine
whom you already know.

FATHER OPINE
The pleasure's wholly mine
We have already confessed our fears in public,
And were only rewarded with the echo of our voices

and the vision of our faces
reflected in polished ebony.
And now we are going to eat: then go.
Perhaps you'll join us, or are you looking for anybody?

1ST WOMAN Yes, A Man. He is dead.

FATHER OPINE Where did he die?

1ST WOMAN
He died here
And he died there.

FATHER OPINE Where Madam?

1ST WOMAN
They stoned him in Rome
They lynched him in Moscow
They bled him in Troy
They broke him at Toledo.
Have you seen my son?

FATHER OPINE No, Madam. How would I know him?

2ND WOMAN
By his eyes which are wet with your tears
By his blood which bleeds from your wounds
And by his scars.

FATHER OPINE Dear lady, what scars?

2ND WOMAN
In Babylon they whipped his back
And in Boston they kicked him
He has a scar on his head
Where they clubbed him at Buchenwald
But it is by the scar in his side that you will know him.

1ST WOMAN Have you seen him?

FATHER OPINE No, Madam.

2ND WOMAN We shouldn't have come here.

1ST WOMAN
Where else can we go?
Now that we are here
Let us kneel, for who knows.
                    They kneel

1ST WOMAN
   I have forgotten all my prayers.
   I do not know what to say.

2ND WOMAN
   Nor I, then how can we pray?
   What shall we say?

CHORUS Tell me your trouble?

1ST WOMAN   I am a woman.

CHORUS Why do you grieve?

2ND WOMAN   I am a mother.

CHORUS For what are you looking?

1ST WOMAN   I am a widow.

CHORUS What is your trouble?

2ND WOMAN   We filled our hearts with love
                           Who'll help us lift our sorrow?

CHORUS No man can.

1ST WOMAN   Is there no hope
                           No one to help?

CHORUS   Only a Son can,
                           Lift a Mother's sorrow.

2ND WOMAN Where is my son?

1ST WOMAN   I am a young woman
                           growing old in grief.
                           Is there no hope
                           no one to help?

CHORUS Only one man can.

2ND WOMAN   I am his widow.

1ST WOMAN   And I his mother.

BOTH WOMEN   There is no other.

CHORUS What do you fear?

1ST WOMAN   That we shall not find

CHORUS For what are you looking?

✻   ✻   ✻

(Canzone)

2ND WOMAN
    The knowledge that death
                        is not a permanent state
    Irrevocable
                and final:
                        a punishment
    A merciless judgment,
                        without the hope of reprieve,

1ST WOMAN
    Passed on us at birth
                        with the intolerance of fate's
    Endless festivals
                of funerals.
2ND WOMAN   Our life is spent
    Keeping this one appointment
                        walking up and down with grief.

1ST WOMAN
    When death was just a parting it was difficult to bear,
    Women left were
                        busied with their dead's clean linen
    For his journey on to heaven;
                            their grief had this consolation
    Death to them was temporary separation.

2ND WOMAN
    Now give us back our faith in heaven and hell
    And it will
                make our mourner's prison open
    And our heavy hearts enliven.
                            Tell us death is a transition
    From life to life. Show us the wheel of recreation.
        The CHORUS *makes a gesture of hopelessness*

*   *   *

1ST WOMAN It's no use kneeling here and not saying a word, I have forgotten how to pray.

2ND WOMAN I also. If only our hearts could speak like a poet, if only Saint Antony could hear my dumb heart's prayer, he would rise from his sepulchre.

1ST WOMAN [*rises*] The trouble with us is that we are too proud for prayer and not wise enough for faith. There is nothing for us but death within and doubt without. Let's go.

2ND WOMAN Where shall we go?

1ST WOMAN Home. There is nothing here but a few postcards of a Saint's sepulchre.

2ND WOMAN [*still kneeling*] For Pity's sake, Christ, give me what I need and do not ask for, lift me into your Mercy.

FATHER OPINE I am sorry you are disappointed. We are too—though not surprised. These myths are picturesque but little more and collapse to ashes on investigation. It's midnight now and we are just going.

Enter an OLD MAN

Who are you?

OLD MAN   My name is Antony.

FATHER OPINE

That's very odd.

Where have you come from?

OLD MAN   I come from God.

FATHER OPINE

Did you hear that?

He's very glib

How long have you been here?

OLD MAN   In and out of time

Five hundred years.

FATHER OPINE

I suppose you'll tell us you're the Saint.

OLD MAN   I was an abbot of Ferrata.

The one who died from too much pride.

FATHER OPINE

Then you do claim to be Saint Antony?

OLD MAN   I am he to whom the woman called.

FATHER OPINE
   Which woman?
   No one here has called

OLD MAN   She who is afraid of death.

MEMBERS OF GROUP
   We all fear death
   That tells us nothing.

OLD MAN   She whose son is dead.

WOMEN OF GROUP
   Many of us have lost our sons
   That tells us little either.

OLD MAN   She who doubted there was life
               After the flesh decays.

MEMBERS OF GROUP
   We all doubt that
   That gets us nowhere.

OLD MAN   She who saw her doubt was pride
               And with faith cried to Christ for mercy.

FATHER OPINE
   It was none of us then
   If we doubt
   It is because we do not know
   and what we do not know we shall discover.
   Doubt is our reverence to the future
   Doubt is our mind's humility.

OLD MAN   Humility to what?
               Humility to your mind's ability?

FATHER OPINE
   We trust our own minds
   We believe in the precision of our instruments
   We have faith in our surgeons' skill.
   With these we will cross the deserts of ignorance
   With these, if we are given time.

OLD MAN   Time is a desert without a clock.
               Knowledge is a desert without the sand.
               Faith is where there is water:
                   You must drink or die.

> A man cannot lead the horse on which he is
> riding
> A man cannot lift the chair on which he is
> sitting.
> A man cannot see the invisible image behind his
> eyes
> Or know the whole of which he's part, however
> wise.
> The deserts of man blow through the heart of God
> The heart of God is incomprehensible
> For only God can understand.

FATHER OPINE Do you or do you not claim to be the saint?

OLD MAN I am to you what you think I am.

FATHER OPINE And that?

OLD MAN

> You think of me as a young man
> Of mental ability and natural vigour.
> A man who had dissolved the pearls of night
> Into the wine of love and drunk
> And drowned within the rivers of her eyes.
> And slept and seen the morning light
> Absolve her breasts from ravishment
> A man who had curbed the hot steed of his virility
> With the rough girdle of impatient chastity
> Restrained within the shafts of his vocation,
> Renouncing love and temporal ambition
> And became a priest, thinking he should be an abbot,
> And became an Abbot, thinking he should be a saint.
> A man who tried to climb to Christ with his own strength
> But did not reach him;
> Who then, from weakness fell and knelt
> And kneeling saw Him.
> Is that not what you think of me?

FATHER OPINE No

OLD MAN

> Do you not recognise me?
> You who were always at my side?

FATHER OPINE I do not recognise you.

OLD MAN

If then, my pride has finally forsaken me
Where is humility to recognise me?

PHILIPPA FORM

Well, I know you're just bogus.
A local guy presuming on our credulity
trying to get some publicity.
Ain't that just so?

OLD MAN You say you know.

PHILIPPA FORM

Of course I know.
They pulled this stunt in Tokio
last week, when I was there
examining some cult of Buddha
A local faked a miracle,
But my camera caught him at it.

    The Group surround the OLD MAN, *who is knocked
    down, where he remains till the group leave*

1ST VOICE Let's photograph him.

2ND VOICE And televise him.

3RD VOICE Let's take him to London and put him on show.

4TH VOICE And feed him to death in a cage in the zoo.

1ST VOICE Let's lionise him

2ND VOICE   and analyse him,

3RD VOICE he's only a beggar scrounging for bread

4TH VOICE a louse ridden parasite who ought to be dead.

1ST VOICE If he's a saint
            Well I'm St Swithin.

2ND VOICE If he's the saint
            I'm just a lemon.

3RD VOICE Let's open the tomb and see what's there.

            They open tomb

    Nothing there! Empty. Not even a bone there

PHILIPPA FORM

Viewers can witness that a fake is proved
No saint or shadow crossed the beam or moved

G

To disturb the circuit round the sepulchre
And science is our impartial arbiter.
This myth of Antony's resurrection
Is merely insular superstition
Persisting on account of bad transport,
lack of research and scientific thought.
I found the same thing in the Hebrides
And in Formosa and in Benares.
And I have proved that all these cults are fake
And none of them have any right to speak
Either for faith or fact and cannot claim
Anything from man but doubt: doubt is our aim
For when the whole world shares the selfsame doubt
The world will have much less to fight about.

2ND VOICE Come on, let's leave here.

1ST MEMBER Where do we go from here?

2ND MEMBER   There.

1ST MEMBER But we've been there.

3RD MEMBER   Where?

2ND MEMBER Where we are going.

3RD MEMBER   Oh there.

2ND MEMBER   We must hurry!
                                The faster we go
                                The longer we have there!

1ST MEMBER The sooner we start
            The quicker we leave there!

3RD MEMBER Where?

2ND MEMBER Where we are going.

3RD MEMBER   Why are we going?

1ST MEMBER   Why are we going!

2ND MEMBER Why are we going!

1ST MEMBER   We are leaving here
                                Because we have been here,
                                We are going there
                                Because we are going there.
                                We are going to see
                                What we haven't seen,

We are going to do
What we haven't done;
When we have seen it
And when we have done it,
We shall have been there
Where we have not been,
And then, then is the time to think
of tomorrow.
Till then, let us hurry.

ANNOUNCER
Ladies and gentlemen, that concludes
Our relay from Zante. We follow with the news.

Exit the ASTRAL GROUP, *after collecting their instruments and remains of feast: the two women follow them. The gauze curtain, which has been down so far, is now lifted.* POSTCARD SELLER *left on stage, he picks up a piece of bread which he hides under his coat as his wife enters.*

WIFE Have they all gone? Did they buy anything? Did they leave anything? I'm hungry. We have eaten nothing today and we have no supper.

POSTCARD SELLER [*looking at remains of feast*]
They haven't left a thing
And they didn't buy a postcard.

WIFE Nothing? How's that, you usually sell a few postcards.

POSTCARD SELLER They had their own cameras and they left in a temper after they opened the tomb...

WIFE ...opened the tomb? Not the tomb of Saint Antony?

POSTCARD SELLER Yes, they opened his tomb.

WIFE And what was there in it?

POSTCARD SELLER They couldn't see anything.

WIFE You mean it was empty! There, how long have I told you there was nothing in it and begged you to leave this island and get a job like a man on the mainland? But no, you had to stay here like your father before you and all of your line to be by your precious Tomb of St Antony.

POSTCARD SELLER Hold your tongue.

WIFE I'm glad they have opened it, I'm glad it is empty. To-morrow you will leave and get a job that will keep us and give us something to eat as regularly as I feel hungry. Now come home and tomorrow we'll leave here. Who's that lying down over there?

POSTCARD SELLER An old man. He said he was St Antony and so they knocked him down.

WIFE [*goes over to him*] He's dead to the world. Who is he, I wonder. He's not from the village. Perhaps he's a servant from the big hotel. A saint! Empty!

She goes off laughing

POSTCARD SELLER *goes to the* OLD MAN

POSTCARD SELLER Come on now. Wake up. They've gone. Did they hurt you? I must say you asked for it. Come on now, wake up, you're not dead yet.

OLD MAN Did you sell any postcards?

POSTCARD SELLER No, they're as mean as sin and you didn't help things by putting them in a temper.

OLD MAN I'm hungry.

POSTCARD SELLER You're hungry! I like that, there's my own wife gone without supper.

OLD MAN Haven't you got anything for me to eat.

POSTCARD SELLER [*taking bread from coat*]
Only this which I picked up.
And I don't mind telling you I'm famished too.

OLD MAN But you can give me half of it.

POSTCARD SELLER None of it.

OLD MAN You wouldn't eat it in front of me and not give me any.

POSTCARD SELLER Who's going to eat? None of this bread will be eaten by you or by me. This is all I have this year, but this is Saint Antony's.

OLD MAN Surely we could have half of it.

POSTCARD SELLER None of it.

OLD MAN But you know his tomb's empty.

POSTCARD SELLER [*goes to tomb*]. Yes, I know his tomb's empty.

OLD MAN [*goes to tomb*]. Then why do you deny yourself and give
the Saint the bread?

POSTCARD SELLER I don't know, but I must. I've done it all my
life and my father before me and now they've opened the tomb
and proved it empty I must kneel here just the same. Why is
that, can you tell me?

OLD MAN Yes, my son.

POSTCARD SELLER Why?

OLD MAN It is faith, Marcus.

MARCUS Father Antony [*He kneels*]

ANTONY
When peasants believe
And Saints appear
What is the poet's comment
Or is the Chorus silent?

CHORUS Are you Saint Antony?

ANTONY
While you are imprisoned in your own passions,
I am merely an old man;
The object alters with the eye.
But if you were to submit
to the voice within you...

CHORUS Then I should sing...

ANTONY Then sing, Julian.

JULIAN [*singing*]
Night is no more
than a cat which creeps
to the saucer of light
    laps, then sleeps.

Night is no more
than the place waves reach
with their hands of surf
    seeking the beach.

Night is no more
than the hounds of fear

with bloody jowl and bark
   bullying the year.

Night is no more
than my love who lies
She dreams of a dream
   lives, then dies.

ANTONY My sons.

MARCUS Take the bread, Father.

ST ANTONY I will divide it.

                              He takes bread. They rise

MARCUS No no, Julian, you divide it. Father Antony will break
   it into three pieces and keep none for himself. I know! I know!

ST ANTONY
   I need none
   I seek the sacrifice and not the feast.
   The single soul wandering through a waste of years
   Wears out its several bodies
      And dissolves the ash in tears
   Searching for its endless sleep
      behind the eyes of tired stars
   And there it creeps into the side of God
   From whence it was torn from, born,
   And back in whom the dream we are, eventually resides.
   I can only be Saint Antony
   When my three attributes
   body, desire and intelligence
   Make me complete by each
   Confounding their own separate frailty.
   My body, Marcus, has denied itself
   and thus fed me, recognised me.
   And in Julian, my senses have found their innocence again
   And stopped the fret of small complaint
   and let the night blow over the chords of the heart,
   to make a song to wake me from the sleep of personality
   into the joy of selfless art.

But yet I cannot be whilst my intelligenc
Enter FATHER OPINE
struts in a state of knowing,
Not wise enough for faith.

FATHER OPINE

I am treading an old path with new feet.
I am standing in footprints already in my mind.
Is not the test of reason to put it to a fear?
And it was here the ferret's tooth of fear struck at my bone
And the draught of alarm blew out my reason.
When I knelt here before
I felt I had knelt here before;
And now this tomb reflects
Secrets beyond the image;
It is as though I am remembering
A dream I had not dreamt;
Or saw the photos on an unexposed and undeveloped film;
now the piano plays the pianist.
If I can remember what I have not known
Then what I know is hardly worth forgetting.
But to kneel to this tomb,
Pray to this stone,
Is to bend the back of reason.

ST ANTONY Is not belief in reason an act of faith?

FATHER OPINE Faith is the end of reason.

ST ANTONY Without faith, Bernard, there is no reason.

BERNARD

It has been a long journey
Those who are given most
Have most to throw away.
How is it that we remember?

* * *

(Canzone)

ST ANTONY

To live is to remember,
   to die is to forget;

Present existence
                        is all reminiscence,
                                            memory
Of our imperishable soul's past journey
                                        woven in and out of time
As strands which never sever,
                            we thread death to birth and get
New feet for the old dance;
                            then, in a trance
                                            of illusory
And receding imagery
                        dream and renew the climb

Back to the mind of God where our deathless soul began
And knew oblivion.
                        Back from death to infancy,
Back from birth to our last exequy
                                    over and over climb to where
We came from and return when He, remembering us,
                                    recalls us, and pities our despair.

Behind the forgotten poem lies the remembered vision.
And this song
                    which I sing in a bewildered ecstasy
Seeks its first silence with loud urgency.
                                        I know who you are;
And you, in recognising me, prove that our souls
                                    remember by forgetting self in prayer.

BERNARD [*kneels*]
    Father.

                        *   *   *

ANTONY
    Man's soul is virtue;
                            his nature evil,

Full of self, brutal,
              material,
                    visible
And therefore perishable.
                  But the ageless soul survives
In so far as it stays pure
                And sustains its vigil
And remains unnatural,
              invisible,
                  indissoluble,
thus immortal,
          the ghost of God walking through our lives

It is easier to question than accept the answer
And there are
          those who deny the spirit
Because they cannot weigh it.
                But beauty is immeasurable
And we perceive it through the projection of our soul's sad eyes.

If we were nothing but fleshy vehicles of small desire
Masked with fear,
              What in us would define desire's limit
Restrain the voluptuary, make the hermit?
                Nor can you say the soul's inseparable
From the body and is to it as harmony to the lyre,
                  death silencing the whole.

BERNARD
And, Father, is the soul immortal?
Is there life after death?

        *   *   *

ANTONY
Everything must renew,
          nothing living is immutable.

The fairest flower
                falls in the hour
                                and becomes dust
As the proudest Emperor must
                    and leave the purple canopies of Rome
For the sepulchre's strict curfew.
                            Nor are the dead unchangeable;
Death's solid splendours
                life devours
                        through the soil's lust
The seed takes, and the thirsty roots thrust,
                —and as a cabbage, Kings re-enter Rome.

If the wheel did not revolve and all life upon this earth
Died in death
                and did not quicken,
Nor reawaken,
                and the severed lay forever fallen
And the buried body were forever broken,

Then in time all life would lie absorbed in greedy death
And no birth
                from the tomb could quicken
Nor from the womb awaken.
                      From Life our death is taken,
From death our life is drawn. So with our souls. Amen.

CHOIR A CAPELLA
Gloria patri, et filio, et spirtui sancto.
Sicut erat in principio, et nunc, et
Semper, et in saecula saeculorum. Amen.

CURTAIN

St Spiv

A COMEDY

CHARACTERS

KATE	A Seller of Flowers
BERT	A Coster
ARCHIE	A Spiv
HORACE	A Pickpocket
MAX	A Newspaper Boy
BEN	A Street Musician
LAZARUS	A Blind Beggar
PENNY	A Street Girl
MADAME SARTRE	A Palmist
LADY RECENT	
THE REV CUTHBERT	
MR SPLEEN	
GABRIEL MUSCATEL	A Film Producer
POLICEMAN	

A Bookmaker, an Assortment of Idiots
A Receptionist, Patients, etc.

Act I

SCENE ONE

A tired, untidy London street, which on the stage can be adequately suggested by a lamp-post, an Underground Tube station sign, two placards, a couple of costers' barrows, and a pub sign. No sets to represent buildings need be used.

It is about 9 o'clock on a fine evening in June.

MAX, the newspaper boy stands at his pitch outside the Tube. He is a ferret of a man; just two profiles stuck together and a placard tied round his middle. KATE and BERT are arranging their barrows. Hers contains white lilac and mimosa; whilst his is heaped with white heart cherries.

KATE is about fifty. A well-bosomed woman who carries all before her. She wears a black apron which has two large square pockets in the front for loose change. As she fusses over her flowers, giving the tired mimosa a good shake, or lifting the lilac out of its bucket and snapping ends off its stalks, she gives the impression of a large broody hen.

About BERT, there is nothing but baldness and belly and a large brass stud in the front of his collarless shirt. He is picking over his fruit, putting the best to the front of his stall and the worst into paper bags. He whistles, or thinks he does.

Against the lamp-post outside the Tube, PENNY, a very pretty gamin of a girl, leans, eating an apple with unashamed pleasure; her teeth are quite obviously her own.

She is certainly not soliciting, but hoping to be picked up. But she is not a tart, nor is she dressed like one. Her hair is combed, but not crimped, set, waved or dressed. She wears a boy's shirt which has been carefully left unbuttoned, and a skirt which has, one suspects, been deliberately torn. Yet for all that, there is nothing in her appearance to suggest that it is calculated. On the contrary, her exposure is so artless as to be almost modest. Nor is her wantonness wickedness. It is just that she is too pretty to be good.

Meanwhile, she is teasing BEN, *a down-at-heel street musician, who is busy tuning his fiddle. The case lies open before him on the kerb. He plays on and off throughout the scene.*

And in the shadow of the pub, a BLIND BEGGAR (HORACE) *stands unobtrusively, a white stick in his left hand, a white enamel mug in the other. He wears dark glasses and a cardboard notice hanging from his neck which reads 'Blind'*

THE CURTAIN RISES

MAX
  Evening Standard! Late Night Final!
  Evening Standard! Late Night Final!
  All the runners for tomorrow!

BERT Waiting for anybody particular, Penny?

KATE I should say! Anybody's to pick up!

BERT Nah then, Ma, don't be jealous!

KATE Jealous? Ain't there enough on this bleeding street without her propping up lamp-posts?

PENNY [*Walking slowly over to* KATE]. You wouldn't be suggestin' anythin' would you, Ma? If you are—I'll slosh your kisser!

BERT Nah then, ladies!

KATE I ain't suggestin' nothing. But mark my words. If you go standing there of an evening the Council might charge you rent for that post.

BERT Leave Penny alone, Ma; she ain't doing no harm.

KATE 'Course she is, stupid, can't you see that? It takes people's
eye away from me stall and Gawd knows this 'ere lilac's looking
limp enough without any competition from 'er. Now where did
I put me aspirin?

> *She searches her stall; then puts a couple of aspirins in the
> pail where the lilac stands. She takes a small jug and
> douches the flowers. One or two people come out of the
> Tube.*

MAX

Evening Standard! Late Night Final!
Derby call-over! All the runners for Epsom!

BERT Half a dollar a pound. Fine Kentish cherries!

KATE Lovely lilac! Three bob a bunch! Lovely lilac...fresh as...

> *The people go off down the street*

KATE My feet. Cor...I ain't sat down since...

PENNY ⎫
       ⎬ [*imitating*]...out of bed I got this morning!
BERT ⎭

KATE You make me laugh—like a drain!

BERT What about pushing the boat out, ducks? I've got a thirst
on me like a bleedin' bishop. I could drink the Thames dry if it
was all turned to stout.

KATE Well, ask Archie to treat yer. He looks as prosperous as a
ruddy brewer.

> ARCHIE *comes in briskly. He carries a small attaché case.
> He is dressed in a flashy coat, pointed shoes and black hat,
> with a white silk muffler round his neck. He takes up his
> stand in the gutter and undoes his case. The others watch
> him with considerable curiosity, out of the corners of their
> eyes.*

BERT What's yer line today, Archie?

ARCHIE This'll fetch 'em. Just you wait and see. It's a cinch.

KATE [*to* ARCHIE] And where do you think you're mussling in?
Can't you keep to yer own pitch down there? This 'ere street's
getting as crowded as Petticoat Lane. No wonder me lilac's all
limp. You move down a bit. Go on now.

ARCHIE All right, all right, keep your 'air on, Ma. I'm going. [*He*

H

moves down a little]. This'll fetch 'em. You see if it don't. [*He takes a razor out of his case and strops it.*]

BERT Cor stone the crows. [*Derisively.*] I thought you said you'd got 'old of somethink noo?

ARCHIE *arranges a few brightly coloured packets on a tray. He is aware of their interest. Then he takes one packet and empties it into a tumbler of water which he has on his tray. The water goes blue. They watch him with respect, suspicion and ridicule.*

KATE Conjurer, eh? Mind yer don't turn yerself into a ruddy rabbit.

A few people come out of the Tube. ARCHIE *immediately begins to lather his face with a shaving brush.*

MAX
Evening Standard! Evening Standard!
All the runners for tomorrow!

BERT
Fine Kentish cherries. Cherry ripe.
Half a dollar a pound.

KATE
Lovely lilac, lady. Buy a bunch of lilac.
Go on, duck, for luck.

The passers by ignore the others but stop opposite ARCHIE *who continues to lather his face.*

ARCHIE [*mounting a box*] Ladies and gentlemen, step up and see the latest invention of Science and...

PENNY [*interrupting*] ...spivery.

ARCHIE [*unabashed*] And I will show you 'ow democratic man has rid 'imself of his last tyranny. I have here... [BEN *fiddles a little louder*]...I 'ave 'ere [*to* BEN] 'ere Ben, will you stop scraping away regardless, there's a chum. [*Continuing*] I 'ave 'ere, as all of you can see, a razor, an ordinary safety razor of a well-known and reliable make, such as any one of you might use. Wot am I going to do? Show you 'ow to shave! [*At this a man turns to go.*] You think you know, sir? 'Alf a mo, cock. Just you show me what to do and take this ten bob for the lesson, sir. [*He hands a ten shilling note over to the man, then continues to lather his face.*] First of all you lather yer face. Correct? Now wot's the next thing we do? We shave. That done, we dry our face. Is that not right? And then? We take the thing to pieces, drop it, dry it on a towel, cut the towel, cut ourselves and this way sharpen our temper and blunt our razor. Is that not wot you do, sir? It is, sir! And that's where we two differ. For when I've shaved I take the darn thing, thus; and drop it so...into this tumbler of clean water. It will rust? It will NOT rust! And why? In this water I've put...VORTAX! One packet, one shilling. It lasts a year. And every morning, VORTAX will save you: Towels, Temper and Time...and time is money! Two minutes saved each day is a week a year. A week spent drying yer ruddy razor! And wot's a week worth to you, or you, sir? Ten quid, I warrant! You can 'ave that for a bob. [*He sells the same man a packet.*] Now give me my ten bob back, sir...yer still nine quid to the good! [ARCHIE *now sells all his packets to the crowd*]

KATE [*rather downhearted*] Lovely limp—er—fresh lilac!

BERT White 'eart cherries, one bob a packet...

MAX *Evening Standard!* All the suckers for tomorrow.

The crowd drifts off

BERT Ain't 'arf got the gift of the gab!

KATE Shouldn't be surprised if he 'adn't been vaccinated with a gramophone needle.

ARCHIE Didn't I tell yer they'd fall for it?

BERT Can see which side of Aldgate pump you were born, chum! Bob a packet! Not a bad line at all. Not bad at all. What is it? Chelsea mud?

ARCHIE That would be telling wouldn't it? But I won't. I had to pay real dough for this formula. Bought it off a bloke called Einstein.

KATE [*shocked*] Wot! That cove wot carved women naked?

BERT Well, now p'raps you'll push the boat out?

A woman comes out of the Tube; she is unobserved by the spivs. She drops a coin into the BLIND MAN'S *mug.*

BLIND MAN Thank you, mum. [*Slight pause*]

WOMAN If you're blind, how did you know I was a lady?

BLIND MAN I didn't, mum. I jest 'oped you were...and still are...

[*The woman sniffs derisively and goes off*]...and I 'eard yer walk, ma'am.

KATE What an 'owler. Who is it? That can't be Lazarus?

BERT Must be his stand-in.

ARCHIE He'll ruin his pitch if he ain't careful.

BERT Cor 'ere's Lazarus hisself. 'E won't 'arf be wild.

Another BLIND BEGGAR *comes up the street. He also has a white stick which he uses to tap on the kerb, and also carries a white enamel mug, and wears dark glasses and a notice round his neck 'Blind'.*

BERT 'Ere, mate, some bleeding cove's been and gorn and pinched your pitch.

LAZARUS Wot?

BERT Yeah, he's making a rare mess out of it too. We didn't turn 'im off. Thought he might be your understudy like.

LAZARUS *stands erect. He no longer taps his way. But using his white stick as a cudgel, strides straight to the other* BLIND MAN, *who cowers in his corner.*

LAZARUS Come orf it! Wot the bloody 'ell d'yer think yer up to, eh?

BLIND MAN [*from his collar*] Nothink!

LAZARUS Nothink! Pinching a pitch from a poor blind old man when he ain't lookin'! [*He drags him out.*] You're nothing but a damned impostor, and I bet you're no more bleedin' blind than I am.

LAZARUS *hits the other* BLIND MAN. *They fight, using their white sticks, the impostor getting very much the worst of it.*

MAX *Evening Standard*. All the latest on the big fight!

ARCHIE Come on little 'un. Give us our money's worth!

PENNY 'It 'im in the...

MAX ...Wall's Ice Cream! Wall's Ice Cream!

KATE Nah then, mind me lilac!

The fight is at its most furious. Unnoticed by the others, a SANDWICH MAN *shuffles up the street. He carries a board in front of him, behind him and one above his head. The top board reads 'ENGLISH MISSION*

SOCIETY' *the other two boards are inscribed* 'GOD IS LOVE'. *Another* SANDWICH MAN *enters from the opposite direction. His top board reads* 'ODEON CINEMA' *the bottom two* 'SHOWING CONTINUOUSLY, 'THIS WAY TO THE RAPE'. Both* SANDWICH MEN *remove their boards and prop them outside the pub. They go into their respective Bars. The swing-doors swing behind them. For a second the pianola is heard inside. The fight continues. Then* MAX *whistles. Everybody freezes instantly. Both* LAZARUS *and the* IMPOSTOR *stand begging, one each side of the pub.* KATE, BERT *and* ARCHIE *rush to their stalls. A woman comes out of the Tube.*

MAX *Evening Standard!* Late Night Final!

BERT Fine English cherries! 'Arf a dollar a pound!

KATE Lovely lilac, lady...

ARCHIE Don't dry yer razor...

The woman passes the costers, but puts a coin into each of the BLIND BEGGAR'S *mugs, then goes off.*

LAZARUS Thank you, sir.

BLIND MAN [*hesitantly*] —er—bless you.

LAZARUS [*looking into his mug*] A bob, struth! [*He rushes up to the Impostor's mug*] Who's pitch is this anyway? Come on now, are yer going to 'and it over, or do I 'ave to tear your teeth out first?

LAZARUS and the IMPOSTOR *fight again over the shilling. During the scrimmage the* IMPOSTOR'S *dark glasses fall off.*

LAZARUS Why knock me down, if it ain't the Squire!

BERT Poor bloody little 'Orace.

PENNY Leave 'im alone.

ARCHIE Kind of sweet on the Squire, ain't you, Penny?

PENNY Shut yer gob. Where you bin, 'Orace? Ain't seen yer anywhere for months?

HORACE I bin away, Penny, down in the country, you know.

BERT H'at your country seat I suppose, Squire. Wot again? Garn, ain't you ashamed of yerself?

ARCHIE Why don't you take yer 'at orf when a lidy speaks to
to yer, eh? [*He yanks* HORACE'*s hat off*] There, why don't you
show 'er where you've bin?

HORACE *feels his shaven head*

PENNY Leave 'im alone! Never mind, 'Orace, I like to see yer
'air short, it shows up the shape of yer 'ead. And if any nosey
parker asks why you wear it like that, just say you bin a monk
for a time.

KATE [*sings*]

'I've been down at me place in the country,
Where the ruddy birds all sing,
I've been down at me place in the country,
As the guest of the King.'

BERT 'Ow long did they send you up for? Six months, wasn't it?
Clumsy lout! You're not smart enough even for bag snatching,
let alone lifting a wallet. Why don't yer go straight, 'Orace?
Yer too simple to make a decent, dishonest shilling.

ARCHIE If yer can't do anything else, why don't yer earn yer
living like other suckers 'ave to?

HORACE 'Ave to wot?

ARCHIE Work, 'Orace.

KATE Some 'ope.

PENNY Surely yer could find something light—like being a night
watchman. You 'ave to be born to it to pick pockets, don't yer,
Archie?

ARCHIE I should say.

PENNY Yeah, born as crooked as a corkscrew. No use having
fingers like a bunch of bananas.

ARCHIE Don't mind telling yer—it's a skilled job, it's a pro-
fession.

PENNY Surely yer could do somethink, 'Orace?

HORACE Wot with?

PENNY Yer 'ands, of course.

HORACE Wot, me navvy, not bloomin' likely.

PENNY Couldn't yer sell things same as Bert and Archie? Why
don't yer 'ire a barrow?

KATE 'E couldn't sell a carrot to a donkey.

BERT If 'e did it'd be a good un and 'ed find 'imself out of pocket. Why don't yer stand for Parleyment?

MAX Or emigrate? Yer could go to Orstralia. I got a cousin dahn there in Quebec.

HORACE I'll show yer, just you wait.

ARCHIE Sure we'll wait, if we live long enough.

PENNY Can't you leave 'im alone?

ARCHIE Orl right, nurse.

BERT Nah wot abaht pushing that boat out, chum?

ARCHIE Come on then, let's drink to termorrow's losers. May all the 'orses be left at the post, especially the Aga Khan's. Cor, there aren't 'arf some dough on it. [*He goes into 'The Cock and Bull'*]

BERT [*following him*] All right, Ma, come and gargle a pint.[*The door swings behind him*]

KATE [*following*] Keep an eye on me lilac, Penny.
　　　LAZARUS *follows the others into the pub. The pianola is heard through the door. A slight pause.*

PENNY Wot's it like there, 'Orace? Outside, I mean, in the country?

HORACE Ain't you ever seen it?

PENNY Course I 'ave—on the flicks and from a bus. It must be 'orribly lonely.

HORACE Why?

PENNY All that space and just nothink but dirt.

HORACE There ain't much dirt, Penny.

PENNY Course there is, miles and miles of nothing only dirt.

HORACE That ain't dirt, Penny—that's soil.

PENNY Wot's the difference?

HORACE Things come out of soil. Beautiful things like lilac and cherries.

PENNY Don't nothink come out of dirt then?

HORACE Nothink.

PENNY I did.

HORACE Wot?

PENNY Grow out of dirt. So there isn't any difference is there, 'Orace? Soil grows lilac and dirt grows me.

HORACE Course there is—all the difference.

PENNY There, you never do say nothink nice—even when I
'ands it to yer. Still yer do keep yer 'ands to yerself, and don't
make a girl feel cheaper than she is. [*She begins to laugh a little
hysterically*] Funny, but that's jest wot yer don't do, isn't it?
Yer don't keep yer 'ands to yerself, do you, 'Orace? They're
always in and out of other people's pockets, ain't they, 'Orace?
And that's why you keep 'aving to go to yer place in the
country, ain't it?

HORACE Now even you're laughing at me.

PENNY I ain't larfing at yer, 'Orace, damn you. You always make
me want to cry. [*She does so*]

HORACE 'Ere blow. Well, wot yer crying about?

PENNY 'Cos yer so 'opeless, 'Orace! Yer like a poor ruddy
sparrow without no wings. If yer like the country so much why
don't you stay there? Outside, I mean, and not come 'ere up-
setting me. Wot makes yer even come to Lundon?

HORACE Easy money 'ere! Eight million suckers—all lined up to
be plucked.

PENNY Yer don't seem to 'ave found it so easy, I bet you'll soon
be wanting to borrow a tanner. As usual for a cup of tea...

HORACE I don't drink tea.

PENNY Better if yer did and lay off the booze for a while. Wot I
means, stupid, is you ain't exactly found yer fortune yet, 'ave
yer?

HORACE No, but yer don't 'ave to rub it in, any'ow it's nothink
to you, is it?

PENNY No, nothink.

HORACE All right, you don't have to shout. I believe yer. You
mean nothink. I got nothink. Add nothink to nothink and wot
d'yer get? Nothink. Still, one thing: if we've got nothink, we
ain't got nothink to lose 'ave we?

PENNY Yes, we 'ave.

HORACE Wot?

PENNY Time.

HORACE Cor, don't talk to me of 'aving time. That's all I do get
is time. Seventeen months out of twenty spent inside.

PENNY Does it drag?

HORACE Sometimes it don't seem to move at all. The seconds drip like rain down a drain-pipe.

PENNY And don't they give you nothink to do there spring, summer or winter?

HORACE No, sometimes we sit and think and sometimes we jest sit. But we can always tell when its summer or when winter's come round again.

PENNY How? Do they decorate your cell with flowers?

HORACE No, but the kids playing against the wall outside. When their voices sound loud and clear we know it's summer, but when they seem distant and faint like a voice that calls down your sleep we know it's winter again.

PENNY Poor 'Orace. 'Spose you gotter be smart like Archie or 'ard like Bert to keep outside and git away with it.

HORACE [*spitting derisively*] They don't know nothink—ignorant, that's wot they are. I'll give 'em somethink one day to make 'em sit up. Jest you wait. I've been doing some 'ard readin' inside—got a cushy job in the prison library I did. And as I couldn't get anyone else to read 'em I 'ad a look at two or three meself.

PENNY Wot were they about?

HORACE Ology, osis and ics—

PENNY What d'yer mean?

HORACE Sociology, zoology, biology, Psychosis, Neurosis and sillicosis, economics, mathematics, acrobatics. Jest as I say, it's all ology, osis or ics. I read 'em all, it's bound to 'ave improved me, ain't it? They can call me ignorant but nobody can say I ain't well read. And it ain't 'alf given me some good ideas. Jest you wait and then I'll make a pile.

PENNY And then will you take me out to the country to see all that dirt?

HORACE Yes, that's wot we'll do Penny, won't we? [*He goes over to* KATE's *stall and returns with a piece of lilac*] 'Ere it looks a bit limp and 'opeless but that'll remind you of me.

PENNY [*pinning it on her*] 'Ere, quick, somebody's coming.

    HORACE *rushes to* LAZARUS' *pitch. A man comes up*

the street. HORACE *adjusts his card round his neck. Then takes a large red handkerchief from his pocket and breathes on the dark glasses and begins to polish them. The man watches him in silence, then snorts derisively and exits.*

PENNY For crying out loud, wot's the use of cleaning specs you ain't supposed to be able to see through?

HORACE Then why do I wear them?

PENNY It's wot they always do. Oh! You'd best go back to the country. Ain't every village supposed to keep an idiot?

HORACE All right—I ain't stupid, it's just that...

PENNY Wot?

HORACE I ain't seen the chance yet. But I've got plenty of ideas in 'ere. I thought 'em out in there.

A prosperous business man who carries a suitcase comes up the street.

HORACE Now jest you watch this one, but don't go and tell Archie [*going to the man*]. Carry yer bag, sir?

The man hands the bag to HORACE *who follows for a few paces and then turns and begins to walk quicker and quicker in the opposite direction. The man continues unawares. Then a* POLICEMAN *appears from the direction in which* HORACE *is going. He turns again and follows the business man who is still unaware. The man calls 'Taxi' turns, takes the bag from Horace and merely thanks him and exits.*

HORACE 'Ere, ain't you going to give me nothing?

POLICEMAN Come 'ere, 'Orace, wot you up to? Trying a kid's trick now? Now look 'ere, mate, I've known yer for twenty years, 'aven't I? I've pinched yer five times meself and I don't want to do it again. So take my tip and keep yer hands out of other people's pockets, there's a sport. Get Penny to 'old yer 'and [*to* PENNY] Can't yer keep 'im out of mischief and find 'im something to do?

PENNY Wot, honest?

POLICEMAN Honest, why of course.

PENNY I know, 'Orace. 'Ow would yer like to make a packet

easy and honest? You run round to old Isaacs—'e might let you 'ave a tray of toffee apples to sell. Tell 'im I sent you. 'Ere's ten bob.

HORACE I don't want you to give me nothink.

PENNY I bet yer don't. I ain't giving you anything. I'm lending it to you for deposit, so as yer can get the toffee apples. Now go on, hurry up or soon it'll be too dark. [HORACE *goes off down the street*]

POLICEMAN That's the trouble with you, Penny.

PENNY Wot is?

POLICEMAN You're too generous—you even give yourself away —seen Archie tonight?

PENNY Wot if I 'ave?

POLICEMAN All right, me girl. I don't want 'im for nothink official...well, not tonight.

PENNY Then why ask if I've seen 'im?

POLICEMAN Don't 'e keep a book and ain't it the Derby to-morrow? 'Spose a bobby isn't allowed to 'ave a bet? But I've got a hot tip at long odds, and I'm going to put a few bob on it. And wot 'orses I back, I watch.

PENNY Wot! Are you really going to Epsom?

POLICEMAN I am—wangles special duty right opposite Tatten-ham Corner. Bit of all right.

PENNY Oh, take me will yer—I've never seen an 'orse race. Oh, go on, do; I'd love to see the Derby.

POLICEMAN What would my missus say?

PENNY Is she going too, then?

POLICEMAN No, she don't hold with 'orses or dogs.

PENNY Then take me...please?

POLICEMAN I'd like to 'ear wot she'd 'ave to say if she 'eard I'd been to the Derby with a...

PENNY With a...

POLICEMAN My wife's a respectable woman, Penny. Why don't you get 'Orace to take yer?

PENNY He ain't got no money.

POLICEMAN Cor I'd never hear the end of it. [*He goes off down the street*] My wife's a respectable woman...[BEN *begins to play again*]

> HORACE *comes up the street. He is walking jauntily and looks spruce in a white coat. He carries a tray and is apparently feeling dangerously optimistic.*

PENNY Lumme! Wot do you think you are—a ruddy surgeon? Wot's the big idea?

HORACE [*hurt*] Don't I look clean?

PENNY [*quickly*] Yes, it does look clean. A good idea, 'Orace. Well, did 'e let you 'ave any?

HORACE [*pulling white napkin off his tray*] Course he did. 'E can tell a smart salesman when 'e sees one. I borrowed the togs from the baker.

PENNY You do look smart. How much did you 'ave to pay?

HORACE A tanner apiece.

PENNY How many did 'e let you 'ave for me ten bob, then?

HORACE How many do you think? Fifteen of course.

PENNY That's all right then. I was frightened 'e'd have done you. 'E would if yer give 'im arf a chance.

HORACE No, he's on the level. I always believe the best till I finds out the worst. And he chucked this tray in for nothink.

PENNY [*sarcastically*] Yes, you'll need that.

HORACE [*proudly*] I 'ad another brain wave too, Penny. It 'it me jest like that, as I was walking along.

PENNY [*generously*] Did yer? Wot was it?

HORACE Jest you turn round. I got a real surprise for yer.

> *She turns her back on him.* HORACE *produces a tall white baker's hat from under his coat. Proudly he puts it on.*

HORACE Now you can look. [*She turns*]

PENNY [*laughing*] Cor, you don't 'arf look f...

> HORACE, *utterly punctured, removes the hat.* PENNY *pulls herself up.*

PENNY Cor you don't 'arf look *fine* 'Orace. Wot yer take it 'orf for? Put it on again. [*She takes it and puts it on his head again*] There let me.

HORACE [*recovering again*] See the idea? People always like to buy 'ome-made things. With this 'at on me 'ead everybody'll think I made these toffee apples all meself and that they're more wholesome.

PENNY Fine idea! Don't they look nice? Ain't yer going to give us one?

HORACE Course not! Don't ye know first thing about business? Yer must never eat first what yer going to sell afterwards! Yer don't see Kate with a bunch of lilac in 'er 'air. Or Bert guzzling cherries do yer?

PENNY [*petulantly*] George often has a pint of beer.

HORACE That's different. That's to show it ain't watered.

PENNY Well, I'll buy one then. 'Ere's a tanner.

HORACE That's wot they cost!

PENNY Who?

HORACE Me.

PENNY Well, 'ow much are they?

HORACE Ninepence.

PENNY Profiteer.

HORACE Profiteer nothing! Ain't I got to pay for hiring these togs and wear and tear and laundry? I think I'll make it a bob and be on the safe side. Let me figure it: twenty shillings are one quid, ought to clear that in 'arf an hour. Just you watch Penny. If I can clean up a quid every 'arf hour, that's two quid every hour ain't it? Must be nearly fifty quid a day...'Struth! I'm in the money, Penny. Jest you watch Archie's face now. Bet he'll be wild 'e never thought of this one. Why it'd pay me to hire him at ten bob an hour, to sèll 'em in another street. I'd be clearing thirty bob even then. I'll 'ave an whole army of blokes selling toffee apples outside every Tube in the city...same as those ice cream fellows do...I'll be sitting pretty. I'm all set. Just you watch. [*Two women come out of the Tube*] Toffee H'apples 'ome-made toffee apples! Take one 'ome to the kids. 'Ere you are, missus, don't disappointment yer kids. Ninepence —er—a bob each...

WOMAN A bob each!

HORACE You can 'ave two for one and elevenpence—they're big apples miss and these 'ere sticks cost money. Good timber's scarce nowadays. Can't use any old bit of firewood else it splinters, see? Has to be proper skewer wood. Comes from China. Junks you know.

WOMAN How interesting. Well, give me two.

> *She hands him the money.* HORACE *goes to give her two toffee apples. The sticks part from the apples, which are left on the tray.*

HORACE Shows how fresh they are, don't it? Sticks ain't hardly set in their sockets yet.

> HORACE *tries several more. Not a single apple comes away with its stick.*

HORACE 'Arf a mo, miss. It's the apples that count anyway. We won't be beat...[*He wrenches one of the apples free from the tray with his hand*] 'Ere you are miss. [*She goes to take it, the apple is stuck to his hand, it sticks to hers, it sticks to everything.*] Like Adam and Eve, ain't we miss? Joined by an apple!

WOMAN Really! [*Wrenching herself free*] I think I'll take a pound of cherries instead.

HORACE [*rushing to* BERT'*s stall*] Certainly ma'am. Fine Kentish cherries, all 'and picked. [*He carefully takes the best fruit from the pile and weighs it accurately to the last stalk.*] There yer are miss. [*The woman goes off*] Fine Kentish cherries!

> BERT, ARCHIE, KATE *and* LAZARUS *come out of the pub. For a second they watch* HORACE *who is unaware of their doing so.*

HORACE Fine Kentish cherries!

PENNY ...sssH!

> BEN *plays louder, trying to blanket* HORACE'*s call*

BERT Well I'll be...Wot's going on 'ere? 'Op it!

ARCHIE Ruddy parasite, that's wot 'e is!

PENNY 'E didn't do nothing, Bert!

HORACE Didn't do nothing? I say I did! I sold a pound of cherries for you, I did!

BERT 'Ow much?

HORACE Two toffee apples.

BERT 'Old me up! D'yer 'ear that?

HORACE I mean the price of two toffee apples, Bert, a bob. 'Ere yer are.

BERT Blimey! 'E not only nabs me barrer be'ind me back but sells me cherries under 'arf price...

KATE Pity 'e couldn't sell me lilac, it looks as if it could do with a drop of gin, too.

BERT [*sarcastically to* HORACE] And I 'ope you let 'er 'ave the best?

HORACE Course I did. I picked 'em out one by one. I saw these 'ere in the bags were a bit bruised like.

BERT That's real observant of yer. And I 'ope you gave 'er full measure too?

HORACE [*pointing to weights*] Course I did.

BERT [*astonished*] That's the pound weight!

HORACE That's right. That's wot I sold, one pound of fine Kentish cherries.

BERT You bloody fool.

ARCHIE 'E's so daft 'e's even honest.

KATE And wot the 'ell yer got that 'at on for?

PENNY Come on, 'Orace.

KATE Shut yer trap!

> ARCHIE *suddenly snatches* HORACE's *tall white hat, treads it in the gutter and shoves it on* HORACE's *head again.*

PENNY Dirty bully...

KATE Bet she put 'im up to it, fast little 'ussy.

PENNY Dirty-minded ole cow!

KATE 'Ear that, Bert? Called me a dirty ole cow, she did.

BERT [*indifferent*] Did she? Why you ain't so old...

KATE Ain't I? Yer bloody ole bull...

> *She chucks her pail of lilac at him. Enter* POLICEMAN *who receives the worst of it.*

POLICEMAN Wot's going on 'ere?

PENNY [*to* KATE] Dirty basket!

ARCHIE Parasite that's wot 'e is...

LAZARUS Penny for the blind...!

POLICEMAN Drunk yer mean.

KATE [*to* PENNY] You bitch, you...

BERT Bin selling me cherries, 'e 'as...

POLICEMAN 'As 'e? Didn't I tell yer to keep yer 'ands to yerself?

KATE Foul-mouthed punt!

PENNY Rotten ole bag!

BERT Ain't yer going to take 'im to the station?

ARCHIE Where's 'is licence?

BERT Ain't there no protection for the poor?

ARCHIE Ask to see 'is street trader's licence.

PENNY Dirty rat, Archie.

POLICEMAN 'E ain't a rat; 'e's a rodent! You'll 'ave to come along, 'Orace. Come on, now, we'll give yer a cup of tea. Kept yer room real tidy, we 'ave.

> *There is a scuffle between* HORACE *and the* POLICEMAN

BERT Mind me stall.

PENNY Leave 'im alone, I'll take 'im 'ome.

KATE Can't you do no better than that, dearie?

> *There is a general scrimmage*

MAX Favourite scratched! Favourite scratched!

OMNES Strewth!

> *With one accord they all rush to buy a paper*

PENNY [*seizing the opportunity*] Quick! [*She drags* HORACE *off, unobserved*]

> *The others are still around the* NEWSPAPER BOY. *It is now almost dark.*

> *The two* SANDWICH MEN *come out of the pub. They put their boards on and as they go off, one sees that the top board of the first* SANDWICHMAN *reads* 'ENGLISH MISSION SOCIETY' *whilst his bottom boards carry* THIS WAY TO THE RAPE' 'CONTINUOUS PERFORMANCE'; *whilst the top board of the second* SANDWICH MAN *reads* 'ODEON CINEMA' *and on the lower board,* 'GOD IS LOVE'.

SCENE TWO

The following afternoon at Epsom Race Course. It is Derby Day, twenty minutes before the big Classic of the season.

For this scene, only a small tent, a barrow, a couple of bookmakers' stands, and a backcloth are needed.

KATE stands on one side of the stage beside her barrow which is now heaped with winkles, their small, dark shells are wet and glisten. She still wears her black linen apron with the two large square pockets in the front; and to mark the occasion she wears, or rather stands beneath, a hat which is so heavily decorated with artificial fruit that it looks like the very image of a cornucopia.

In the centre of the stage stands a fortune-teller's red tent. It is open at the front, a small notice is inscribed 'Madam Sartre, Palmist' and a picture of a painted hand leans against a postboard. MADAM SARTRE is a colourful, dark woman of about forty; that is, as years go; but if you were to look into her black, blasé eyes, you would see such cynicism and indifference that only 4,000 years could have accumulated. A cigarette smokes itself in the corner of her mouth. She is, of course, filing her nails. Perhaps her confidence in being able to foretell the future of others derives from the knowledge of her own, unhappy, past. Anyhow, there she is, as she always was, and always will be as long as men have hands and women hopes.

BERT has his bookmaker's stand to the right of the tent. He is now wearing a bowler hat and busily shouting the odds and marking them up with a piece of chalk. He rubs some figures on it, using a small wet sponge which hangs on a string. His CLERK, a rather weedy youth, stands beside him with a large, open ledger. Behind him, also on a stand is a smartly-dressed TIC-TAC MAN, whose white

I

gloved hands are never still as they signal the odds to and fro to his boss in Tattersall's ring. Occasionally, he whispers to BERT.

Just behind BERT, *a little man, a professional* RELIGIOUS MANIAC, *with long white hair and a black cloak—stands on a platform which bears the inscription 'REPENT' 'The day of Judgement is at Hand'. He appears to talk to the crowd throughout the scene. Nobody pays the slightest attention to him. His remarks are occasionally heard and are seldom comprehensible. His lack of audience appears to cause him no distress.*

The following calls are, of course, repeated with variations, throughout the scene and run together. The actors may improvise.

BERT 5 to 4 the Field; 5 to 4 the Field! 6 to 4 bar one. [*ad lib he takes a bet*] Ten bob each way, Dil Fareb. 'Ere y'are lidy, quick. [*He hands the woman a card*]

PREACHER And the Lord God said...

KATE Fresh winkles, bob a pint! Luvly fresh winkles! [*ad lib.*]

PREACHER And said unto Israel...

VOICE [*off*] I gotta horse! I gotta horse!

Enter the PRINCE. *A colourful Zulu tipster. He wears an Arabian blanket draped over one shoulder and on his head he proudly bears three rich ostrich feathers which, he claims, were given to him by H.R.H. the Prince of Wales. He carries a genuine gold-headed cane—a gift from the Earl of Derby. He holds a number of small envelopes.*

PRINCE I gotta winner—[*ad lib.*]

PENNY and HORACE *come on the scene. She is dressed very prettily in a printed frock with a very full skirt and wears a large brimmed hat.* HORACE *has his one and only suit on, but has affected a stock for the occasion. He carries an extraordinarily large umbrella.*

HORACE 'Ere's a quiet corner, Penny. Now then, jest you watch, give me five minutes and we'll clear a packet.

PENNY No, 'Orace...

HORACE Come on, can't miss a chance like this. You keep your eyes peeled for a copper.

He opens his large umbrella which he puts on its side in front of him, resting the handle between his feet. He now uses one sector of the top to serve as a table. From his pocket he produces a soiled pack of cards. He selects three. Two or three people gather round him.

HORACE [*whispering*] Go on, Penny, lend me ten bob. Look at 'em already like wasps round a pot of jam.

PENNY Oh, 'ere Y'are. [*She hands him a note*] Wish it came as easy as it went.

HORACE puts three cards face upwards on the umbrella. The centre card is the Queen of Spades. He rolls his cuffs up.

HORACE Nah then: spot the lady! No trick to it! Just sharpness of your eye against the quickness of my hand.

He puts the two side cards one above the other in the palm of his right hand; and then picks the Queen up with his left. Very clumsily he performs the trick. The resulting position of the Queen of Spades is obvious.

Spot the lady, nah, then; which is it, guvnor?

The man points to the card

Are you sure that's 'er?

He turns it over—it is the Queen of Spades. HORACE *now puts the ten shillings on to the umbrella and picks up the rest of the cards.*

Nah then, guvnor, ten bob at evens—if you can spot 'er again.

The man puts another ten shilling note on the umbrella.

HORACE *repeats the trick—this time more neatly.*

Nah spot the lady, guvnor.

The man points to a card. HORACE *turns it over. It is not the Queen of Spades. He pockets two ten shilling notes.*

[*Whispering to* PENNY] See? Easy! Lend us another quid, ducks, to shove up the stake money.

PENNY *produces the note and* HORACE *puts the pound note and the two ten shilling notes on to the umbrella.*

Like to take two quid off me guvnor? Come on, be a sport—
no trick to it. Just the sharpness of your eye against the quickness of my hand. [*He performs the trick very clumsily and turns
up the Queen*] Are you game guvnor?

> *The man produces two pound notes and puts them on top
> of* HORACE'S *money.* HORACE *picks up the cards and
> repeats the trick.*

Nah then, guvnor, spot the lady!

> *Instantly the man puts one hand on each of the two
> outside cards.*

MAN There she is—in the middle. [*He turns over the two outside
cards—neither is the Queen of Spades*]

HORACE 'Ere mate, wot yer up to?

MAN Come on now, turn her over! She must be lying there
mustn't she—if she ain't up yer shirt?

> HORACE *looks helplessly at* PENNY

MAN What are you waiting for? *He turns over the centre card. It
is not the Queen*] Can't think where she could have got to, can
you, Horace? [*He pockets the four pounds*]

PENNY Cor, there goes my two quid.

HORACE [*speechless*] Only a bleedin' plain-clothes man knows
that one.

MAN That's right Horace.

> *The* PLAIN CLOTHES MAN *goes off.* PENNY *drags*
> HORACE *over to* KATE'S *stall.*

PREACHER And the Lord said unto Israel...

BERT 10 to 1 Dil Fareb; 6 to 4 the Field. I'll take 10 to 1 Dil
Fareb.

PENNY Buy me a pint of winkles, 'Orace. 'Ere you are. [*She
passes a shilling to him under cover*]

KATE 'Ello, ducks, ain't it luvly out 'ere. Does you fair good to
git out for a blow once in a while don't it? But I see you've got
yer 'ands full—wot you come wiv 'im for?

PENNY And wot's wrong wiv 'im?

KATE None of my business, I'm sure.

PENNY So am I!

KATE Bit short ain't yer? Nobody can say I poke me nose into other people's business—that they can't.

PENNY Not 'arf yer don't. Any'ow, give us a pint of winkles. Ain't seen the likes of 'em for a long time. Wot yer been down to Southend and scraped 'em off the pier?

> *Enter* ARCHIE *very flashily dressed, brisk and carrying a shooting stick. He is accompanied by a* LITTLE MAN *in a raincoat to whom he passes a couple of notes on the sly, and then mounts a portable stool which his stooge produces from under his raincoat.* HORACE *watches him;* KATE *and* PENNY *continue as if they have not noticed his entrance.*

BERT I'll lay 6 to 4 the Field, *etc.*

KATE [*handing* PENNY *a plate of winkles which are still unshelled*] Well, they're fresh enough. Still smell the sea on 'em. [*She shoves a plate under* PENNY'S *nose*] Smell!

PENNY [*sniffs then sighs*] They always remind me of me Dad—he was in the Navy you know.

KATE [*sighing*] 'The Noos of the World' in an easy chair, a cup of tea, a pint of winkles—all alone, me feet in soak—me stays undone. Cor, if there's a Paradise, that's me own!

PENNY Come on, 'Orace, pay for me winkles. Wot yer gaping at? [HORACE *pays*] And give me a pin.

> HORACE, *still staring at* ARCHIE'S *preparations, removes a pin that serves his braces. The crowd gathers round* ARCHIE.

KATE [*to* PENNY] 'Ere, there's Archie, I bet 'e's going to work the windbag.

ARCHIE I 'ave 'ere [*holding up a watch*] a gent's wrist-watch, fully-jooled. Eight quid. I tell yer it's as stiff with rubies as a pomegranite's pips.

PENNY Coo! 'E ain't 'arf poetic.

ARCHIE Wot's more, it's got a strap of genuine...

MAX [*going across stage*] Paper! Paper! *Evening Standard*! Fust three winners!

ARCHIE Five quid this gent's wrist-watch—it's a gift!

HORACE [*holding his trousers up*] Yer mean y're giving it away?

ARCHIE 'Old me up! If it ain't 'Orace hisself...

HORACE Yer mean you'll give us it as a present?

ARCHIE Nothing of the sort, wot I said was: it's a gift! Well, metamorphorically speaking.

HORACE Don't tell me I can't understand me own finicular! That's wot 'e said didn't 'e? A gift?

PENNY Course 'e did.

ARCHIE All right mate, if you will take me literally you can 'ave the ruddy watch for nothink. Just to show there's no 'ard feeling. 'Ere you are. [*He holds the watch out to* HORACE] That's 'ow I gets me living; standing 'ere giving gent's wrist-watches away by the hour...I tell yer, I'm a real philatelist. Come on then, wot yer waiting for? 'Ere yer are. Go on chum, open it! Now 'old it up, chum, and let them listen to its silent innards: tick tock, tick tock...[*He produces another exactly similar*] Anyone who buys another such as this buys much more than a watch...it's self-winding! And what is time without a stop? I'll tell yer: it's eternity, it's immortality! It is—all yours for a five pound note!

ARCHIE's STOOGE *in the crowd hands up £5*

ARCHIE Well guvnor, you at least knows a bargain when it stares you in the face, you're a proper gambler, one who'll speculate—and just to show me 'igh regard fer you, I'll chuck in this razor sir, as a gift—a present, free, gratis, for nothink, nix, 'ere you are, sir.

The STOOGE *takes both watch and razor.* ARCHIE *produces another watch.*

Now who wants another speculation? Here's jest another watch, same make, same price, same jewels. Nah then. Who'll give me five quid—will you?

A member of the crowd hands it up to ARCHIE *who keeps it in his hand.*

Are you quite sure, sir? [*sarcastically*] I see this speculation's contagious. Such enterprise deserves encouragement—so I'll tell you what I'll do; here's a watch, five quid and another safety razor. Now sir, will you give me ten quid for the lot?

The same man hands up another two fivers

You will, sir? You're a proper ruddy sport.

> ARCHIE *hands over the five pound note, watch and razor,*
> *pockets the two fivers, jumps down, picks up his stool and*
> *goes off quickly.*

KATE [*to* PENNY] And they say there's one of 'em born every minute! 'E'll wake up one day, but it fair make me 'eart bleed to see a poor soul pay out ten quid to buy back his own five pound note...

BERT I'll lay 5 to 1 Dil Fareb [*ad lib.*]

PREACHER And the Lord God said unto Israel...

> *An* OLD WOMAN *in the crowd goes up to the* PREACHER
> *and hands him a ten shilling note.*

OLD WOMAN [*timidly*] Five bob each way Black Tarquin, please.

> THE PREACHER *pockets the note and hands her a tract.*
> *He is quite unaware of the* OLD WOMAN's *intentions.*

PREACHER Bless you. And the Lord... [*He burbles on*]

OLD WOMAN Bless you too, sir. [*She turns to her companion*] Did you hear that? What a nice man.

BERT [*who has observed this dumbfounded*] Cor Blimey! If John the Baptist ain't taking bets! I'll report you to Tattersalls, that's what I'll do!

> *During this interlude,* HORACE *has been holding his*
> *watch in his hand and silently rehearsing to himself the*
> *trick known as 'working the windbag' which* ARCHIE *has*
> *just done.*

PENNY 'Ere, wot you up to, 'Orace?

HORACE Ssh! If he gives me five quid and I gives him five quid...

PENNY Oh no, you don't try that. Look, 'Orace, let's go an 'ave our fortunes told...perhaps she can tell us 'ow we're going to get 'ome. [*To* MADAME SARTRE] Can you do us one 'and for a bob like, instead of the two?

> MADAME SARTRE *stops filing her nails; they enter the*
> *tent which is well open in the front.*

SARTRE [*gabbling*]

You were born under the star of Venus de Milo,
Though Sagittarius is in the ascendant;

I see the planet Virgo has passed you;
From now on the constellation of Phallus guides you,
While Aubergine is your favourite jewel.
Now as to your lucky colour: it's scarlet.
And remember your magic numeral is three!
There you are dearie, now let's look at your hand. The left one.
I see the line of your heart's a deep one. Your wealth line too, is
most marked, that means you'll be rich [*under her breath*] Or
perhaps it comes from too much scrubbing...

PENNY And ain't I going to 'ave any children?

SARTRE [*dropping professional manner*] Not if you're careful.

PENNY I am going to get married, ain't I, and live in the country?

KATE [*producing field glasses from under her barrow*] There
they go now out into the ring...can't see the French horse,
Bert.

SARTRE What? [*she rushes out of the tent and grabs* KATE'*s
glasses*] 'Ere, let's 'ave a squint.

BERT [*also looking through glasses*] Looks as though they've
scratched him.

SARTRE No, there 'e is. No. 13 [*she runs off*]

KATE [*to* BERT] I think I'll 'ave a bob each way on 'im, seein' as
'ow she's psychic.

> KATE *and* BERT *follow* MADAME SARTRE. *The*
> PRINCE *does likewise after chucking his envelopes on to
> the ground.*

PENNY Well, I'll be...she's gone and left me all unfinished—
now 'ow are we going to get 'ome. That's our last bob gone.

HORACE Leave it to me, Penny. Leave it to me. Here's our
chance.

> HORACE *seizes the coloured table cloth from the Palm-
> ist's tent and drapes it round himself.*

PENNY Now what yer up to?

HORACE There!

PENNY And what yer supposed to be?

HORACE An arab!

PENNY What for?

HORACE Just you watch. Here, help me pick up these envelopes.

HORACE *starts collecting the small envelopes which the tipster has thrown down.*

PENNY [*helping him*] Oh Horace, what are we doing this for? We shan't see the race if we don't hurry.

HORACE Now then, shove a pinch of sand in each of them. [*He fills two or three packets with sand which he takes from the ground*] It's the chance of a lifetime, Penny, and it came to me just like that.

PENNY Now, 'Orace, if you're going to try and sell your watch for nothing, I'm going.

HORACE 'Ere, take your 'at off. [*He hands her a white cloth which he takes from the tent*] Shove this round your 'ead.

PENNY Wot, am I supposed to be in your 'arem?

HORACE Course not, I believe in mahogany.

PENNY Wot's this for then?

HORACE Makes yer look like a nurse, see?

> He takes MADAME SARTRE's *board down and scribbles on the back of it. Then he climbs on to a chair and hangs the board above him—it now reads 'Dr Buchman'.*

Hokey pokey. Abracadabraca! Here in this packet I've got the Elixir. All the mystery of Asia, all the science of America in one packet. Hokey pokey. Abracadabraca! At last. At last. Now here it is: one hundred and ten per cent pure pandemonium in this little packet. Step up. Step up!

PENNY Oh 'Orace, that was wonderful. I've never 'eard so many words I never understood. You must 'ave done an awful lot of reading...

HORACE Hokey pokey! Abracadabraca! Step up! Step up!

YOUNG WOMAN Can it cure headaches?

PENNY Course it can, can't it, doctor?

HORACE Yes, nurse, it can cure 'eadaches, earaches, toothaches 'eartaches...why there is nothing it won't budge.

YOUNG WOMAN 'Ow much?

HORACE Sixpence.

PENNY [*quickly*] For two. Threepence each.

YOUNG WOMAN I'll take half a dozen. I suppose it's full of vitamins?

HORACE From A to Z lady. It'll buck you up no end who'll buy a packet?

A roaring trade is done. PENNY *serves packets as fast as she can.*

HORACE There you are, Penny, didn't I tell you? And it's all for you. Now 'ow about a day in the country...

Unobserved by HORACE *a young* CRIPPLE *comes on. He uses two crutches.*

Hokey Pokey! Abracadabraca...

PENNY Ssh!

HORACE What's up?

The CRIPPLE *stops to the right of* HORACE. *The crowd make way for him.*

PENNY I think we'd better 'ave that day in the country right now, 'Orace...come on.

HORACE *turns and sees the* CRIPPLE

HORACE Yes, p'raps you're right.

CRIPPLE Can you cure me? [*quietly*]

HORACE [*shouting the* CRIPPLE *down at the same time as he prepares to leave*] Hokey Pokey! Abracadabraca! etc.

CRIPPLE Can it cure this?

PENNY [*kindly*] Well...any'ow we ain't got none left...

CRIPPLE Yes, you have. I'll buy a packet. Never know your luck. Can't do me any harm.

HORACE [*kindly*] No, can't do any 'arm...

CRIPPLE 'Ere's a tanner.

HORACE No, chum, you keep it, no. I'll tell you what I'll do, I'll give you a packet just for luck. 'Ere you are, take three.

He lays his hand casually on the CRIPPLE'S *shoulder as he hands the packets to him.*

And I hope to Gawd it 'elps yer...anyway, can't do no 'arm.

HORACE *turns to give a look of helplessness to* PENNY. *She shows her relief at the way* HORACE *got out of the situation. The* CRIPPLE *turns to go. He drops his crutches.*

[*rushing to pick them up*] 'Ere chum, let me 'elp yer.

He goes to replace the crutches under the CRIPPLE'S *arms*

CRIPPLE You have. Can't you see? I don't need them any more. Look. [*He walks away*]

PENNY He's walking!

HORACE Blimey!

> HORACE *and* PENNY *are frightened. The crowd turn and watch the* CRIPPLE *who goes off.*

ONE IN CROWD D'yer see that?

ANOTHER Look!

ANOTHER He's running!

ANOTHER Jumping!

ANOTHER It's magic!

ANOTHER A miracle! [*ad lib.*]

PENNY [*now terrified*] Wot you done, 'Orace? Wot's 'appened?

HORACE I done nothing. Honest, I didn't. [*with bravado*] I got it. He wasn't lame at all—no more lame than I am. [*Indignantly*] Just some cove trying to make a fool of me, that's wot 'e is...

> The CROWD *turn from watching the* CRIPPLE *and seethe round* HORACE.

ONE IN CROWD Saw it with me own eyes I did.

ANOTHER Would never 'ave believed it.

ANOTHER An 'ealer. [*ad lib.*]

> KATE *and* BERT *come in,* ARCHIE *follows*

KATE Wot you been up to, 'Orace?

ONE IN CROWD A cripple cured.

ANOTHER Dropped 'is crutches.

KATE I wish 'ed cure my feet...

BERT Muscling in on someone's pitch again, that's wot 'e's doing.

ARCHIE E'll get you into trouble, Penny.

HORACE I done nothink, did I, Penny?

PENNY No, nothink.

ONE IN CROWD He's an 'ealer.

ANOTHER Got the gift.

ANOTHER Works in wondrous ways.

ANOTHER That cripple was in our coach. Told me hisself 'ed been like it for years. Crashed at Dunkirk, 'e did.

POLICEMAN Wot's going on 'ere. Penny I'm surprised at you.

Didn't I tell you to keep 'Orace quiet, at least so as I could see the race in peace?

ONE IN CROWD Can you cure me?

ANOTHER And me? [*ad lib.*]

Enter LADY RECENT *and the* REV. DEAN CUTHBERT. *The former is a most masculine woman, the latter an effeminate man. She wears a homburg-type hat, tweeds and her stance suggests that there is either the deck of a battleship cruiser beneath her or the saddle of a seventeen-hand hunter. She is addicted to good works and suffers under the delusion that the people are to be improved, mainly through her direct agency. The* REV. CUTHBERT *wears a dog collar—but is not on a leash. He is a self-appointed founder of the Lowest Common Denominators, a new set which is all-embracing and seeks to unite all beliefs into one church. He is, for all that, quite a well-intentioned little man.*

LADY RECENT Ah, that's what I like; the people. It does you good to get amongst the people. Cuthbert, what's going on? [*She stands at the edge of the crowd*]

POLICEMAN Nah then, 'Orace, pack it up and come along now. Pack it up...

ONE IN CROWD Wot's 'e done?

POLICEMAN Come on mate, get cracking...

ANOTHER He ain't done nothing, leave 'im alone. [*ad lib.*]

POLICEMAN Trying to obstruct the law, are you?

ANOTHER Is it a crime to heal a cripple?

ANOTHER Saw it with me own eyes I did.

POLICEMAN Saw wot?

ANOTHER Saw 'im eal the cripple with one of them packets.

POLICEMAN Wot, one of these? [*Picking one up*] This looks serious. 'Orace. Purveying dangerous drugs. What is it?

PENNY He ain't done nothink.

POLICEMAN Wot's in it 'Orace?

HORACE Nothink!

POLICEMAN Bit 'eavy for nothink, ain't it?

HORACE It's only sand, ain't it, Penny? Sand ain't a drug is it?

POLICEMAN So, you're selling sand at twopence a packet eh? That's misrepresentation...about three months you'll be up the line this time.

ONE IN CROWD Dirty shame!

ANOTHER 'Ere 'e comes now. You ask 'im if these ain't 'is crutches.

Enter CRIPPLE *again*

POLICEMAN Are these yours, chum?

CRIPPLE They were. I don't need them now. He healed me.

POLICEMAN Wot! Wiv one of these packets of sand?

CRIPPLE No, I haven't even opened it.

POLICEMAN Then 'ow was it 'e 'ealed you?

CRIPPLE He laid his hand on my shoulder.

HORACE I didn't do nothink, did I, Penny?

PENNY No, nothink, reely.

CRIPPLE But bless you for what you did do.

CROWD Proper miracle! [*ad lib.*]

ARCHIE Come orf it! Don't pull that stuff 'ere. He's just 'Orace's stooge, placed in the crowd, same as I...

PENNY No 'e wasn't, so there.

BERT All right then, if 'Orace can heal, why don't 'e do some more?

ARCHIE Yeah, why don't you straighten that kid's arm?

A woman pushes the child forward

WOMAN Go on, sir, please 'ave a try. Never know what yer can do wiv a bit of faith. Poor little basket's been like it ever since 'e was born.

CROWD Go on, 'Orace, 'ave a try.

HORACE No, I can't do nothing. Come on, Penny.

MOTHER Just lay yer 'and on 'is arm and see.

HORACE I tell yer it'll do no good.

LADY RECENT Go on, my man, don't keep me waiting.

    HORACE *touches the boy's arm which straightens. Crowd exclaim suitably.*

PENNY Strike me... [*She is struck dumb with surprise but nobody notices her*]

CUTHBERT He's a Saint, a sign made manifest.

LADY RECENT He's a psychotherapist.

HORACE [*turning on her*] I'm not. I'm as good as you are. I ain't done nothing 'ave I, Penny? Tell 'em 'ow it was: we ain't got no money to get 'ome and I wanted to…Go on, tell 'em, why don't yer?

> HORACE *thinks* PENNY *has let him down since she does not support his statement.*

POLICEMAN 'Ere, look at this crowd. 'Olding everything up yer are. I can't have this. And if I catch yer selling sand…

LADY RECENT Leave him alone, Officer. I'll be responsible.

POLICEMAN Who are you?

LADY RECENT I am Lady Recent. Perhaps you will let me stand surety for this man? He has obviously great gifts.

POLICEMAN You can stand bail if you like but he's bound to come with me. Come on 'Orace. [*He goes to take* HORACE]

ONE IN CROWD They're off! They're off!

> The ENSEMBLE, *including the* PREACHER—*rush, as one to the footlights, and, as it were, watch the race with suitable exclamations.*

CROWD They're they go. Black Tsar, Dil Fareb. Go on Dil. Black Tsar on the rails. Come on Dil.

> LADY RECENT *and* CUTHBERT *take* HORACE *off unnoticed except by* BERT *who nudges* ARCHIE.

BERT See that?

ARCHIE Nice little racket. Come on. Let's be in on it. [*They follow*] Wait a minute, Your Ladyship, can't leave us behind. [*They exit*]

CROWD Come on Dil! Hurrah! [*ad lib.*]

> PENNY *rushes across to* KATE *who apart from the mumbling* PREACHER *is the only one now left on stage.*
> PENNY *points desperately to her mouth, trying to speak.*

KATE Wot, you backed it too?

> PENNY *shakes her head, still pointing to her mouth.*

KATE Go and have a drop of gin, ducks, you'll be all right.

> KATE *goes off leaving* PENNY *alone,* PENNY *turns in despair, sits down disconsolate, fishing in her purse which contains only one coin.* MADAME SARTRE *enters.*

SARTRE Course you'll live in the country. Very soon too! That'll
be one shilling dearie.

She takes the shilling from PENNY'S *lap and starts filing
her nails.*

CURTAIN

Act II

SCENE ONE

Evening of the same day. A Derby Day Cocktail Party at LADY RECENT's *house in London. A box is not necessary; furniture will be sufficient. But for those who insist on realism on the stage, let me describe the set if they must have one.*

It is a 'modern' room in the best of taste—though it would be difficult to describe the taste. At any rate it is quite plainly the salon belonging to what is known as a woman of culture. The chairs are Heppelwhite, the inlaid cabinet in Italian Renaissance; a Chinese gong adorns one wall and a Burmese image of Buddha in black teak sits on the mantelshelf. India is represented by several small tables of Benares brass whilst an old Russian ikon hangs above a polished Welsh dresser.

A cocktail bar has been cunningly contrived as an inlet into one corner of the room. It is in the style of a wheelhouse on a British destroyer. Round mirrors give the effect of portholes; a telescope and an admiral's sword hang above a row of bottles. The barman wears a white naval coat. The only incongruous details are the stools in front of the bar; these have riding saddles for seats and stirrups for footstalls.

But the pièce de résistance *of the salon is a very large painting of a female nude in the manner of Fragonard, which hangs back stage centre.*

When the curtain rises, the cocktail party is in full swing. The room is crowded with people all being most animated, yet it preserves the atmosphere of still life. Some of the occupants are men, some women— their clothes distinguish them.

The door is opened imperiously

Enter LADY RECENT, *followed by the* REV. CUTHBERT, HORACE, BERT, ARCHIE, *who all push their way, unnoticed, to the bar.*

LADY RECENT Dear me, I see I am late for my own party. [*Nobody notices her. Then to herself*] But I know none of you will have missed me. [*forte*] Ladies and gentlemen, friends, pray silence. I wish to make an important announcement, for this afternoon I have discovered a man...

MR SPLEEN Which by itself is no mean achievement [*to himself*]...

LADY RECENT ...a man with exceptional powers...of healing! The Reverend Dean Cuthbert and I saw him perform a series of miracles. Curing the lame and sick by laying his hand upon those who were ailing. And I have brought him here—here he is now with two of his associates—disciples! Ladies and gentlemen, it is my privilege to introduce the Twentieth Century Saint!

She turns to bring HORACE *forward but he is otherwise engaged with* BERT *and* ARCHIE *at the bar. The party turn and observe him.*

HORACE ...wot, no mild and bitter?

LADY RECENT As you observe, he is 'of the people'.

HORACE is to be observed draining other people's glasses. A cocktail cherry on a stick takes his eye.

HORACE Cor, stone the crows, Bert, look 'ere, same principle as the toffee apples. You could sell all your cherries separately if you stuck 'em on a stick—slow, that's wot you've bin.

LADY RECENT Now Master, allow me to present you to my guests.

ARCHIE Go on 'Orace, she means you. Lay off the licker.

BERT And say somethink they can chew on!

HORACE [*surfacing from drinks*] Hokey pokey! Abracadabraca!

LADY RECENT I beg your pardon?

K

ARCHIE Don't worry, mum. That's 'is way of blessing yer. The lingo's Romany, though he ain't never been to Rome—it came quite natural to 'im—like 'is 'ealing...

CUTHBERT After considerable meditation in absolute solitude, no doubt?

ARCHIE No doubt.

BERT No doubt at all. You've got somethink there, guvnor, for the Master always was one for going away into the country, in retreat, where he's wont to sit for weeks, yea, even months in lonely solitude. And once he's in, there don't seem no way of getting him out.

CUTHBERT You mean he's in a trance?

SOMEONE IN CROWD He's a Yogi, that's what he is!

HORACE I ain't, don't insult me!

BERT No, he's all right. He's only had a couple of gin and limes.

SOMEONE I tell you he's a Yogi. I bet he's been dipping into the Upanishads.

HORACE I tell you I ain't, I've kept me 'ands to meself.

LADY RECENT Will the Saint eat something? I hope the three of you will partake of dinner. I will go and order it—if you will excuse me. Vegetarian of course?

BERT Of course, and a trifle underdone.

LADY RECENT Mr Spleen, as you know everybody here, will you please introduce the Saint to those he might wish to meet?

SPLEEN Certainly, Lady Recent. [*She goes off*]

SPLEEN [*to them*] First, let me introduce myself; I'm Spleen, and at your service.

HORACE Who's that old girl?

SPLEEN Your hostess? That's Lady Recent. She's a woman who, as you see, carries all before her.

ARCHIE And wot's she do?

SPLEEN She holds the keys of the metropolis. Those whom she asks here, despise her, those who are uninvited, hate her. She is a remarkable hostess and she's a woman of considerable culture. [*Looking round the room*] As you see, she collects objets d'art, specialising in pekinese and poets.

ARCHIE And which are you?

BERT Come on, Archie, let's leave this cove who's too educated to have any manners—talking like that behind the lidy's back, and let's drink to 'er 'ealth in her strongest lickers before she comes yattering back again.

SPLEEN Is there anyone here you would care to meet?

HORACE Who's that over there?

SPLEEN That man talking Austrian with a Hungarian accent is Gabriel Muscatel the film producer. Don't worry, you're bound to meet him—he'll probably want you to play St Joan.

Enter LADY RECENT

LADY RECENT Now Master, perhaps you will oblige me and perform.

HORACE Wot 'ere?

LADY RECENT Why not? Isn't the atmosphere conducive? [*leading him off*] There were more people around you this afternoon on Epsom Downs when you performed the miracle.

HORACE I didn't do nothink!

LADY RECENT Nothing but cure an incurable cripple!

HORACE But I ain't got no more magic sand.

LADY RECENT I see you hide your divine gift with modesty. Ladies and gentlemen, the Master has generously consented to heal anyone of any ailment. [*Pause, nobody steps forward*] Surely you can't all be in good health? [*Pause*] How tiresome! Has no one here a broken leg or arm or something? [*Pause*] Why, of course! We have our three eminent critics. Now then, Mr See-no-Good the art critic, let the healer lay his hands upon your eyes. [*She drags him forward*]

SEE-NO-GOOD No, no, Lady Recent, I beg you. It's better for an art critic to be blind than...

LADY RECENT Well, Mr Speak-no-Good, the literary critic, let the master cure your stutter.

SPEAK-NO-GOOD N...N...No!

LADY RECENT It seems that people cling to their misfortunes like limpets to a rock. But I'm sure you, Mr Hear-no-Good, the drama critic, will be more sensible and let our healer return to you the gift of hearing.

HEAR-NO-GOOD No, God forbid. Tomorrow I have to go to
'The Lady's Fit for Burning'.

   LANCASTER, *the butler, enters and limps toward* LADY
   RECENT.

LADY RECENT Yes, Lancaster.

LANCASTER There is a young woman here...

LADY RECENT Well, who is it? What is her name?

LANCASTER I don't know, she seems too excited to speak.

LADY RECENT There are several people here I do not recognise,
   one more stranger won't make much difference so show her in.

   LANCASTER *goes to the door as* PENNY *enters, looking
   for* HORACE.

LADY RECENT [*to* PENNY] How d'you do? So good of you to
   come.

   PENNY, *who is still dumb, gesticulates, pointing towards
   her mouth.*

LADY RECENT Lancaster, the young lady seems rather hungry,
   please pass her a plate of food. [*He does so*] Surely somebody
   here has some ailment which the healer can cure? [PENNY
   continues to point to her mouth] And thirsty too? Give her
   something to drink.

   He does so. Meanwhile HORACE *is surrounded by other
   guests The* REV. CUTHBERT *engages him in earnest
   conversation.* ARCHIE *and* BERT *spot* PENNY *and try to
   shoo her out.* HORACE *turns and notices her. He immediately makes his way towards her but is buttonholed by*
   LADY RECENT.

LADY RECENT Ah, one minute. Lancaster, tell me how is your
   gout this evening?

LANCASTER No better, milady. As you see, I can hardly crawl
   about.

LADY RECENT Good.

LANCASTER I beg your pardon?

LADY RECENT Come here. Into the centre, so everybody can see
   you. Now, Master, pray lay your hands upon him.

HORACE Where abouts...?

ARCHIE No, not on his hip pocket...

LADY RECENT Just touch him as you did the cripple. [HORACE
does so] Now, Lancaster, let us see you walk across the room.

He does so, no longer limping

LANCASTER Is there anything else, milady?

LADY RECENT No thank you, that will be all.

They all watch him walk out

BERT Blimey!

ARCHIE Must be worth five quid a time.

LADY RECENT Master, let me kiss your hand.

She does so. Everybody crowds round HORACE. PENNY
is still pointing to her mouth, and is unable to reach him.

LADY RECENT There! With our own eyes we saw it...the man's
a saint...

SPLEEN ...Saint Spiv!

LADY RECENT Here with this hand alone, he did it. It was a
miracle.

CUTHBERT A miracle of grace! I must talk to the Bishop. You
must be ordained!

MUSCATEL Shut up all of you! This man is mine. This man has
talent! Consider yourself under contract! We'll fix you up at
Lourdes in Technicolor. Have a cigar! [*All exit except* PENNY]

SCENE TWO

Several weeks later. SAINT SPIV's *Harley Street Sanctum. It is a cross between an atomic laboratory and a
Russian Orthodox Church. It attempts to suggest a
happy synthesis between religion and science. Yet for all
that, the room is clinically clean and prosperous.*

*A door backstage leads to the hall and waiting room;
another, stage right, to the* SAINT's *inner sanctum. A
large figure of an alabaster angel stands on the mantelshelf, the halo above the figure is made of a tubular neon
light which flicks on and off throughout the scene. On the
opposite wall, an ebony panel with several knobs and*

switches. Front stage left, a desk containing a dictaphone, a telephone, press-button bells and a large crystal.

A pretty blonde RECEPTIONIST, *dressed in transparent plastic and wearing rubber gloves sits at the desk. She is playing patience.*

ARCHIE, *wearing a surgeon's white coat, sits by the little table beside the door leading to the* SAINT's *inner sanctum. He is hidden behind 'The Greyhound Gazette'. The table bears an enormous cash register; it is flanked by lighted candles. The phone rings.*

RECEPTIONIST [*She opens a large appointment book*] Welbeck 1869, the Saint's Sanctum. No, I'm sorry but the Saint cannot see anyone without an appointment...not for two months at least. The earliest would be 2.15 p.m. on the twenty first of September. You may die before then? In that case perhaps you will phone to cancel your appointment.

She replaces the receiver and continues with her game of patience. ARCHIE *does not stir until suddenly a red light above the door back stage flicks on. Immediately he stiffens, stuffs his racing paper behind the cash register.* BERT, *who is now the Butler, enters.*

BERT Step h'up miss. [*A cross-eyed woman follows him*]

WOMAN I can't see any steps.

BERT There aren't any, I mean you're 'ere.

BERT *withdraws,* ARCHIE *leads the woman into the inner sanctum.*

ARCHIE This way lady. [*He returns to his paper*] Ain't it supposed to be lucky to see a cross-eyed dame? I think I'll try a double...

HORACE [*off*] Hokey pokey! Abracadabraca!

ARCHIE That was a quick 'un.

Quickly he places his paper again behind the cash register. The cross-eyed woman reappears.

WOMAN [*still cross-eyed*] I'm cured! I'm cured! A miracle!

ARCHIE Congratulations! That'll be twenty quid—I beg your pardon—guineas.

The WOMAN *hands the money to* ARCHIE. *He turns and*

approaches the cash register almost reverently. *As he
turns the handle of the machine, the drawer shoots out and
it plays a little hymn.* BERT *appears at the door, he stands
to attention and waits till the hymn stops.*

WOMAN Bless you both. [BERT *shows her out*]

ARCHIE I think I'll make it a treble. [BERT *returns*]
    BERT *rushes over to the electric panel and from behind
    the volt meter produces two bottles of stout.*

BERT Quick! Before His Eminence comes in [*He pours*]

ARCHIE [*toasting*] To all incurable complaints.

BERT And imaginary diseases.
          They drink. BERT *goes to the cash register*

BERT Wot's the box-office like?

ARCHIE Not bad, not bad returns at all...

BERT And mind it all goes in.
    HORACE *now appears. He wears a dog collar in place of
    his stock. His manner is both indignant and a little
    pompous.*

HORACE What's going h'on 'ere? How can I meditate amidst
  h'all this fracasse?

ARCHIE Nothink, 'Orace, 'onest.

HORACE You've dropped something.

ARCHIE What?

HORACE A haitch. Two Haitches! [*He sniffs*] H'and the h'air is
  laden with h'alcoholic h'odours. One of you has been boozing
  —drinking. [*He finds the bottle behind the cash register*] Which?
  Who? [*both look penitent*] Brother Bert you will be fined half
  your rake h'off! [*He now retrieves 'The Greyhound Gazette'*]
  Brother h'Archibald, I see you are going to the dogs both
  metamorphorically and laterally speaking.

ARCHIE Crikey!

HORACE And no blasphemy.
          A bell rings. BERT *sidles off*

ARCHIE Can't we 'ave a drop of beer now and again just to keep
  body and soul together?

HORACE No! We must mortify our flesh. Beer will not help h'us,
  but Spirit will.

ARCHIE Ah, that's more like our 'Orace. [*He produces another bottle*] There's nothing like a nip of gin as a chaser. [*He goes to pour it*]

HORACE No, let me pour it.

> *He takes the bottle and begins to pour its contents on to the floor.*

ARCHIE Strewth! Bert, quick 'ere! 'Orace 'as gorn orf 'is 'ead!

> *Before* ARCHIE *turns round,* HORACE *takes a long swig from the bottle but with a final effort empties the remains on the floor.*

HORACE This will go down to history!

ARCHIE More likely to the flat below! Bloomin' sin I calls it.

HORACE [*sententiously*] There's more rejoicing in Heaven when a drunkard denies himself a gin than when a teetotaller orders another tomato cocktail.

ARCHIE I must write that one down.

HORACE Yes, here's a pencil. And you may add this, which I culled from my meditation this morning.

ARCHIE Wot?

HORACE All is not wot it would appear to seem. [*Closing his eyes*]

ARCHIE Not 'arf it ain't.

HORACE You don't understand. But you will when you've had the same spiritual experience as I, as me, as us! Do you know this morning I heard voices, Voices crying my own name?

ARCHIE What did they say?

HORACE Simply 'Horace, Horace'.

ARCHIE It must have been your conscience.

HORACE No, it was far too clear. It must have bin an angel.

A VOICE [*through the desk phone speaker*] 'Orace! 'Orace!

HORACE There it is again! Or do you not hear it? Perhaps you are not attuned.

VOICE 'Orace. 'Orace.

HORACE Yes! I hear you. I vow to sign the pledge today.

VOICE Cor Blimey!…Any'ow there's a certain young lady to see you. She ain't got no appointment. Shall I show 'er up?

ARCHIE [*into desk speaker*] Yes, Bert, just show the spirit up. [*To*

HORACE] We 'ad these gadgets fixed this morning. There's one in your Sanctum too. Useful box of tricks.

HORACE Ho! Ho! An 'oax! But no gadget can explain my powers away, can they?

ARCHIE No.

HORACE I 'ave the powers of a saint yet I have lived like a sinner.

ARCHIE Oh! I dunno, 'Orace, you've lived a pretty reg'lar life... stretches of 'ard labour and plenty of solitude.

HORACE And henceforth I intend to live a life more fitting to my powers lest they be taken from me.

ARCHIE Wot are you going to do?

HORACE It's wot we're not going to do! Henceforth you will stop knocking orf my clients' gloves, handbags and umbrellas whilst they are in the Sanctum with me. From now we shall be a charity!

ARCHIE I got yer, no income tax.

HORACE And to continue; that consulting couch must only be used for consultants...

ARCHIE [*indicating* RECEPTIONIST] And who's going to keep Betty 'appy?

HORACE Leave her to me, I will guide her.

ARCHIE Mind she don't guide you.

Enter BERT *followed by* PENNY

BERT [*whispering to* ARCHIE] How is 'e? Any better?

ARCHIE No.

BERT An old friend to see you, 'Orace, one you might be able to help.

HORACE So I will—if she will let me. Tell me, have you renounced your wanton ways? [PENNY *is still unable to speak*] As I feared; and can you deny that on Mondays, Wednesdays and Fridays you walk out with one, and on Tuesdays, Thursdays and Saturdays you go out with another?

PENNY *remains silent though she makes a great effort to speak.*

ARCHIE You got Sunday free, Penny?

HORACE Your silence is an eloquent confession of your guilt.

The red light flicks on

BERT Cavey!

HORACE You mean somebody is at the door. Show them in.

    BERT *opens the door to admit the* REV. CUTHBERT *and*
    MR SPLEEN, *then withdraws.*

CUTHBERT My dear Horace, how nice to see you. Tell me, how
are your supernatural powers today?

ARCHIE [*pressing cash register*] Fifty-eight pund.

HORACE ...guineas.

CUTHBERT Well, I'm relieved to hear the 'fluence is no less.
Lady Recent is most anxious that your potency should be at its
zenith for your Jamboree—the day she launches you and gives
London its own Lourdes. She and Gabriel Muscatel are in
committee discussing the financial ways and means of this
spiritual revival—being a film producer, Gaby's just the man to
get your message over, he exudes ideas—as you'll see, he said
he'll be along.

HORACE Have they booked the H'albert 'All?

SPLEEN Yes and Lady Recent has agreed to take the Chair.

ARCHIE I'll 'elp to 'old it up.

HORACE Shall I be on the air?

CUTHBERT Why yes of course, television too, to show each cure
before and after you have laid your hands upon them. Now
Master, there is one question I must ask you; what is your
baptismal denomination?

HORACE Eh?

CUTHBERT Are you C. of E.—or Non-conformist?

        HORACE *looks bewildered*

SPLEEN He means to what religion do you belong? What is your
belief?

HORACE I believe in *the* Commandment.

CUTHBERT Indeed—which one?

HORACE Don't steal—why, are there any more?

ARCHIE It's just as well you never 'eard of them.

CUTHBERT There are another nine—ten in all.

HORACE [*self-pity*] Any'ow that is quite enough for me [*aggressively*] or any other man, I 'ope!

CUTHBERT [*genuinely impressed*] How true and how extraordinarily profound! I have been thinking along those lines for years but have not been able to express it with the same brevity or your lucidity.

> *The red light goes on,* GABRIEL MUSCATEL *enters with appropriate flourish. He stands framed in the doorway and looks round the room. The others seem almost hypnotised.*

MUSCATEL Be at your ease, I am ingognito. Well? What is it you all want? Why have you come to see me? I can give you five minutes before I fly to Rome. [*He comes into the room*] No! That's where I was this morning—at the Vatican...I have applied for the Papal blessing on my new picture, 'The life of Saint Francis' in technicolor. In ten minutes we leave for Hollywood.

SPLEEN With His Holiness or Saint Francis?

MUSCATEL Neither, I fly alone.

SPLEEN But you said 'we'.

MUSCATEL Quite so, my friend, I have the genius for two.

SPLEEN How you do get about.

MUSCATEL This interview is finished.

SPLEEN I'm not of the Press.

MUSCATEL Then do not waste my time. [*To all*] Now the way to put this show over is first of all to script the thing. [*To* RECEPTIONIST] Can you take shorthand? With those legs you should. Well, give me a couple of dictaphones and in ten minutes we'll have it all lined up, ready for a run through. I guessed you'd need my help so I brought the choir along— show them in.

> BERT *goes to the door.* THREE WOMEN *enter, they constitute the* VOX POPULI CHOIR.

MUSCATEL [*to* HORACE] Now just run through a cure or two as you'll do it on the Day. It'll give us the proper timing. Now, stand there. [*He drags* HORACE *into position*] Then what happens? You lay your hands on the cripple? Where the Hell's the cripple? [PENNY *tries to volunteer and seize this opportunity to be cured*] What you? No, you won't do. You don't look lame enough. [*To* RECEPTIONIST] We'll use you as

a stand-in. [*The* RECEPTIONIST *replaces* PENNY] Right do
your stuff. [HORACE *lays his hands on the* RECEPTIONIST]
No, no, that's flat. We'll have to hot it up. Do your tricks
again. [*to* CHOIR] And take your cue from me.

> HORACE *repeats his movement.* MUSCATEL *makes a*
> *gesture to the* CHOIR *who commence to chant.*

CHOIR Halleluja! Halleluja! [PENNY *exits unnoticed*]
MUSCATEL Yes, yes, that's what we'll do. After each cure a
chorus. Nothing like music to move the feelings. That'll get
'em. Now—one, two...

> *The phone rings*

RECEPTIONIST Welbeck 1869. The Saint's Sanctum...yes...
HORACE If that's Lady Recent, tell her I cannot lay hands on her
tonight...!

CURTAIN

Act III

SCENE ONE

A week later. The Inaugural meeting of the Lowest Common Denominator. The stage represents the platform of the Hall. It is decorated with appropriate banners and bunting. An extraordinary large photograph of SAINT HORACE *hangs back stage centre. In front of this is a long table decorated with flowers and draped to suggest an altar—behind this sits a motley crowd of Sponsors. There is an empty chair in the centre; the* REV. CUTHBERT *sits to its right. A Mohamedan sits beside a Catholic priest, whilst a Chinese Buddhist and a Plymouth Brethren are doing their best to find a common viewpoint. Everybody wears earphones. The neon-lit alabaster figure is on the table. The musical cash register, still flanked with burning candles stands on a small side table, stage right.*

To the left, front stage, sit several people who are to be cured—though one might suspect that this is against their best interests. Amongst these are a girl with St Vitus Dance; a Dipsomaniac; a Depressive; and an old man playing the violin—but neither his bow nor violin have any strings, nevertheless the inaudible melody moves him to tears, another man wears shorts and an open neck shirt and sits with a butterfly net, sometimes he gets up and catches an imaginary specimen which he triumphantly thrusts into his specimen box. And there is a large, obstreperous type who wears a Russian red stock and boots, he carries a hammer and sickle and is constantly bruising himself with one and cutting himself on the other. Sandwiched between these assorted idiots are LAZARUS *who sits slyly wearing his dark glasses, label and with his white stick, and finally* PENNY, *who is still dub with the shock of* HORACE's *first healing at Epsom.*

At one side of the Proscenium stands a Radio Commentator who is in the person of SPLEEN: *at the other side, an engineer with a television camera. Steps lead from the central aisle of the auditorium on to the stage.*

When the CURTAIN RISES there is loud applause coming from the stage—because of the somewhat colourful delegate from Mecca, the CALIPH *of* KATHWAT, *who has just delivered his speech. For a second he stands beaming, then he continues speaking in Arabic:*

KATHWAT [*still standing*]

Inmud eelsare

Inclaynoneis!

Infir taris

Inoaknoneis!

He pauses—more applause

SPLEEN As listeners heard, the Delegate from Islam the Caliph of Kathwat, ended his address with an apt quotation from the Koran [*he put on his earphones*] which translated means:

In mud eels are

In clay none is

In fir, tar is

In oak none is.

Enter LADY RECENT, *alla marcia*

SPLEEN Now, everybody stands to greet the Chairman as Lady Recent appears. Here she comes leaving a wake of admiration before and after.

There is appropriate music as the Procession following LADY RECENT *and headed by* GABRIEL MUSCATEL *dressed as a Buddhist and swinging a censer enters up the aisle of the auditorium.* BERT *and* ARCHIE *are smartly dressed and walk each side of* HORACE. *They carry banners. The* VOX POPULI CHOIR *bring up the rear.*

SPLEEN And now the Saint arrives. Gabriel Muscatel leads the procession.

*The Procession reaches the platform. The Sponsors stand
for a second, then the* REV. CUTHBERT *rises.*

CUTHBERT Before the Saint performs a miracle and lays his
hands on those gathered here to be healed or cured, it is my
privilege to ask his Eminence to address us to give us that
guidance which we seek. This is the moment for which the
silent Universe has listened. Now Master, give us thy word.

> CUTHBERT *sits.* HORACE *is motioned towards the
> central dais. He clears his throat, he feels his dog collar.*

HORACE Don't.

> *There is an awkward pause. Then the* SPONSORS *begin
> to examine their headphones straining to hear what is not
> being said. The* TECHNICIANS *frantically attend to
> their instruments.*

CUTHBERT [*removing his headphones*] I beg your pardon, but
owing to some technical hitch we did not hear...pray give me
your message once again.

HORACE Don't.

> *Another pause. Then* HORACE *descends*

SPLEEN Seldom has wisdom been imparted with such celerity
or with more commendable brevity.

> THE SPONSORS *are embarrassed, the* IDIOTS *restive.*
> LADY RECENT *takes all in hand.*

LADY RECENT Commence the Cures!

CUTHBERT Begin the Miracles!

MUSCATEL [*to* CHOIR] Bring up the Music!

> *The* CHOIR *begins a low chant whilst* MUSCATEL *goes
> over to the* IDIOTS. *He selects* ONE *which he leads
> forward.*

MUSCATEL This schizophrenic suffers under the delusion that he
is Napoleon Bonaparte. May the Saint now reveal his true
identity and restore him to the grace of human sanity.

> *The* IDIOT, *who maintains the well-known position of
> Napoleon, now kneels before* HORACE *who lays his hand
> on the Emperor's head.*

HORACE Hokey pokey! Abracadabraca!

> *The music of Jubilation commences*

CHOIR Halleluja! Halleluja!

> *The* IDIOT *stands, turns and confronts the audience. He now appears as* ADOLF HITLER *complete with moustache and arm band. He gives the Hitler salute and is about to commence a frenzied peroration.*

NAPOLEON Meinen Damen und Herren...

MUSCATEL [*to* CHOIR] Ssh! [*To* ARCHIE *and* BERT] Take him for a ride!

BERT I've been waiting for this chance...

> ARCHIE *and* BERT *frog march the Fuehrer off as he begins his oration.* MUSCATEL *hastily selects a young man who is a Depressive and who looks doped, he kneels before* HORACE.

HORACE Hokey pokey! Abracadabraca!

> *The* CHOIR *chants—the young man instantly falls asleep. Still snoring he's carried off by* BERT *and* ARCHIE, *who have returned.* MUSCATEL *selects another* IDIOT *and leads on the catcher of non-existent butterflies. This man kneels, the ceremony is repeated and when he rises he breaks his net in two. At this the* CHOIR *chant enthusiastically and even* MUSCATEL *joins in the singing.*

MUSCATEL A miracle! A miracle!

> *The* ENTOMOLOGIST *slowly goes over to* MUSCATEL *and carefully removes a non-existent specimen from his coat, and putting it in his box, he goes off—as* MUSCATEL *produces the* DIPSOMANIAC. *This unfortunate gentleman drinks from a bottle of Scotch and sings in between mouthfuls. He is forced to kneel before* HORACE.

HORACE [*sympathetically*] Hokey Pokey! Abracadabraca!

> *The* DIPSOMANIAC *rises. He passes his bottle, still half full, to* ARCHIE. *The* CHOIR *chant most energetically, then the* DIPSOMANIAC *produces a hip flask and drinks from this. Pandemonium now reigns on stage.*

LADY RECENT Bring down the curtain!

CUTHBERT House lights!

LADY RECENT Charlatan etc. [*ad lib.*]

> *They* ALL *go off as the curtain goes up and down and the*

lights on and off. ARCHIE *and* BERT *rescue* PENNY
from the riot and exit though she still gesticulates towards
HORACE *who is left alone on stage except for the* DIPSO-
MANIAC. *He is most dishevelled and broken. Slowly he
removes his dog collar. Then with his old skill, he removes
the hip flask from the* DIPSOMANIAC'*s pocket. He
drinks deep on the darkened stage.*

HORACE The worst of these dipsomaniacs is they get us drun-
kards a bad name!

SCENE TWO

*Several nights later. The same street scene as in Act I,
Scene Two. It is a dark November evening. The street
traders stand in their usual positions.* MAX *is selling
newspapers outside the Tube.* KATE *has a couple of pails
full of chrysanthemums.* BERT *is roasting chestnuts
whilst* ARCHIE, *wearing* MUSCATEL'*s coat, is lounging
against a wall.* BEN *continues to play his fiddle and
from his old corner,* LAZARUS *views the charity of
man.*

MAX
Evening Standard! Late night Final!
All the runners for Aintree.
   A woman comes out of the Tube and goes down street
KATE Lovely chrezants! Buy a nice bunch of chrezants ducks...
BERT Chestnuts all hot...[*ad lib.*]
                BEN *begins to fiddle*
BERT Cor, still playing the same old tune? Anybody'd think
your fiddle only 'ad five notes.
BEN Well, and how many fingers do you think I 'ave, eh?
KATE [*to* BERT] We all know you've bin to the H'Albert 'All
once, but you don't 'ave to go all 'ighbrow now you're back in
the gutter again.
ARCHIE And now you're both working for me you don't 'ave to

L

waste your breath chewing the rag either. If you don't sell those chrezants soon, they'll take root in yer ruddy bucket.

KATE Ain't easy to sell at your price, Archie. People who've got that amount of money ain't interested in bunches of flowers, only wreaths seem to take their eye.

LAZARUS 'Ere, look who I see.

BERT Who?

LAZARUS 'Orace! He's just come round the johnny horner.

BERT Not the Saint hisself? Wonder wot 'e's bin up to?

ARCHIE Pity 'e forgot how to do that trick of 'is. We were sitting pretty for a time.

BERT You couldn't 'ave done so badly out of it. More like only 'arf went into that kitty.

> HORACE *slouches in very disconsolate. His hands in his pockets, his coat collar turned up; he lacks both his stock and his buttonhole.*

BERT Hokey Pokey! Abracadabraca! [HORACE *makes no sign*] What 'appened to yer? Proper riot it was. We waited for yer quite a time, didn't we Archie?

ARCHIE Yer—a good minute it was. Any'ow, 'ows yer principles, 'Orace?

BERT 'Ope you've given up wastin' licker? Well, what made you crawl back 'ere?

> HORACE *still makes no response*

KATE I expect 'e came back 'ere cause 'e'd nowhere else to go— same as most of us do most of the time. [*She goes and sticks a flower in his lapel*] [*To* ARCHIE] All right, you can take it out of me wages...why don't you sign 'im on?

ARCHIE I ain't running no circus nor home for fallen angels.

> *Meanwhile* HORACE *has been looking round unobtrusively. He now sidles furtively into the gutter and takes up a pitch. He hopes nobody has noticed his move and begins to whistle with studied unconcern and of course, out of tune.*

LAZARUS [*seeing him*] Oh no you don't...this is my territory!

> *The others turn and notice* HORACE'*s move. They begin to laugh at him whilst he continues to whistle putting on a*

brave front and quietly confident of something up his sleeve.

BERT Now what's he up to?

ARCHIE Bet it's ice cream—it's cold enough for him to have thought of that.

BERT Wot's yer line, 'Orace? More magic sand? Come on, tell us what it is.

HORACE [*proudly*] Truth.

ARCHIE Wot! Ruddy tracts. Can't 'ave that dope in this street, can we Bert?

KATE Perhaps 'e's going to sell his old haloes.

They are all laughing at him whilst he proudly produces a little board which he hangs round his neck. The board bears the inscription 'DOWN AND OUT'. The others look at it—then stop laughing.

BERT [*genuinely embarrassed*] Well you look yer part chum. Not a bad line at all, is it, Archie?

ARCHIE No future to it, not unless you've got a wife in rags by your side. 'E ought to ask Penny to 'elp 'im. She don't do much nowadays.

BERT Any'ow, let's 'ave a pint to drink to Private Enterprise.

ARCHIE Yes, but better not ask him, too.

BERT and ARCHIE go into the pub and as PENNY comes up the street, HORACE hides his board inside his coat as though suddenly ashamed of his plight. And he bends down as if to do his shoe lace up, pretending he was in the gutter for that purpose. She misunderstands the move and thinks he is merely trying to avoid seeing her, so she passes on to the lamp post where she stands looking the other way. Immediately she passes HORACE he begins to shamble off in the opposite direction.

KATE Where are you orf to? What's she done to you, eh?

HORACE Even Penny's turned against me now.

KATE What gives yer that idea?

HORACE She don't even speak to me no more.

KATE Don't she indeed?

HORACE No, not a word since I took 'er to the Derby.

KATE [*sarcastically*] I wonder why?

HORACE Dunno. She knowed all along that I was only selling sand but when I asked her to tell the copper she didn't say nothing—ratted on me she did! If only she's explained to them, maybe I wouldn't have got taken up, then dropped so bloomin' 'ard.

KATE Didn't you know she was as dumb as a gatepost? Struck dumb she was.

HORACE With what?

KATE Why surprise of course! The shock at finding you were an 'Ealer—or whatever it was you was. It gave 'er a nasty turn it did, I can tell yer to find you were a sort of saint.

HORACE But she never told me.

KATE How could she, stupid? Didn't I tell you she was dumb but she tried to see yer, but yer'd got so many toffs round yer she couldn't get a word in edgeways and when she pointed to 'er poor mouth they thought she was just 'ungry or thirsty—like I am!

> *She follows the others to the pub. After a moment's hesitation* HORACE *goes over to* PENNY *and hands her his buttonhole.*

HORACE 'Ere Penny—it looks a bit ragged but it'll remind you of me.

> *She takes the flower. Together they sit on the kerb*

HORACE Seems as if I shall 'ave to do all the talking, don't it. I'm sorry, Penny, I didn't know then, when I 'ad the power to cure yer. Too late though now, ain't it a pity. Don't seem to be able to do that trick no more, however much I tries. Can't understand how I ever could; can you? God must be a queer sort of bloke—He gave me powers when I was nothing and then, when I tries to pay Him back by stopping drinking and thieving, He just took 'em away again. Don't make no sense does it? P'raps He likes us better when we're wicked and 'umble, than when we are good and with swollen 'eads. Still there it is, Penny, and nothink makes much sense to a fool does it?

> *He puts his arm affectionately but awkwardly round her*

PENNY If I could speak I'd tell yer.

HORACE Wot would yer tell me?

PENNY Oh, 'ow I'd missed yer...[*she realises*] Good Lord, I said it...didn't you 'ear?

HORACE [*quite unaware*] Wot?

PENNY Me! Me speak! You've done it again. Cured me you 'ave!

HORACE Oh dear.

PENNY Ain't you pleased? Kate! Bert!

> *She gets up to call the others.* HORACE *puts his hand over her mouth.*

HORACE Ssh! Please don't tell 'em. I don't want to go through all that again.

PENNY Yer, [*sitting down*] they'd only take you away from me again...well, take me into the country, as you promised. Come on, let's enjoy ourselves.

HORACE Yes but...[*he feels in his pocket*]

PENNY Are you broke?

HORACE [*proudly*] No, I got a good line now, Penny, regular too.

PENNY Honest!

HORACE Of course.

PENNY I mean—really?

HORACE Yes, job for a lifetime.

PENNY [*hopefully*] And somewhere to sleep?

HORACE Yes, a flat all to me own. [*Pause*]

PENNY You can come 'ome with me if you like, 'Orace seeing as you've nowhere to go.

HORACE I tell yer I got a nice place, proper cosy it is, and ever so cheap.

PENNY [*now believing*] Well, can't I come with you?

HORACE No.

PENNY Don't you want me?

HORACE There's only room for one. It's a small place.

> *He gets up, wishing to stop her curiosity. Then with resolution he continues.*

Any'ow, if I'm going to save up to take you to the country, I'd better get along so I can get up early tomorrow and put in a double shift.

PENNY [*touched*] Work overtime for me?

HORACE Yes, that's it—you'll 'ave to wait a bit.

PENNY [*getting up*] Oh, well, I dare say it'll still be there.

HORACE What?

PENNY The country of course—all that dirt—nothing but dirt.
Well...good night, 'Orace.

HORACE Good night.

> *She goes off.* HORACE *picks up the flower she's forgotten.
> He makes sure that she has gone. Then he goes into the
> phone box still carrying the flower. He takes his coat off
> and lifts the receiver.*

Will you please call me at 7.30? This number is HOPE 0100...
> *He kicks off his boots and carefully places them tidily
> together outside the door of the phone box. Then he hangs
> his board on the outside door handle. He curls up and
> goes to sleep.*

> LAZARUS *taps his way along the street. As he passes the
> phone box, he stops and peers at the board, moving it
> towards the street light. It can now be seen to read 'NOT
> WORKING'.* LAZARUS *turns the board back to
> DOWN AND OUT. He goes off tapping his way
> along the kerb.*

CURTAIN

Our Lady's Tumbler

Es vies des anciens peres
La on sont bones les materes
Nos raconte on d'un examplel;
Jo ne di mie c'alsi bel
N'ait on oi par maintes fois
Mais cil n'est pas si en desfois
Ne face bien a raconter
Or vos voil dire et aconter
D'un menestrel que li avint...

Del Tumbeor Nostre Dame
Anonymous French twelfth
century. Text taken from
article by Wilhelm Foerster
in *Romania* (Libraire A.
Frank, Paris 1873)

This play was commissioned by the Salisbury and
District Society of Arts as part of the celebrations
for the Festival of Britain 1951. It was first performed in Salisbury Cathedral. The decor for the
original production was by Cecil Beaton.

The music was composed by Arthur Oldham and
is obtainable from Messrs Boosey & Hawkes Ltd.,
295 Regent Street, London W1.

CHARACTERS

FATHER MARCELLUS   an abbot

BROTHER SEBASTIAN   a poet

BROTHER JUSTIN   a composer

BROTHER GREGORY   a gardener

BROTHER ANDREW   a novice

The scene is set in a chapel. The action takes place before a statue of the Blessed Virgin.

The period is not specified.

The play is in one act and is so designed that, if necessary, it may be performed in a church or hall without a stage or house curtain. The statue is the only essential property.

Our Lady's Tumbler

Before the statue of the Blessed Virgin. To the right,
BROTHER SEBASTIAN *is seen, seated on a step. He is*
writing, the paper is held on his knee, a broom beside him.
A mixed choir sing (off)

HYMN OF DEDICATION

If love is made of words,
    Who can love more than I?
If love is all self-love,
    Who's more beloved than I?

If love is made of faith,
    Who can love less than I?
If love is to submit,
    Who's less beloved than I?

If love is made of tears,
    Who could love more than she?
If love is to betray,
    Who was beloved as He?

Oh may my fickle heart
    Be faithful to my soul;
Deceiving jealous Death,
    Betray my life to Thee.

*

ARIA [*Tenor solo off*]
    O Virgin Mother,
        Your arms were made a cradle,
    And that cradle
        was for Him.

Your care was as gentle,
                        gentle as the candle
Lighting the low stable;
                that high throne at His birth.

O Virgin Mother,
   Your heart was made for sorrow,
And that sorrow
   was for Him.
            Your grief was as heavy,
                        heavy as the thunder
Rending the high hill to
                that valley of His death.

O Virgin Mother,
   Your lips were made for gladness,
And that gladness
   was for Him.
            Your smile was as happy,
                        happy as His Spirit
Leaving the sepulchre,
                that palace as He rose.

O Virgin Mother,
   Your eyes were made for pity,
And that pity
   is for Man.
   Your love is as gracious,
                        gracious as a river
Flowing through this desert,
                this desert which is Man.

*   *   *

BROTHER SEBASTIAN [*reading his composition over to himself*]
He stands as a beggar, yet it is I who am blind,
  Nor does he seek for alms, but to give me sight;
For my sin is self-love and all my days are darker than the
  night...'

That's clumsy!...I don't like the inversion: 'nor does he seek for
  alms'.
It's terribly clumsy...
Let's try: 'He does not seek for alms but to give me sight.'
Yes, that's clearer and has got rid of that inversion.
Now how does it run?
'He stands as a beggar, yet it is I who am blind,
  He does not seek for alms but to give me sight;
For my sin is self-love and all my days are darker than the
  night.'
Still not right. The last line stumbles like a centipede that's out
  of step.
'For my sin is self-love...' another inversion—that's the worst
  of knowing too much Latin;
Must alter that, somehow...

> BROTHER ANDREW *comes in carrying a pail. He starts
> to scrub the aisle, and seems unaware of* BROTHER
> SEBASTIAN'*s presence.*

'For my sin is self-love'...No: 'for self-love is my sin.'
BROTHER ANDREW [*to himself as he noisily pushes his pail
about*]
'Amo, amas, amat,
Amamus, amatis [*pause*] amant.'
'amabo, amabis, amabit,
amabimus, amabitis...[*pause*]
BROTHER SEBASTIAN
'For self-love's my sin'
No, 'For my eyes are blind with self-love'—yes, that's better.
BROTHER ANDREW
'Amabo, amabis, amabit,
amabimus, amabitis...[*pause, then almost proudly*] amabint!'

BROTHER SEBASTIAN [*correcting him without looking up*]
  'Bunt.'
BROTHER ANDREW
  'Amabunt.'
BROTHER SEBASTIAN
  'For my eyes are blind with self-love and my days are darker
    than the night.'
  That's worse. Now it sounds as if that centipede's got gout!
BROTHER ANDREW
  'Amabam, amabas, amabat,
  amabamus, amabatis, ama...[*pause*]
BROTHER SEBASTIAN
  'Bant.'
  'For my eyes are blind with self-love and all my days are night.'
BROTHER ANDREW [*moving his pail as emphasis*]
  'Amabant.'
BROTHER SEBASTIAN
  'He stands as a beggar;
     He does not seek for alms, but to give me sight;
  For my eyes are blind with self-love and all my days are night.
  Night that is darker than darkness
     night that...'
BROTHER ANDREW
  'Amavi, amavisti, amavit,
  amavimus...
BROTHER SEBASTIAN
  Do you mind?
BROTHER ANDREW
  Ssh...'amavimus, amavistis'
BROTHER SEBASTIAN
  Brother Andrew...
BROTHER ANDREW
  Yes?
BROTHER SEBASTIAN
  Do you mind?...
BROTHER ANDREW
  What?

BROTHER SEBASTIAN

Oh, nothing. I thought perhaps I was interrupting you.

Are you sure I'm not disturbing you or preventing you from
  concentrating?

BROTHER ANDREW

No, not at all, Brother Sebastian.

I don't mind in the least.

BROTHER SEBASTIAN

Indeed, that's very good of you.

BROTHER ANDREW

Not at all. I'm used to working with people watching me.

BROTHER SEBASTIAN

Are you? Why, of course—I was forgetting.

But you see, Brother Andrew, I am not so fortunate:

I lack your professional experience...

So do you mind not imitating a parrot,

And taking your amo amas amat elsewhere,

So that I get on with my work?

BROTHER ANDREW

I'm sorry. I didn't know you were doing anything.

I thought you were just sitting down.

BROTHER SEBASTIAN

So I am 'just sitting down'...

Why must everyone, especially in a monastery,

assume that unless you've got a pail in one hand

and a hammer in the other—you're not doing anything?

As a matter of fact, I was thinking.

BROTHER ANDREW

Why, have you lost something?

BROTHER SEBASTIAN

Do I look as if I have?...

Ah, I see what you mean...dear Brother Andrew.

No, I've not lost anything; I was just thinking of something

I've never had—

well, never long enough to lose.

BROTHER ANDREW

Yes, good money is very hard to come by, isn't it?

BROTHER SEBASTIAN
Is it?
BROTHER ANDREW
Well, it was—
I can't get used to the fact that I don't need it no more...
BROTHER SEBASTIAN
If you must know:
I was trying to finish a poem
which I've been trying to write
with a broom in one hand and...
BROTHER ANDREW
You made it up yourself?
I wish I could write poetry.
BROTHER SEBASTIAN
Don't you?
I have yet to meet anybody who doesn't.
The reason why nobody reads poetry today is:
Everybody's too busy writing it.
You should—it's most relaxing.
BROTHER ANDREW
No, I can never find a rime,
But I did once make up a song, a sort of a ballad...
BROTHER SEBASTIAN
What a pity! I hoped you were unique.
BROTHER ANDREW
What's your poem about?
BROTHER SEBASTIAN
It's a canzone.
BROTHER ANDREW
Is it in Latin?
BROTHER SEBASTIAN
No, though that would have been easier.
BROTHER ANDREW
What's it called?
BROTHER SEBASTIAN
'A Prayer for Our Lady's Intercession'.
I've written it for the Celebration.

BROTHER ANDREW
  What celebration?
BROTHER SEBASTIAN
  This evening's, of course.
  I shall recite my poem before the statue,
  As an offering to Our Lady.
BROTHER ANDREW
  She'll like that.
  Do you always read your poems to her?
BROTHER SEBASTIAN
  No, of course not.
  Don't you know what day it is? Can't you read the calendar?
BROTHER ANDREW
  No, I can't make Latin out yet.
BROTHER SEBASTIAN
  But hasn't anybody told you?
  Don't you know why you're giving the floor an extra scrub?
  And why I'm sweeping with one hand and writing with the
    other?
BROTHER ANDREW
  To brighten the place up, I suppose.
BROTHER SEBASTIAN
  Yes, because today happens to be
  The feast day of the Blessed Virgin.
BROTHER ANDREW
  And your poem's a sort of birthday present?
BROTHER SEBASTIAN
  One of three offerings.
BROTHER ANDREW [*to statue*]
  Nobody told me it was your birthday,
  Or I'd have done something too.
BROTHER SEBASTIAN
  Never mind, Brother Andrew, you can watch with the others.
  The chapel will soon be full—
  Everybody in the village will be here,
  And people come from miles around
    to see whether the statue will move.

M

BROTHER ANDREW
    Does she really?
BROTHER SEBASTIAN
    Don't you know? I thought everybody knew.
    It's a legend: when the perfect offering is made, the statue will
        make a sign.
BROTHER ANDREW [*to statue*]
    You see, I wasn't here last year. And nobody told me.
    So I haven't got you anything.
BROTHER SEBASTIAN [*interested and touched by* BROTHER
ANDREW's *simplicity*]
    Brother Andrew, tell me what made you become a novice?
BROTHER ANDREW
    My heart.
BROTHER SEBASTIAN
    You mean, you had a vocation—
BROTHER ANDREW
    Yes, my heart used to go pit-a-pat
    Whenever I did my...
    Whenever I did anything vigorous.
BROTHER SEBASTIAN
    Ah, palpitations...
BROTHER ANDREW
    That's it; so I had to stop...
    so I had to give the profession up
    right in the middle of the season.
    Three years next Christmas it'll be.
BROTHER SEBASTIAN
    I understand: a vacation more than a vocation...
    But what made you become a novice?
    Couldn't you have retired to a little farm or...
BROTHER ANDREW
    It wasn't because I hadn't any money, don't think that.
    But I was sort of lonely, you see
    —Always having moved around in a troupe...
BROTHER SEBASTIAN
    Yes, I see—so you just joined another?

BROTHER ANDREW
Why, the Abbot's not going to make me leave, is he?

BROTHER SEBASTIAN
No, I don't think so—not if you learn your conjugations silently, and let me try and finish this poem.

BROTHER ANDREW
Won't you read me a bit?

BROTHER SEBASTIAN
No, it needs polishing.

BROTHER ANDREW
I'll make allowances. Don't be shy.

BROTHER SEBASTIAN
Thank you. But you'll hear it later.

BROTHER ANDREW
I suppose you think I wouldn't understand it?

BROTHER SEBASTIAN
No, it wasn't that.
I'll tell you what I'll do: I'll read some if you stand down there and then you can tell me if you can hear it all right. The acoustics are a bit erratic; one's voice certainly goes up to heaven—
for nobody can hear you on earth.

BROTHER ANDREW [*going back*]
Here?

BROTHER SEBASTIAN
No, farther back. There, that'll do.
'Night that is darker than darkness,
    Night which no gentle evening
Leads in,
              nor dawn
                        alleviates,
nor sun penetrates;
                        night of no shadow;
Night...'

BROTHER ANDREW
Right, I'm ready.

BROTHER SEBASTIAN
  But I've read it. Didn't you hear it?

BROTHER ANDREW
  Not a word.

BROTHER SEBASTIAN
  I'll have to stand farther from the statue.
  I'll try again...
  'Night that is darker than darkness,
    Night which no gentle evening
  Leads in,
            nor dawn
                     alleviates,
  nor sun penetrates;
                night of no shadow...'
  How's that?

BROTHER ANDREW
  Not very good.

BROTHER SEBASTIAN
  You mean the poem? Or can't you hear it?

BROTHER ANDREW [*returning to him*]
  You want to throw your voice. Look, like this:
  And use your lips more and imagine you are talking
    to some person right at the back of the audience.

BROTHER SEBASTIAN
  ...You mean 'congregation'.

BROTHER ANDREW
  YOU WANT TO SPEAK LIKE THIS,
  or half the sound gets lost in the roof of the marquee...

BROTHER SEBASTIAN
  ...cathedral.

BROTHER ANDREW
  But of course, it's easier if you've got a good house.

BROTHER SEBASTIAN
  A what?

BROTHER ANDREW
  If it's a good day...if the takings...
  I mean, if you've got plenty of people in the tent...

BROTHER SEBASTIAN
  Cathedral.

BROTHER ANDREW
  Then the sound carries better, see?

BROTHER SEBASTIAN
  Yes, I think we'll get a good house...
  But I'll throw my voice as you showed me.
  Thanks very much for the tip.

BROTHER ANDREW
  That's all right—we artists have got to help each other, haven't
    we?

BROTHER SEBASTIAN
  Yes, that's true...
  I wonder if you'd mind doing this sweeping for me while I
    finish this poem?

BROTHER ANDREW [*taking the broom and sweeping*]
  Not at all,
  I don't suppose I could help with the poem.
        BROTHER GREGORY *comes in carrying some roses*

BROTHER GREGORY
  Brother Sebastian...

BROTHER SEBASTIAN
  Yes, what is it now?

BROTHER GREGORY
  As you're not doing anything, could you hold these flowers for
    a moment while I get some water?

BROTHER SEBASTIAN [*not looking up*]
  Why, of course. I hate being idle.

BROTHER GREGORY [*holding the flowers out*]
  Well, come on then.
  What are you doing now?

BROTHER SEBASTIAN
  I'm just writing an inscription.
  I've dedicated my poem to you.

BROTHER GREGORY
  Really! I'm touched.

BROTHER SEBASTIAN

You will be [*reading it*]: 'To my friend, Brother Gregory, with
whose help this poem would never have been written.'

He goes to hold the flowers

And you needn't thrust the thorns into my hands quite so
viciously.

BROTHER ANDREW [*going to them, still holding his broom*]

Aren't they beautiful [*pause*]

There's nothing like flowers, is there? [*pause*]

To cheer a place up, I mean.

Though, of course, they always remind me of funerals...

Do they remind you of funerals, Brother Sebastian?

BROTHER SEBASTIAN

Yes, that's why they cheer me up.

BROTHER ANDREW [*coming closer*]

They are lovely.

BROTHER GREGORY

Do mind your broom...

BROTHER ANDREW

I'm sorry. Yes, they're the most beautiful roses I've ever
seen.

They're almost too perfect, don't you think? [*pause*]

What's your favourite flower, Brother Sebastian? [*pause*]

I said: 'What's your favourite flower, Brother Sebastian?'

BROTHER SEBASTIAN

Black roses.

BROTHER ANDREW

Is it? How interesting!

Now, I've never seen a black rose.

Have you seen a black rose, Brother Gregory?

BROTHER GREGORY

They're all black at night.

BROTHER ANDREW

Are they now? How interesting.

But my favourite rose is a sweet brier rose.

BROTHER SEBASTIAN

Is it now?

BROTHER GREGORY
  How interesting.
BROTHER ANDREW
  Is it? Why, many people like the sweet-brier rose.
  They're quite common in the hedges: indeed, they grow wild.
  In fact I suppose they're not a rose at all.
BROTHER GREGORY
  Not at all. They're a species of flowering thorn.
BROTHER ANDREW
  How interesting. Still, they're very pretty...
  But, of course, not as beautiful as yours—
  Did you grow them all yourself?
BROTHER GREGORY
  Nature took a hand here and there. [*He finishes arranging the
    flowers*]
  Now which is best—which is the most perfect rose of all?
BROTHER SEBASTIAN
  What about this?
BROTHER GREGORY
  No, it's a little too full.
BROTHER SEBASTIAN
  Or this red one?
BROTHER GREGORY
  Yes...or this white?
  Now which of these two...?
  It's very difficult.
BROTHER ANDREW
  Why must you choose only one?
BROTHER GREGORY
  To offer Our Lady the best, of course.
BROTHER ANDREW
  Couldn't you give her all of them?
BROTHER GREGORY
  No, her hands can only hold one rose;
  And that must be the most perfect rose of all.
BROTHER ANDREW
  Then let me help you.

BROTHER GREGORY [*ignoring him*]
Now, shall it be the white or the red, Brother Sebastian?

BROTHER ANDREW [*excitedly running up*]
The red! The red!

BROTHER GREGORY
Don't touch it!
Oh, now you've soiled it.

BROTHER ANDREW
I'm sorry. [*He returns to his sweeping*]

BROTHER GREGORY
Now it will have to be the white!

BROTHER SEBASTIAN
No; choose the red.

BROTHER GREGORY
Why?

BROTHER SEBASTIAN
It's more appropriate. [BROTHER GREGORY *places the red rose
in a bowl to the left of the statue.* FATHER MARCELLUS *and*
BROTHER JUSTIN *come up the aisle.*]

FATHER MARCELLUS
The boys should, of course, lead the procession.
Now, show me where you want them to stand.

BROTHER JUSTIN [*taking up a position to the left of the statue*]
Here, Father—when I rehearsed them yesterday,
I found that if they stood farther back,
Most of the sound got lost in the transepts.

FATHER MARCELLUS
Yes, yes, I know...

BROTHER GREGORY
But if the choir stand there, Brother Justin,
None of my flowers will be seen.

FATHER MARCELLUS
Is that the difficulty? Well, surely some compromise could put
     that right.
Let them stand forward, but more to the left.
If they're here, they will not hide the flowers—

Which reminds me, Brother Gregory, see that all the gardens
are open to the villagers this evening.

BROTHER GREGORY

But...

FATHER MARCELLUS

Yes, I know we unaccountably lost all our pears last year;
But if you open the gates, the boys might get out of the habit of
climbing the wall.
The flowers are beautiful. Have you chosen the rose?

BROTHER GREGORY

Yes, Father.

FATHER MARCELLUS

Then all is ready. And just in time.
Now the three of you should retire
And prepare yourselves for the ceremony. [*They turn to go*]
And, Brother Justin, remember:
your anthem should be heard and understood;
I cannot tolerate slovenly singing.
Tell your boys to bite their consonants as though they were an
apple.
I'm sure Brother Sebastian agrees with me
—otherwise his lyric's wasted.

> *The three monks go.* FATHER MARCELLUS *examines
> the flowers.* BROTHER ANDREW *is still sweeping.*

BROTHER ANDREW

Father Abbot...

FATHER MARCELLUS

Yes, what is it?

BROTHER ANDREW

Isn't there anything I can do?

FATHER MARCELLUS

For what, my son?

BROTHER ANDREW

For her...I hear it's her birthday.
Nobody told me before,
Or I'd have done something special.

FATHER MARCELLUS
  But you have! You've scrubbed the chapel...
  I've never seen it so clean.

BROTHER ANDREW
  Please, Father, isn't there anything I can do in the ceremony, I
    mean?

FATHER MARCELLUS
  I'm afraid not, my son.

BROTHER ANDREW
  Nothing?

FATHER MARCELLUS
  No, you see, only three offerings are made each year;
  And they are already chosen.
  Besides, you can't write music or poetry, can you?

BROTHER ANDREW
  No, but...

FATHER MARCELLUS
  But what, my son?

BROTHER ANDREW
  Couldn't I light the candles for her?

FATHER MARCELLUS
  Why yes, of course. You light the candles.
  Our Lady will be grateful for anything you can do.

BROTHER ANDREW
  Anything, Father?

FATHER MARCELLUS
  Of course.
  And perhaps the more humble it is,
    the more she is pleased.
  Yes, you light the candles, Brother Andrew.

BROTHER ANDREW
  Thank you, Father. Shall I light them now?

FATHER MARCELLUS
  No; wait until you see the procession coming up the aisle.
  And don't forget to snuff them immediately the ceremony's
    over.

> FATHER MARCELLUS *goes up the aisle, leaving* BROTHER ANDREW *alone. Still holding his broom, he addresses the statue.*

BROTHER ANDREW

I'm sorry. Nobody told me it was your birthday,
Or I'd have got you a present.
But I suppose it doesn't help to be told that now.
—Now it's too late to do anything about it?
But I'll make it up to you next year, you see if I don't.
I'll tell you what I'll do...
No, we'll keep it as a surprise, we will.
It's too late this year...isn't it? [*pause*]

If you'll excuse me, sweet Lady, I'll put the broom away and
   go and smarten myself up a bit.
Then I'll be right back to light your candles.
I shan't be a minute.

> BROTHER ANDREW *goes off, right*

*

ARIA [*tenor solo off*]
I tried to grasp it in words,
                I failed.
Had I found it in words,
                it would have been enough.
I tried to grasp it in song,
                I failed.
Had I found it in song,
                it would have been enough.
I tried to grasp it from love,
                I failed:
Had I found it in love,
                it would have been enough.
I tried to grasp it from Christ,
                I succeeded.

Christ gave. I succeeded.

          It is enough.

                    *

THE CELEBRATION OF THE FEAST DAY OF
OUR LADY

BROTHER ANDREW *returns and lights the candles
before the statue of the Virgin.*

*A choir of boys proceeds up the aisle in silence. It is
followed by the three monks who are to make offerings;
and lastly by the* ABBOT *himself.*

The full choir, which has remained in position, sings:

THE HYMN FOR A FESTIVAL

Now larks and linnets lift
Into the autumn sky,
And sing as though it's spring.
    Her day renews the year.

                    Dies Mariae
                    Mater Laudanda.

The fallen leaves fly up
On to the oak and beech,
And furl themselves again.
    Her life renews the year.

                    Vita Mariae
                    Mater Aeterna.

Frail blossom and firm fruit
Are seen upon one branch,
And daffodils return.
    Her love renews the year.

                    Amor Mariae
                    Mater Amanda.

And where the stallion stamps
There, violets reappear

And all the earth is glad:
  Her Son renews the year.
                    Puer Mariae
                    Mater Divina.
The boys' choir at the left of the statue; the three monks
on the steps before it. The ABBOT *ascends the pulpit and*
addresses the congregation.

FATHER MARCELLUS

Once again, my children, we have met to celebrate
The Feast Day of the Blessed Virgin.
Here, in this chapel which bears her name,
And before this statue made in Our Lady's likeness,
It is the custom of our ancient Order
  to offer of our best
  to her who gave the world its best.
                    As you all know, the Legend is:
That when the perfect offering is made,
This statue will move and make a sign.
  Most of you will have witnessed this ceremony many times.
Those of you who are old men saw it as young men.
And those of you who are here for the first time will be
  children—
For no one in this part of the country
  fails to celebrate the Feast Day of Our Lady.
  All of you know that though we have made
These humble offerings so many times before:
  the statue has never moved.
And consequently some of you ask: how a statue made of stone
Can ever be expected to move. It is a reasonable question.
And I will answer it by asking you another question which is
  also reasonable.
It is this: Is it not more difficult for man
  To make a perfect offering out of his imperfect heart
Than it is for a statue to move
  Though its muscles be of stone?
And not until that perfect offering is made
Can this legend be disproved.

When a miracle does not occur, it does not mean
That God has not the power to perform it,
But rather that we have not the virtue to deserve it,
Nor the faith to perceive it.
    Last year, as you will remember,
I chose three people from the village to make the offerings.
And so this year, as is our custom, I have given the privilege
To three brothers of this Order:
    Brother Sebastian has written a poem, Brother Justin has
        composed a song;
    and Brother Gregory, our gardener, has grown a rose.
Let us pray that Our Lady, the Blessed Virgin,
May graciously receive these humble offerings;
And that the imperfections of the gift
May be redeemed by the humility in which it is given.

> *The* ABBOT *kneels,* BROTHER GREGORY *rises and
> stands before the statue.*

FATHER MARCELLUS
    Laetabunda canant pie
        Corda cuncta cor Mariae
    Cor amandum omni corde,
    Cor laudandum omni mente.

> *The* ABBOT *rises,* BROTHER GREGORY *kneels*

BROTHER GREGORY
    Consors patris Dexterae
    Fit Matris Deiparae
        Cor et natus

    Flos cordis Altissimi
    Flos cordis Virginei,
        Flos et fructus.

> *He rises and takes the rose from the altar. Then stands
> before the statue again.*

BROTHER GREGORY
    Thou, who grew so pure
        On this earth,

That Jesus was thy flower
   At His Birth;

Thou, who stood alone
   At the cross,
And wept for thy own
   And the whole world's loss;

Thou, who saw their spears make scarlet flowers
   In His side,
Wounds which were His, yet scars that were ours
   As He died;

Now take this rose that was so white
   And is so red
Stained with the blood which from Him bled.
   O Mary Mother,
              it was thy own they shed.
   He places the rose in the statue's hands, kneels for a
   second before it, then resumes his place on the steps
   beside the two other monks.

FATHER MARCELLUS
  What is there more fitting
  Than that a rose should be given
    To her who is the Rose of all the world?
  Yet Our Lady's statue did not move.
  What imperfection can there be
  In those frail petals which enclose
    All that grace which is a rose?
  There can be none: for imperfection implies the potentialities
    of perfection.
  Nothing is perfect unless it is immortal.
  And since everything in nature is material and mortal,
  Nothing in nature is perfect.
  Only man can be perfect;
  For he alone has an immortal spirit.
  Only man could be perfect.

Therefore it is he, alone, who is imperfect.
>*The* ABBOT *kneels,* BROTHER JUSTIN *rises and stands*
>*before the statue.*

FATHER MARCELLUS
Cor aeterni numinis
En factum est Virginis
    Cor aeternum.
>*The* ABBOT *rises,* BROTHER JUSTIN *kneels*

BROTHER JUSTIN
Haec est Virgo sapiens
Haec est Virgo rapiens
    Cor divinum.
>*He rises and conducts the choir of boys who sing his*
>*Anthem*

ANTHEM TO THE VIRGIN
O Holy Mary
    who, for thy chastity,
Was chosen to bear
    Him whose birth was God's own birth,
Pray that He may forgive us our sin
As thou, in His infancy, comforted Him.

O Holy Mary
    who, for thy piety,
Was chosen to bear
    Him whose life gave grace to life,
Pray that we may be freed from our pride
As He, in humility, was at thy side.

O Holy Mary
    who, for thy purity,
Was chosen to bear
    Him whose death was death's own death,
Pray that He may grant us that rest
Which he, in His gentleness, gave to thy breast.
>BROTHER JUSTIN *turns and places his manuscript*
>*at the foot of the statue; then kneels for a moment*

*before resuming his place on the steps. The choir also
kneel.*

FATHER MARCELLUS

In music man reaches beyond his height
And makes a frail cathedral of sound,
A monument of a moment, transient
As himself.

It is an insubstantial edifice of order
Challenging the chaos of the night.

It is the spire of the human spirit.
Silence surrounds it, echo its answer.

Music is that sound to which a rose is shape.
Yet still the statue does not move.

Perhaps that is because nothing which delights our senses
Can be perfect.

For, since our senses are both mortal and imperfect,
That which delights them must be imperfect also.

The ABBOT *kneels.* BROTHER SEBASTIAN *rises and
stands before the statue.*

FATHER MARCELLUS

Infundatur omnibus
Ros ille pectoribus
Accendatur cordibus
　Flamma sacra.

The ABBOT *rises,* BROTHER SEBASTIAN *kneels*

BROTHER SEBASTIAN

O Jesu cor Mariae
Ros, ignis, fons gratiae
Ure, purga, posside
　Corda cuncta.

He stands before the statue and delivers his canzone

* * *

BROTHER SEBASTIAN

As a small boy can
　　　　　run to his mother

N

and admit his naughtiness,
    certain of her forgiveness;
                so are we
In all our ageless infancy
            able to come to thee,
Whose child was more than man,
            making thou the Mother
Of us all. So now we can confess,
            with childish artlessness,
            To thee, O Holy Lady,
Who stood so lonely,
   and heard Him forgive that sin which was our sin,
      that pain which was His pain—though the agony

Was yours then, and must be now, since we deny Him hourly;
And crucify Him daily:
            The Cross, the axle;
Humanity, the wheel,
           turning from birth to death,
Returning from death to birth,

While our circumference is sleep as we move from dream to
                dream, and wearily
Wake to dream again. Only
        He, alone, is still
Beyond this mortal wheel
           which turns from birth to death;
Returns from death to birth.

               *

O Holy Lady intercede for us
    that He may forgive us, not only those sins
Which we confess,
    but those we do not confess;
      not only those things we do against each other,

But those things we do not do for our Saviour,
                who was thy Son, O Holy Mother,
Intercede for us
     that He may grant us, not only that mercy
       which we seek,
         but that grace which we cannot even imagine;
Since we are chained to our own shadows,
         and our eyes are blind with our own sight,

As we stampede through the forest of our dreams, fleeing
From what we pursue; evading
       what we seek; always fearing to find
What is not lost, but lies within our mind;
         As a lake beneath the curtain of the night,
Sleeps concealed, till it is woken, and its surface broken,
             by the thirsty foal of light.

So is He within us. O Holy Mary, thy Son is waiting
Outside my empty heart, walking
       up and down my mind.
He stands as a beggar; yet it is I, who am blind.
       He does not seek for alms; but to give me sight;
For my eyes are blind with self-love, and all my days are night.

*

Night that is darker than darkness,
night which no gentle evening
Leads in,
       nor dawn
          alleviates,
Nor sun penetrates;
         night of no shadow;
Night which is our loneliness,
           loneliness of being,

Yet never living,—
                    for to be comes after being born
             as does our death, so many times, so many years
                    before the moment of our dying,
                          and in between our life's a state
Of loneliness which is not solitude; of being separate
  From Him, whose death we mourn, but to whom we are the
                                                    sorrow.

Sorrow that is not anger, sorrow that falls
As summer rain falls,
                so lightly over,
So gently to cover
                field, thorn and flower. Then lies like a pearl
Of Joy, set in the crimson petal.

Joy that's a lark, joy that's a linnet, joy that falls
Out of the sky, a waterfall
                              of song for ever
Singing, and never
                Silent. His joy is His love: both eternal.
It is we in our loneliness, who, in the crutch of the night,
      clutch ourselves to ourselves, and mourn for ourselves,
                              who are mortal.

                              *

O Holy Mary,
          only Virgin
To be mother;
          the only mother,
                    out of all the labour
In all the world,
          to see a son die, yet rise from the dead.
O Holy Mary,
          only Virgin

To be mother;
>> yet there is no Mother
Who does not weep with your tears,
>> who does not pray with your words. Intercede

For them, for us, that our sin of self-love may be forgiven;
That we be not forsaken;
>> Pray through His compassion
We may partake of His Resurrection;
> O Holy Mother, with thy prayers and His pity, even
Man might live, and death might die,
>> Through Jesus Christ, *Amen.*
*He places his manuscript at the foot of the statue, then
kneels before it before resuming his place beside the other
two monks on the steps.*

* * *

FATHER MARCELLUS
Where music failed how could poetry succeed,
When it is lamed with words,
Words that are worn with our complaint?
And all our complaint is pride.
> Perhaps poetry lies only in piety
> And perhaps the spirit is articulate only in its tears.
The statue has made no sign; and that is just.
For we cannot expect to move God by our achievements;
It is only when man is humble
That he is worthy of God's pride.
> Let us pray that Our Lady, the Blessed Virgin,
Who has graciously received these offerings,
May intercede for us who are not worthy. [*He kneels*]

Amor, Amor, Amor propera,
Ubique imperia
> In terris ut super sidera.

He rises and leads the Recession down the aisle to the
accompaniment of the 'Hymn for a Festival' sung by the
full choir. Only BROTHER ANDREW *is left. He snuffs*
the candles. Then turns and looks down the church to
make sure he is alone and unobserved. Then, while the
following song is sung (off), BROTHER ANDREW
removes his habit to reveal a clown's smock beneath.

ARIA [*tenor solo off*]
　　Love that is passion
　　And all compulsion
　　　　　　　　devours me.

　　Love that is treason,
　　Betraying reason,
　　　　　　　　deceives me.

　　Love that is mercy,
　　Tender as Mary,
　　　　　　　　evades me.

　　Love that is gracious,
　　Gentle as Jesus,
　　　　　　　　awaits me.

　　　　BROTHER ANDREW, *now dressed as a clown, kneels*
　　before the statue of the Virgin.

BROTHER ANDREW
　　Ave Maria, Gratia Plena,
　　Dominus tecum, Benedicta tu in mulieris...
　　I mean, 'in mulieres', no, 'in mulierorum'
　　Dear me, that's not right either...
　　You see, I cannot even pray to you as the others do.
　　Though I've learned your prayers by heart,
　　They will not stay within my head,
　　But come and go, in one ear and out the other
　　With nothing to stay them in between.
　　The only phrase I know
　　Is 'quia amore langueo'—
　　Anyhow, Latin's no language to talk to a young woman in—

begging your pardon, O Holy Mother...
He rises

Sweet Lady, I mean no disrespect;
You see me as I am.
I put this on especially for you.
It's five years if it's a day since I wore them—
But I daresay you've guessed all along
   that they call me Brother Andrew
Only because I was once Merry Andrew,
   the circus clown, juggler and tumbler
known half the world over—
   well, in this part of the country.
And now that we're alone, I've a surprise for you,
A special treat for your Feast Day.
Father Marcellus told me himself only this morning
That you, in your graciousness, would receive
   any offering I made, however humble.
I can't write poetry, nor compose a song
(never having had much time for either)
But tumble, juggle and vault I can do
(though self-praise is no recommendation
   as we say in the Ring).
I can stand on my head till the cows come home.
I can balance a chair on the end of my nose.
As for juggling, I can keep five balls in the air
   with one hand tied behind me back
(though between you and me there's nothing to it,
merely a knack and ten years' practice).
   But it was for the Roman vault
that I used to be called again and again.
I can do the Roman vault, the Spanish vault
and the French double turn.
I can somersault forwards.
I can somersault backwards
   and clap me hands in mid-air
   and land where I left the ground.

All this I'll do for you.
It'll be your own Gala Performance,
'By Special Command', as they say.
I hope you like it, for there's nothing else I can do.
And O Sweet Lady, how I love you,
    After my own fashion, how I love you.
Though others may worship you with words,
See, Mary, I adore you with my heart
                        and with my hands
                                                and with my feet.
*He begins to tumble energetically but clumsily. The more
he tries, the more he fails. He attempts every kind of
somersault and botches each. Finally, he kneels, breathless
and dishevelled, before the statue.*

I'm sorry. It wasn't very good, was it?
Don't tell me. I know. It was terrible, terrible.
I messed up every one.
Some acrobat—as agile and awkward as a rheumatic crab.
It's only that I'm out of practice.
Yes, see how breathless I am.
Not so young as I was—getting old...
And an old clown's as useless as an old egg.
    I suppose that's how it always is:
When we at last find someone worth loving,
We've nothing left worth offering. [*He stands*]

But I have it!
I know what I can still do for you:
I can do my Pierrot's Dance.
I used to do it while they were fixing up the cage
    for the man-eating lions...
It used to go over quite well...
It's rather a sad dance—but I know you'll understand it;
Sadness comes as easy to a clown as it did to the Mother of
    Jesus (meaning no offence, of course).
Yes, I'm sure you'll like it...
It is slow and graceful...[*He begins to dance*]

Or it's meant to be.
I made it all up myself.

Let me see now: one, two and three; one, two and three,
One 'pas de chat', one 'battement';
Now a 'pirouette'—no, that comes later...
                    He stops and begins a second time

One, two and three; one, two and three...
As you see, it's not a Pavane,
And it's not a Chaconne;
But slower that the first, and more graceful than either—or
    meant to be.

I made it all up myself.
        It's all about a man who fell in love with a lady who was
            beyond his reach.
        I suppose he was a dwarf and she was very tall.
        So the poor little man courted her by standing on his
            toes...
(ah, that's where the pirouette comes in)
        and, having deceived his Lady this way,
        the poor little man had to go on walking on his toes...
            doing everything on his toes.
        And, as his toes got tireder and tireder,
        he sank smaller and smaller...
                    He overbalances
    Sorry, I haven't got the time quite right
Yes, I'm sure the tempo used to be steadier...
One, two and three; one, two and three.
As I was saying:
        As the little man got older and older,
        he got smaller and smaller...
That was meant for a full pirouette
But I lost my balance...

    And as the little man got older and smaller,

the higher he had to stand on his toes
      which got tireder and tireder,
so he had to jump and spring into the air.
                    He tries a tour en l'air
Yes, that's where I did a 'tour en l'air'...
Wait, I'll try it again.
                    He goes across to repeat the step
And the tireder and smaller the little man got,
the more his lady seemed beyond his reach;
as his shoulders were bent and his legs were doubled
I'm sure the tempo used to be steadier...
    He goes across to repeat the step almost sobbing the lines
    which precede it.
And the tireder and smaller the little man got
the more his lady seemed beyond his reach
as he sank down on his knees.
                    He ends clumsily
No use, I can't do it!
                    He goes to the statue
That's the worst of fairy stories.
They always come true,
especially when you make them up yourself.
                    He kneels to the statue
Sweet Lady, forgive me.
Treat me not with utter contempt.
Oh the pity I had not you to dance to
      when I was young enough to dance.
Then I would have had all the grace in all the world.
But now, there is nothing I can do.
And here am I, sorry for myself,
When I should be sorry for you—
For it's your birthday, isn't it. And now you're disappointed,
And look like a child looks when nobody has come to her party.
No, we can't leave things like that, can we?
Merry Andrew won't give in yet; he'll cheer you up
And bring not only a smile to your lips—
      (for that's easy)

He'll make you laugh with your eyes;
  and that's difficult, especially for your eyes.
Though I can't tumble or dance, I can sing!
I'll tell you what I'll do:
I'll sing you a little song which used to make the children laugh.
It's all about your feast day, so I hope you won't take offence.
I made it all up myself—and it rimes, too
(though, of course, I don't pretend to be no poet.)
It's called 'Poor Old Me'.
    He begins to croak the following ballad, holding his knee
  On the Feast of Our Lady, I'd hurt my poor knee;
    Ah me, I'd hurt my poor knee.
  On the Feast of Our Lady, I'd hurt my poor knee
  On a gate,—what a penance a bruised knee can be!
    He turns to the statue to emphasise his rime
  Good Saint Peter, come and put a poultice on
  Poor old me.
So I stood on my feet to pray.

  On the Feast of Our Lady, I'd hurt my poor foot,
        He clutches it
    Ah me, I'd hurt my poor foot.
  On the Feast of Our Lady, I'd hurt my poor foot
  On a rock,—and the swelling split open my boot!
    He almost nudges the statue lest his rime be missed
  Mary, aid me!
  Good Saint Peter come and put a poultice on
  Poor old me!
So I lay on my back to pray. [*He does so*]

On the Feast of Our Lady, I'd hurt my poor back;
  Ah me, I'd hurt my poor back.
On the Feast of Our Lady, I'd hurt my poor back
With a log. And I felt I'd been laid on the wrack.
  Father Abraham, Isaac and Esau.
  Mary, aid me!
Good Saint Peter, come and put a poultice on

Poor old me.
So I knelt on my shoulders to pray.
                    He arches his back
On the Feast of Our Lady, I'd hurt my poor shoulder;
    Ah me, I'd hurt my poor shoulder.
On the Feast of Our Lady, I'd hurt my poor shoulder
At work. That's a serious thing when you're older!
            He raises a foot to emphasise his double rime
Bell, book and candle, incense, water!
    Father Abraham, Isaac and Esau.
    Mary, aid me.
    Good Saint Peter, come and put a poultice on
    Poor old me!
So I stood on my head to pray!
                    He attempts this position
On the Feast of Our Lady, I'd hurt my poor head;
    Ah me, I'd hurt my poor head.
On the Feast of Our Lady, I'd hurt my poor head
On a beam. May Our Lady forgive what I said!
    Mary, aid me...no, that's not right...
    He realises he's got muddled and starts shouting wildly
    Bell, book and candle, incense, water!
    Good Saint Peter...No, that comes after...
            He tries to catch up with the music
    Isaac, Esau, Father Abraham!
Wait, Wait, Oh, don't go away!
    *Still standing on his head, he tries to remember the words
    whilst the accompaniment continues...Slowly, he gets to
    his feet.*
I've forgotten it!
O sweet Lady, is there nothing I can do
    to show my love for you? Nothing? Nothing?
I can't pray. I can't dance. I can't sing.
I can't even somersault. Can't I?
    *He now throws himself violently and hysterically about,
    trying to somersault. The accompaniment gets quicker
    and quicker.*

Watch, watch...this time...
> *He crashes against the altar but picks himself up to try*
> *again. The noise brings in* FATHER MARCELLUS *and*
> *the three monks. The music ceases.*

BROTHER SEBASTIAN
What's that noise?

BROTHER JUSTIN
Look!

BROTHER GREGORY
Quick! Stop him! Stop him!
> *They rush up the aisle while he continues to hurl himself*
> *about. The music starts again.*

BROTHER ANDREW
When Merry Andrew can no longer tumble
What's the use of Merry Andrew eh?
This time, I'll do it, or...or...
I'll curl myself into a ball
And throw myself away. [*He takes a run in silence*]

BROTHER SEBASTIAN
It's sacrilege! Stop him! Stop him!
Brother Andrew...
> BROTHER SEBASTIAN *goes to stop the clown but the*
> ABBOT *prevents him.*

FATHER MARCELLUS
No, let him try again.
He offers all he has, and with what humility.

BROTHER ANDREW [*taking another run in silence*]
See, Mary, I adore you with my heart
> and with my hands
> and with my feet...

FATHER MARCELLUS
No, leave him.
Who are we to say how God would have us worship.
He tries for her sake and not his own sake.
> *Now the clown makes a final, violent effort and falls at the*
> *foot of the statue. He is broken.*

BROTHER ANDREW
  Sweet Lady, I can never reach thee
  Unless thou reach down to lift me...
    Quia amore langueo.
      He collapses. BROTHER SEBASTIAN *goes to him*
FATHER MARCELLUS [*as if to himself*]
  Seek not to embrace Me
  But rather that I should embrace thee.
BROTHER SEBASTIAN
  He is dead.
      The statue of the Virgin drops the rose upon the body.
      The monks kneel. The full choir begins to sing the 'Hymn
      for the Dead'.
FATHER MARCELLUS [*He goes to the body and takes the rose*]
  Rose of pity, flower of passion,
  Bleeds for ever, petals crimson;
  Rose of Mary, Christ's compassion.
      He places the rose on a white cushion and stands before
      the statue.

  Stabat Mater dolorosa
  Juxta crucem lacrymosa
  Dum pendebat Filius
  Cujus animam gementem
  Contristatam et dolentem,
  Pertransivit gladius.
                  He returns to the body

  O Holy Mary, Virgin Mother,
  Is there no way for love to enter
  A man's small heart
  Unless he first breaks that heart?
      The monks rise and lift the body. FATHER MARCELLUS
      turns again to the statue.

  Eja Mater, fons amoris
  Me sentire vim doloris

Fac, ut tacem lugeam
Fac, ut ardeat cor meum
In amando Christum Deum
Ut sibi complaceam.
> *The monks begin to bear the body down the aisle. The* ABBOT *follows, carrying the rose. The choir continue to sing the Hymn*

HYMN FOR THE DEAD

Hour of mourning, day of sorrow;
See the river drags a shadow:
Velvet grief and hollow echo.

Close his eyes and bring clean linen;
Bear this body which is broken;
Let these obsequies be spoken.

All that dances, dances to us;
All that's growing, grows towards us;
All that's chaste, is wanton with us.

Heloise found us her lover;
Lovely Helen we embroider;
Flesh our fabric, we the weaver.

Nothing's born, but we're born with it;
Nothing lives, but we live on it;
Nothing dies, but we devour it.

Every battle is our conquest;
Pestilence and plague our harvest;
We the termites in death's forest.

As a leper in the gutter,
See his shadow stalks its master:
Phantom sentry, lonely mourner.

Now his dreams like wolves are baying
Over him, beyond all dreaming,
Since in death there's no desiring.

Death embraces all that's vital;
Death is jealous of Death's rival;
Death is endless, Christ's eternal.

Wake this man whom Death has taken;
Take this heart which life has broken;
Break this web which Death has woven.

May he rest, not be forgotten;
May he sleep and yet be woken;
May his faith be not forsaken.

Rose of pity, flower of passion,
Bleeds for ever, petals crimson;
Rose of Mary, Christ's compassion.

May the gentle earth enclose him;
And the wind and rain embalm him,
Till the day when Christ redeems him.

Virgin Mary, Holy Mother,
Intercede with God our Father,
To receive his soul for ever.

Amen.

* * *

Ensi fina li menestrex:
Bur i tuma, buer i servi,
Car haute honor i deservi,
A cui nule ne se compere.
Ce nos racontent li saint pere
Qu'ensi avint ce menestrel.
Or prions Deu, il n'i a tel,
Qu'il nos doinst lui bien servir,
Que s'amor puissons deservir.
Explicit del Tumeor.

The Rehearsal

CHARACTERS

DAVID MAUGHAM, aged 47
PATRICIA, his wife, aged 42
THEONA, his daughter, aged 24
TREVOR, aged 26

Time: Present
Place: The Maughams' home at Henley-on-Thames

Act I

The living-room is dead. Every detail might be the subject for a still-life painting. It is womb-like, web-like and oppressively feminine. It is a room dominated by things, and all of them expensive. It might be the subject for an illustration in the 'Connoisseur'. But in spite of the luxury, the room is without elegance.

Only two incongruous objects are of any interest; a cheap card table and a mirror, such as one might see in the dressing-room of a theatre. DAVID *sits beside the former.* PATRICIA *in front of the latter. It is as though they were camping in a museum. He is in his shirt-sleeves, she wears a house-coat.*

DAVID'S *card table is his work bench. A small vice is clamped to one edge, a reading-lamp to another. A candle burns in a cigarette-tin. Several jam-jars are filled with different kinds of feathers. It is the paraphernalia of his hobby.*

PATRICIA'S *large shoddy mirror stands on a table. As usual, she is not far from it.*

All the windows, including the French window which leads out to the garden back stage, are open. An electric fan is on a table. There is a heat-wave. It is sultry, making for thunder.

When the curtain rises both DAVID *and* PATRICIA *appear self absorbed and oblivious of each other. They do not speak for at least a minute. She is examining herself in the mirror. He picks up the tail of pheasant from the card table, scrutinises the feathers carefully, then eventually selects one and pulls it out.*

*He then pares the feather with a pair of scissors, snips off
a bit which he holds with a pair of tweezers.*

PATRICIA [*putting her comb down and addressing her own reflection*]
I don't want him to come.

> DAVID *does not appear to hear her. He applies the piece
> of feather to one which is already in the vice. Then cuts off
> a piece of black thread and begins to run it over a lump of
> wax.*

I don't want him to come.

> PATRICIA *turns and observes him with sullen irritation
> while he meticulously binds his feather to the hook. Then
> she goes to the window and draws the sunblind down.
> This obstructs his vision.*

DAVID [*quietly*] Why did you do that?

PATRICIA [*indicating card table*] For the same reason you do
this.

DAVID [*switching on the reading-lamp over the vice*] I'm sorry if it
annoys you.

PATRICIA It doesn't. I like having my sitting-room festooned
with feathers, scattered with fish-hooks.

DAVID I refuse to rise. Besides all my clutter is on this table.

PATRICIA I pulled the blind down because it's insufferably hot.

DAVID Then let's have the fan on. [*He switches it on*]

PATRICIA [*she switches it off, then looks at herself in the mirror*]
That thing only creates a draught. I pulled the blinds down
because...

> *She has no need to finish the sentence.* DAVID *drops his
> work and goes to her immediately.*

DAVID Darling, you don't look a day over...

PATRICIA Over?

DAVID Wasn't it only yesterday that somebody mistook you and
Theona for sisters?

PATRICIA [*more cheerfully*] He'd got his sunblinds drawn.

> *He pulls her up. Leads her towards the window. Raises
> the blind and lets the sun shine on her face.*

DAVID Theona is pretty. But you are still beautiful. [*He kisses
her*]

PATRICIA [*she breaks away and faces the mirror*] A pity you said 'still'.

DAVID [*gives up effort*] Does it matter what I say?

PATRICIA No, it doesn't matter what you say.

DAVID I suppose sympathy between two people is possible, but conversation is impossible. We achieve nothing but soliloquies.

PATRICIA [*indicating mirror*] It's what it says that matters.

DAVID [*back at table*] Where did I put those scissors?

PATRICIA And do you know what it says? It says I'm finished. [*Pause*] I don't want him to come.

DAVID Can you see them?

PATRICIA Yes, I can see them. What is time waiting for? Time must be very bored to spend its time doodling round my mouth, scribbling its name all over my neck and across my brow. Still, no one can say its 'signature' is not legible.

DAVID [*quietly*] For Christ's sake, Patricia stop staring into that bloody mirror.

PATRICIA Why? Do you remember when I made you carry it out of my dressing-room at the Haymarket?

DAVID It was the Lyric, Hammersmith. It was the best part you ever had.

PATRICIA Yes. Gina in *The Wild Duck*. The last show I ever did.

DAVID That's what I said.

PATRICIA The last part I ever played.

DAVID Hardly.

PATRICIA You don't think I would have been a great actress?

DAVID I don't know. You married me because you yourself were uncertain of it. But as soon as we married you were confident you could have been.

PATRICIA I sacrificed my career to you.

DAVID Yes, yes, I know; you gave me the best week-end of your life.

PATRICIA I hope Theona won't make the same mistake: throw up her career for a man.

DAVID You make me feel like a cul-de-sac...

PATRICIA Then when her children grow up, find she's nothing

but her own reflection...You know I think she's got quite a talent and might develop into a useful little actress, if only...

DAVID If only?

PATRICIA If only she'd stop wasting her time with young men like Trevor, and stay in London instead of coming down here to play the lead in some amateur set-up, merely because that creature's playing opposite her.

DAVID You don't seem to like Trevor?

PATRICIA No, I do not. And I don't want Theona to bring him here again this week-end.

DAVID You've left it rather late. He'll be here within an hour. Why didn't you say something before?

PATRICIA If I had, nobody would have listened: you knew what I felt about him.

DAVID I certainly did not.

PATRICIA Anyway, I didn't want to interfere. It's your job to make the decisions.

DAVID That's what you always say when you don't want to make them yourself.

PATRICIA You don't want to see your daughter throw away her career and marry a man like that?

DAVID And repeat your mistake?

PATRICIA I was thinking of Theona.

DAVID Of course. Anyway I didn't know they were 'serious'.

PATRICIA Don't be flippant. This will be the fourth week-end this summer he's been down here.

DAVID Theona's had her boy friends—a whole succession—down here before. They come for the tennis, your conversation or perhaps my claret. At any rate, none of them have ever asked me for Theona's hand. Trevor certainly hasn't.

PATRICIA Wake up. Today they don't ask you for your daughter's hand until a week before they're about to present you with your first grandchild.

DAVID You mean?

PATRICIA Ah, I see you are interested? You needn't worry. Trevor's ambitious; he's far too calculating and mean to give himself, if he's anything to give, which I doubt.

DAVID Didn't I say he likes to come here for the tennis? I thought you liked him. You seemed to be getting on very well with him last week-end. You certainly made a fine pair...

PATRICIA [*pleased at the suggestion*] Nonsense.

DAVID ...On the court. Theona and I didn't win a game. And you seemed to like dancing with him too.

PATRICIA Naturally I made an effort to entertain him. Theona gets these young men down then leaves them sitting around. You know how shy she is. I tried to make things go. It wasn't easy... Trevor's certainly not the man for Theona.

DAVID Why?

PATRICIA He's not sensitive enough for her. And he's cold. Theona's a girl who needs affection, a great deal of affection.

DAVID That's true.

PATRICIA And besides they haven't...I know it sounds silly...

DAVID That generally means you think something or other's true.

PATRICIA They haven't the same background. He's a social climber.

DAVID You mean he wants to get on in the world? No harm in that. He wants to become an hydraulic engineer. I see no reason why he shouldn't end up as a most successful hydraulic engineer, so long as he doesn't compromise and become a prosperous plumber. Ambitions are easily achieved, the difficulty is to remember what they were.

PATRICIA You're very bitter.

DAVID We're very comfortable.

PATRICIA You mean all this is a mess of pottage?

He goes and winds the clock

DAVID I mean all this is a diffidence which faltered. Anyhow don't let's talk about me. We were discussing Trevor. Why don't you like him?

PATRICIA I hate him.

She pulls the blind down

DAVID That doesn't tell me why.

PATRICIA He's a snob for one thing.

DAVID Doesn't he come from what is now erroneously called the working-classes?

PATRICIA That's what I mean. He boasts that his mother was a barmaid in the same way people used to claim remote connection to a duchess. He makes me feel ashamed because I don't eat peas with a knife. And he despises you because you merely had a private income whereas he was state subsidised.

DAVID I can see his advantages...

PATRICIA He wears that row of pens in his top pocket as if they were medals entitling him to enter the proletarian paddock. He was at Exeter University.

DAVID What's wrong with that? I dare say they've got plenty of books there.

PATRICIA At least I'm being honest. Don't pretend you like him any more than he likes you.

DAVID All the more reason why I shouldn't be prejudiced. I don't have to like him, nor do you. He's Theona's boy-friend, not mine, not yours.

PATRICIA You mean you're going to let him come here again?

DAVID Of course. He'll be here within half an hour. Do you expect me to pull the drawbridge up and flood the moat?

PATRICIA We could get him a room at the George. I could say one of your partners had had to come down for the week-end to talk business.

DAVID You could. But he knows you've eight bedrooms.

PATRICIA I could pretend that our car was being repaired and we wouldn't be able to drive in and out to take him to rehearsals. You know what a good liar I am.

DAVID Yes. But what about Theona?

PATRICIA Darling, she could stay at the George too.

DAVID To hell with this.

PATRICIA You mean you'll let him come?

DAVID Of course. What else can I do? You shouldn't have covered up your animosity so well, or left this move so late. Why did you?

PATRICIA I tried to like him. When I found I couldn't I said so. I'm not such a hypocrite as you are, always bending over backwards so that you can approve of your own reflection. Why are you such a hypocrite? You didn't hide your disapproval of Theona's other boy-friends. Why are you so tolerant of this one?

DAVID Because I think Theona likes him.

PATRICIA Because you think Theona doesn't care for him, that's the real reason. How dishonest can you be?

She goes out. He continues at his table. He whistles tunelessly to himself. Enter THEONA. *She raises the blind.*

THEONA Daddy, what are you doing?

DAVID The usual. Making another salmon fly.

He continues to whistle the phrase

THEONA I mean why are you whistling?

DAVID Am I? I didn't know...I suppose it's because I'm angry.

THEONA I've never heard you whistle before.

DAVID Haven't you, darling? That's because you've never made me angry.

THEONA Never?

DAVID Not really angry...

THEONA [*picking up pheasant's tail*] I suppose Mummy...

DAVID [*He whistles the phrase again*] Yes.

THEONA Isn't this pretty?

DAVID Very...'Autumn, like a pheasant's tail
            Lifts over the hedge...'

THEONA That's pretty too. Did you write that? Daddy, why did you stop writing? [DAVID *doesn't answer. He whistles the phrase again*] What is it you're whistling?

DAVID I don't know. I haven't the faintest idea.

THEONA But it sounds very gay. Not like you at all.

DAVID Gay? I don't feel gay.

He whistles the phrase again, repeating it consciously to himself. Then suddenly he stops in the middle of the phrase and puts one hand to his face.

Bloody bully.

THEONA What's wrong.

DAVID I can feel that slap now. With the back of the hand right across my face. It knocked my glasses off.

THEONA Who hit you? You never wear glasses.

DAVID I used to.

THEONA When?

DAVID When I was nine. At my prep school...Proof that one never grows up, one simply grows old.

THEONA What happened?

DAVID One of the form rooms was a sort of army hut. It was a day like this. The windows were open. He was the geography master. I liked geography. I liked him too. He was called Blake. He was drawing a map on the blackboard. Borneo...An errand boy came down the drive, stopped outside our form room to put his cycle clip on. Blake turned from the blackboard and asked which of us was whistling. He then continued with his map. The errand boy got on his bicycle. Blake put his chalk down again, walked straight up to me, cuffed me across the face, knocking my glasses on to the desk. I was angry, very angry. [*He whistles the phrase*] And that's what the errand boy was whistling...as you say, it's quite a gay little tune, isn't it?

THEONA You mustn't let Mummy upset you. She doesn't mean...

DAVID I know...her age. That's the pity. If we didn't have to make so many allowances for other people, we'd be able to make some for ourselves.

THEONA Bad as that?

DAVID Bad as that. A man hopes that marriage will provide him with a background. He ends in becoming a background to his marriage.

THEONA Why have you never left her? Because of me?

DAVID You were an excuse. Hardly the reason. The reason is more complicated than that. I've often thought of leaving your mother. Just as I suppose she's often thought of leaving me. But always just when I was about to do so, she would do or say some trivial thing which touched me, and would puncture my resolution. So we'd go round and round again. People stay together not because they love each other, but because they haven't the vitality left to hate...

THEONA Hardly an encouragement for me to marry, is it?

DAVID [*pulling himself up*] I swear I didn't tell you this because of that. I want you to marry. As a matter of fact that's what your mother and I were quarrelling about...

THEONA But the question hasn't arisen. You know I don't want to leave home yet. I want to be somebody myself first, not just become some man's shadow.

DAVID I know, it was all very premature. But your mother was saying that she didn't think Trevor should come here.

THEONA Why? She's never been stuffy over my other boy-friends. She always seemed to like having them down here. She used to say it livened things up, didn't she?

DAVID Yes.

THEONA I thought she was getting on terribly well with Trevor last week-end. It was I who was playing gooseberry.

DAVID I know; but the truth is she doesn't like him. I suppose that's why she made an extra effort to be sociable for your sake.

THEONA For my sake...

DAVID We all do that at times. Your mother better than most. It's not for nothing she was an actress.

THEONA I wish I'd known this before. I wouldn't have asked him here. He could have stayed in Reading. It would be nearer the rehearsals anyway. I suppose there's still time to fix it... Trevor won't mind. He's more at home in a pub anyway. He says he feels out of place here...

DAVID You'll do no such thing.

THEONA Daddy, don't you start pretending. I know you don't like him. Do you?

DAVID I don't have to.

THEONA He's clumsy, arrogant, intolerant and rude, isn't he?

DAVID I didn't say so.

THEONA He's also rather sweet.

DAVID Then let's drive down to the station to meet him.

THEONA Darling Daddy. But you don't have to like him. I don't suppose I'll be seeing much of Trevor anyhow after this show. You needn't worry.

DAVID Who said I was worrying?

They make to go as PATRICIA *enters. She has changed her clothes.*

THEONA What a pretty dress, darling. It makes you look terribly young.

PATRICIA You mean an old ewe dressed up as lamb? Is that what you mean?

THEONA I mean it's lovely.

PATRICIA I had to put something on for your sake. You don't want your mother to look like a slut.

DAVID And you don't. Well, we'd better get down to the station. It's 5.30.

Exit DAVID *and* THEONA. PATRICIA *goes to window, draws blind down and returns to mirror.*

PATRICIA Well, Pat what did you think of that? How was that for a bitchy remark? Gina does look terribly young doesn't she? Not a day over...be honest, darling. Gina doesn't look a day over thirty, does she? No she doesn't Pat. And she doesn't feel it either, do you hear?

She leaves mirror goes across room, lights a cigarette and after a second or two is drawn back to the mirror again.

I said she doesn't feel it either. [*Pause*] Pat, now do be honest, tell me, do you think Gina should wear a scarf, and maybe a clip. [*She puts one on*] You see the question is if Gina does wear one it spoils the line of her dress. But if she doesn't, he might mistake her wrinkled neck for a salt cellar, or an ash tray. Certainly he could strike a match on Gina's skin. She who was the armourer's daughter etc., Dust has closed Helen's eyes, etc. Lord have mercy on us, etc., Well, Pat, I think this calls for a drink. Can Gina have a drink? You can't say she didn't try to stop him coming, can you?

She goes and pours out a drink, then sits down far from the mirror. In an agony of solitude she goes and picks up a silver hand mirror.

PATRICIA You can't say Gina didn't try. She tried to avoid it. She kept her promise to you, Pat. She did say something. She did try.

> *Enter* TREVOR *at back. He can only see the back of* PATRICIA's *head.*

But what shall Gina do now? Tell me that. If she does, she'll get hurt, if she doesn't, she'll hurt herself. What do you advise? If only it weren't so hot.

TREVOR I don't remember those lines.

> *She freezes and does not turn. He walks across the room towards her.*

Darling, you might wait for me before you rehearse our scene. No wonder you're always word perfect.

> *He pulls her head back to kiss her. She turns*

I thought you were Theona.

PATRICIA Of course...

TREVOR You looked just like Theona sitting there.

PATRICIA [*pleased*] Did I?

TREVOR Yes. Your hair...

PATRICIA Yes?

TREVOR I thought you were Theona from the back. You're wearing her scarf. It was that.

PATRICIA For Christ's sake don't apologise. It was a mistake any man might make in the dark. I drew the blinds...

TREVOR It isn't exactly light in here.

PATRICIA ...to keep the heat out. I hate this heat.

TREVOR Then why don't you turn on this fan? [*He does so*]

PATRICIA That's a good idea. I like that. [*She stands with her back to him, letting her hair out*] Our hair is rather alike isn't it?

TREVOR Yes. In many ways you and Theona might be sisters.

PATRICIA [*delighted*] What ways? Tell me.

TREVOR Things you say, things you do...Where is she?

PATRICIA Theona and David went down to the station to meet you. Didn't you see them?

TREVOR No. I came by car. A friend gave me a lift.

PATRICIA They'll only wait for an hour. They'll be back here soon. So don't worry.

TREVOR Do I look worried?

PATRICIA I mean you can relax.

TREVOR I'm sorry if I embarrass you.

PATRICIA I didn't say you did.

TREVOR Not directly.

PATRICIA I suppose you think every woman…Why don't you sit down?

TREVOR I'm not tired.

PATRICIA You don't like this room, do you?

TREVOR I didn't say so.

PATRICIA I asked you a question.

TREVOR Because you think you know the answer.

PATRICIA You don't like it. Do you?

TREVOR Do you want me to be polite or honest?

PATRICIA Be yourself.

TREVOR You mean be rude? No I don't like this room. It makes me feel clumsier than I am. It has luxury but no comfort. Elegance but no taste.

PATRICIA You mean it's not your own.

TREVOR I mean that it is yours.

PATRICIA Splendid. That's what I like to hear. Go on…

TREVOR It's like a web. It's the epitome of the predatory female.

PATRICIA It is Theona's home.

TREVOR That's what I said. Why do you goad me to insult you?

PATRICIA What else can I expect from you? And I want you to feel at home. Tell me what you think of this portrait. I've just had it reframed.

TREVOR Why?

PATRICIA Do you like it?

TREVOR What, the frame?

PATRICIA No, the portrait.

TREVOR By Kodak, I presume. And who's the beauty?

PATRICIA You like her?

TREVOR Certainly.

PATRICIA Don't you recognise her?

TREVOR No. Should I?

PATRICIA I suppose not. I've changed in twenty years. It was painted when I played Viola.

TREVOR I'm sorry.

PATRICIA Don't apologise.

TREVOR But I do. It was stupid of me not to recognise the costume. I didn't know you had played in Shakespeare.

PATRICIA You did.

TREVOR No. Theona is always talking to me about you, but she has never told me that.

PATRICIA But I remember telling you myself. It was the first time you came here. We were having a picnic down by the river. Theona had been talking about her Othello rehearsals.

TREVOR Yes, I remember.

PATRICIA And then I told you of my experience when I'd played Beatrice with John at the Old Vic. And after I'd told you, do you know what you said?

TREVOR No.

PATRICIA You said, 'Do you mind passing the mustard'.

TREVOR No, it was the salt.

PATRICIA Love-thirty. You never miss a point. So, Theona's always talking about me, is she?

TREVOR Yes, otherwise we get on very well.

PATRICIA That was just rude.

TREVOR Was it? Then I think you'll agree I've deserved a drink.

PATRICIA Yes, I suppose you have. [*She goes and pours it*] I like you because you say what you think. You're uncouth, uncompromising and clumsy. I hope you'll always remain uncouth, uncompromising and clumsy. I hope you'll say what you think. I hope you'll do what you feel.

THEONA *enters behind her*

TREVOR [*seeing her*] Yes, I can promise you that.

He crosses and kisses THEONA

PATRICIA [*turning to herself*] But not too clumsy...

THEONA I suppose you got a lift down?

TREVOR It saved me ten shillings.

THEONA Plus the bob you didn't use to phone us.

TREVOR I hoped to get here before you went to the station.

P

THEONA You clot.

TREVOR I'm sorry.

THEONA Good. Just you stay that way. You can't have been here long. I can't see anything broken.

PATRICIA Just bruised. He's been on his best behaviour. We played a game of tennis or rather a few shots, didn't we? What have you done with your father?

THEONA Done? Daddy is sitting down by the river.

PATRICIA Then I'd better join him. I know you two will want to be alone.

THEONA Oh no...

PATRICIA You mustn't be so shy, Theona—or inhospitable.

THEONA Who said I'm shy?

PATRICIA Well you know you are a little. Why don't you take Trevor for a walk. You could go and show him Farlingham or perhaps you could both have a bathe before dinner?

THEONA It's too hot to bathe or walk.

TREVOR And I don't think I mind not having been to Farlingham.

PATRICIA Well, I suppose you could sit in here. It's cool in here.

THEONA That's what I thought we'd do. We've got to rehearse. That's why Trevor came: to rehearse.

PATRICIA I know.

THEONA So that's what we're going to do—if nobody minds.

PATRICIA [*at door*] Darling, I don't mind what you do. So long as you two don't get bored. [*She goes*]

TREVOR Which means she hopes we will be.

THEONA What?

TREVOR Bored. People like your mother say precisely the opposite of what they mean.

THEONA Poor Mummy, you mustn't mind what she says.

TREVOR I don't. Her remark was aimed at you. The implication was: you lack her personality, charm, and maturity and I would find you dull compared to her.

THEONA Unfortunately that's true.

TREVOR She wants me to think it and you to fear it, but she's right. I enjoy meeting her.

THEONA [*surprised but pleased*] Do you? I'm so glad. Why?

TREVOR She helps me to remove one of the chips on my shoulder. Knowing your mother makes me pleased I was an orphan.

THEONA That's unkind; you hardly know her.

TREVOR Why is it unkind to speak the truth? In this house kindness means turning a blind eye to the facts; and good manners consist in pretending facts don't even exist. This whole house is a fabric of lies, furnished by Liberty's and upholstered by falsehood. It's very comfortable of course. Illusions generally are for a time till you find the cushion is a rake sticking into your ruddy arse. And I suppose this is a Renoir? Genuine, of course?

THEONA Yes. Daddy gave it as a present to Mummy for their silver wedding.

TREVOR That ought to be his epitaph, poor chap.

THEONA Glad you like it.

TREVOR I didn't say I did. What I admire is the money he paid for it. He ought to have had the cheque framed. I could have stood here looking at that for hours. I'd have respected him if he had done that. Money's the only thing that counts in this house: the whole place is papered with fivers. But some of it is turned into art. Art is so respectable. That's another of the lies...'Portrait of a Woman with a Looking-glass'. Appropriate gift.

THEONA Daddy's name for it is...'Hedge against Inflation'. I'm sorry, darling. I see it's a ghastly mistake.

TREVOR Which mistake are you talking about?

THEONA My making you stay here again.

TREVOR On the contrary, it does me good. It removes another chip from my shoulder. I used to be sore that I never had a home of my own as a child. Seeing yours makes me glad I didn't. It gives me a feeling of claustrophobia. It's not a home. It's a womb that refuses to give birth. If I had put up at a pub in the town, we could at least have had a tumble of an afternoon. We can hardly do that here. Sex is another fact this house pretends doesn't exist. Why did you insist I stayed here?

THEONA It's usual.

TREVOR What is? To meet your parents, etc. For God's sake, you're not going to propose to me, are you? You said there'd be no strings. You know I don't want to get married to you or anybody else. Or is it impolite for me to say so.

THEONA Manners don't enter into it.

TREVOR If that's what you want, I'd better go—now.

THEONA Don't be silly. All that can wait. I wanted you to stay here because...

TREVOR Because?

THEONA It's impossible in the town in this heat. We can bathe here.

TREVOR But it wasn't hot when you insisted.

THEONA And because I wanted you to get to know Daddy. You hardly saw him last week. And he's naturally curious to know anybody I know.

TREVOR Is he? Why?

THEONA And I want him to like anybody I like.

TREVOR Do you? Why?

THEONA You're impossible. Let's rehearse. It'll be a relief; drama's so much less dramatic than living: it's also much tidier.

TREVOR All right. Which bit do you want to do?

THEONA [*moving chairs*] Our scene in Act Two. The watch scene. Tony said it dragged. Let's try and lighten it up and see if we can't get some pace into it. After all it's supposed to be a comedy.

TREVOR Is it? I think it's a bloody silly little play.

THEONA Then why did you agree to play it?

TREVOR Because you bullied me into it.

THEONA Hardly. Anyhow, it can't be that bad. It ran two years in the West End.

TREVOR It's still a bloody silly little play.

THEONA A million people saw it.

TREVOR Morons.

THEONA Come, I thought you respected the majority view or is the mob only infallible when it comes to politics? Or do you

believe in social democracy but cultural autocracy? People like
you are hilariously inconsistent.

TREVOR Shut up.

THEONA Anyway it's better than those priggish social realist
plays you rave about.

TREVOR At least they're about something.

THEONA H. Bombs, child delinquency or drains.

TREVOR What's wrong with drains?

THEONA I was forgetting you're training to be a plumber.

TREVOR An hydraulic engineer.

THEONA Same thing on a bigger scale. Anyhow we're 'committed' to *Marriage à la Carte* at the moment so let's run the
scene from your entrance. [*Reads from script*] 'It is mid-
November.' This fan then can be the gas fire. Mummy's
precious chippendale can be the front door. [*She moves*] So—
for God's sake don't slam it. And we shall need some glasses.
[*Fetches them*] Can't possibly rehearse a modern play without
glasses. Now, as I'm your mistress, I dare say Tony will have
the inspired idea of placing me waiting for you curled up on a
sofa reading a novel, and wolfing chocolates. [*Looks at script*]
No, it's her flat in Notting Hill. Of course, I shall be ironing,
and wearing a pony-tail.

TREVOR Without scripts?

THEONA Without scripts. Remember: pace. Pick up the cues.

She mimes: ironing

TREVOR 'Il trouve dans adulterie toutes les platitudes de mariage'.

THEONA What?

TREVOR Flaubert. It's what this scene's about, isn't it?

THEONA I don't understand French. I haven't read Flaubert.

TREVOR I'm sorry. I was forgetting that you're rich enough to
afford to be illiterate.

THEONA Do you mind?

She 'irons'. He 'knocks'. She goes and 'lets him in'

'I thought you were never coming?'

TREVOR [*looking at his wrist-watch*] 'I'm sorry. But I said five
o'clock'.

THEONA 'One.'

TREVOR [*looking at watch again*] 'I'm only ten minutes late.'

THEONA 'Two.'

TREVOR '...No more than ten minutes late?'

THEONA 'No more? You've never waited. How long have we got?'

TREVOR 'She's got some people coming to dinner.'

THEONA 'I didn't ask about her social engagements. How long have we got?'

TREVOR 'So I shall have to get home early to dress.' [*He looks at his watch again*]

THEONA 'Three. Give it to me.'

TREVOR 'What?'

THEONA 'Your watch. You've already looked at it three times. I can't bear it. Last time, you looked at your watch more often than you looked at me, although I was prancing about naked.'

TREVOR 'I'm sorry.'

THEONA 'Give it to me.'

TREVOR 'Don't be silly.'

> THEONA *goes to remove his watch*

'If I'm late, she'll ask questions. Give it back to me.'

THEONA 'No. [*She goes to imaginary phone*] I'd rather have our time torn across than continuously punctuated. [*Into phone*] Will you please give this number a ring at 7 o'clock. No, I'm not going to sleep, I'm going to bed.' [*She replaces phone*]

TREVOR I'm sorry, I've dried.

THEONA Then get your script.

> *She sits in exactly the same position which* PATRICIA *had when* TREVOR *arrived.* TREVOR *registers the repetition but plays the kiss.* THEONA *turns as* PATRICIA *had done.*

'Aren't you confusing us?'

TREVOR What?

THEONA What do you mean 'what'? That line's not in my script. I go straight on [*She reads*] 'Aren't you confusing us? Maybe your wife likes being kissed on the back of the neck. It merely tickles me.' You see, you don't come in with any 'what'.

TREVOR Theona, who was Gina?

THEONA I don't know. Gina? The only Gina I know of is the
Gina Ekdal in *The Wild Duck*. Mummy's favourite part. Why?

TREVOR She was talking to me about the part before you came
in.

THEONA Was she? Yes, she played it, now it plays her...Any-
how, are we rehearsing or are we not?

*She returns to position on sofa. He takes up the cue, enters
and kisses her on the back of the neck again.*

'Aren't you confusing us? Maybe your wife likes being kissed
on the back of the neck. It merely tickles me.'

TREVOR 'I'm sorry.'

THEONA 'And that's the third time you've said you were sorry.
If you feel so damned apologetic, why do you come here?'

TREVOR 'To sleep.'

THEONA 'Don't be insulting. Or don't you want to come to bed?
Is that why you stand there wasting time talking about your
wife?'

TREVOR 'You're a bitch.'

He kisses her on the ear

THEONA 'That's better. I like that. I suppose she hasn't got one.'

TREVOR 'What?'

THEONA There, that's where your 'what' comes...'An erotic
zone. I wish I were your wife.'

TREVOR 'I'm sor...'

THEONA 'Don't say it. You clot, I didn't mean I wish I were
married to you. I meant I wish I were over forty like your wife
is.'

TREVOR 'Why?'

THEONA 'It must be so restful to reach that flat plateau of middle
age. Life must be like a li-lo then: comfortable with no frustrations...'

TREVOR 'Now who's being insulting? I'm 46.'

THEONA '...With all passion spent.' Sorry, I get up on that line
and cross...'at last out of the jungle of emotions; finally free
from the tyranny of sex. Yes, I wish I were forty; I am jealous
of your wife.'

TREVOR 'You shouldn't be. You'll notice little change.'

THEONA 'Swine. Are you telling me I'm already unresponsive?'

TREVOR 'I'm telling you you'll notice little change.'

THEONA 'You don't mean she feigns that she still thinks she has
to make demands on you, which you satisfy rather than hurt her
feelings? My poor sweet, how hideous for you. Why don't you
tell her about me? It would come as a relief, then she wouldn't
have to pretend to those desires any more. She could relax...'

TREVOR 'On the li-lo? How old are you?'

THEONA 'Twenty two.'

TREVOR 'You'll notice little change. Except that when you are
forty-two you will find that vanity has become pride, and
desire has become desperation. The tragedy of a woman is that
when she has found out how to live she finds she has no longer
the means of attracting life towards her. You're on the foothills;
the plateau, as you call it, is only another mountain. We never
climb it, we simply slither off its sides.'

THEONA 'It's not—all habit then?'

TREVOR 'Not exactly.'

THEONA 'Then stop talking about that bloody woman...If it's
still like that why do you come to me? What have I got that she
hasn't?'

TREVOR 'Me. And you want me to tell you?'

THEONA 'Yes.'

TREVOR 'I don't come here for that. I come here for you.'

THEONA 'Not just to...?'

TREVOR 'No. I don't find you in the least attractive. I come here
to relax: I find your conversation so banal it never disturbs my
thought.'

THEONA [*fondly*] 'That's the foulest thing any man ever said to
me. [*She kisses him*] Now for heaven's sake pick me up and
throw me on that bed: I feel terribly sleepy.'

                    He picks her up and staggers

TREVOR We'll certainly get a laugh on this.

THEONA Clumsy lout. I'm not as heavy as that. Put me down.
[*He does so*] And your embrace was as amorous as a fireman's.

TREVOR I felt I was transporting a hunk of Henry Moore.

THEONA Now look, if I stand here...

TREVOR You'll mask me completely.

THEONA Then here...Now try it again. Take it from your line about the mountain. And let's get some edge into it. We're supposed to be so much in love that we can insult each other with impunity. Our banter reveals our intimacy. It is a kind of embrace.

TREVOR Etcetera...'You're on the foothills; the plateau, as you call it, is only another mountain. We never climb it, we merely slither off its sides.'

> *Enter* PATRICIA. *She stands, unobserved by the door watching their rehearsal.*

THEONA 'It's not all habit then?'

TREVOR 'Not exactly.'

THEONA 'Then stop talking about that bloody woman. If it's like that, why do you come to me? What have I got for you that she hasn't?'

TREVOR 'Me. And you want me to tell you?'

THEONA 'Yes.'

TREVOR 'I don't come here for that. I come here for you.'

THEONA 'Not to...'

TREVOR 'No. I don't find you in the least attractive. I come here to relax. I find your conversation so banal it never disturbs my thought.'

THEONA [*fondly*] 'That's the foulest thing any man ever said to me.'

> *Before* THEONA *moves to the embrace* PATRICIA *comes into the room.*

PATRICIA My dear child, just what are you supposed to be doing?

THEONA Rehearsing.

PATRICIA I gathered that. It was awful. You can't possibly say that line like that. 'That's the foulest thing any man ever said to me.' In that tone, and look as though you want to be kissed.

THEONA But that's the whole point of it!

PATRICIA Let me show you.

THEONA Mummy, please...

PATRICIA Don't you want to learn? I'm sure Trevor does.

THEONA Mummy, this is a modern play...

PATRICIA It's true I played with Noel in *Bitter Sweet* but that hardly makes me an antique, or him a classic. Now let me show you. Give me your script.

THEONA But you don't know what the play's about.

PATRICIA None of us knew what *The Eagle has Two Heads* was about. But we played it with complete conviction.

THEONA But you can't possibly play a scene cold.

PATRICIA That's just what an actress can do, can't they, Trevor?

TREVOR So I'm told.

PATRICIA The scene is obvious; two women after one man; not so very modern. You'd like me to help you, wouldn't you, Trevor?

TREVOR I'd be most grateful.

THEONA [*pleading*] Trevor...

TREVOR Let's take it from the top of page 38.

PATRICIA Right. Top of page 38. Give me your script, Theona. [*She reads*] Lavinia is seated on sofa etc....

> She takes up the position then becomes aware that she has been trapped. TREVOR *plays. He enters, and kisses her on the back of the neck.* PATRICIA *overplays the entire scene.* TREVOR *responds with an edge which was lacking when he rehearsed with* THEONA. *He sadistically forces* PATRICIA *to make a fool of herself.*

'Aren't you confusing us? Maybe your wife likes being kissed on the back of the neck: it merely tickles me.'

TREVOR 'I'm sorry.'

PATRICIA 'And that's the third time you said you were sorry. If you feel so damned apologetic, why do you come here?'

TREVOR 'To sleep.'

PATRICIA 'Don't be insulting—or don't you want to come to bed?...'

THEONA I told you it was modern.

PATRICIA Beds were invented before your time, Theona. Indeed if they hadn't been—you wouldn't have any time. [*She continues*] 'Is that why you stand there wasting time, talking about your wife?'

TREVOR 'You're a bitch.'
> *He kisses her ear*

PATRICIA 'That's better. I like that. I suppose she hasn't got one?'

TREVOR 'What?'

PATRICIA 'An erotic zone. I wish I were your wife.'

TREVOR 'I'm sor...'

PATRICIA 'Don't say it. You clot. I didn't mean I wish I were married to you. I meant I wished I were over forty like your wife is.'

TREVOR 'Why?'

PATRICIA 'It must be so restful to reach that flat plateau of middle age. Life must be like a li-lo then. Comfortable with no frustrations...'

TREVOR 'Now who's being insulting? I'm 46.'

PATRICIA 'With all passion spent. At last out of the jungle of emotions, finally free from the tyranny of sex. Yes, I wish I were forty. I'm jealous of your wife.'

TREVOR 'You shouldn't be. You'll notice little change.'

PATRICIA 'Swine. Are you telling me I'm already unresponsive.'

TREVOR 'I'm telling you you'll notice little change.'

PATRICIA 'You don't mean she feigns? That she still thinks she has to make demands on you which you satisfy rather than hurt her feelings? My poor sweet, how hideous for you. Why don't you tell her about me? It would come as a relief then she wouldn't have to pretend to those desires any more. She could relax...'

TREVOR 'On the li-lo. How old are you?'

PATRICIA 'Twenty-two.'

TREVOR 'You'll notice little change, except that when you are forty-two you will find that vanity has become pride, and desire has become desperation. The tragedy of a woman is that when she has found out how to live she finds she has no longer the means of attracting life towards her. You're on the foot-hills; the plateau, as you call it, is only another mountain. We never climb it. We simply slither off its sides.'

PATRICIA 'It's not all habit then?'

TREVOR 'Not exactly.'

PATRICIA 'Then stop talking about that bloody woman…If it's still like that, why do you come to me? What have I got—that she hasn't?'

TREVOR 'Me. And you want me to tell you?'

PATRICIA 'Yes.'

THEONA [*to herself*] Oh no.

TREVOR 'I do not come here for that. I come here for you.'

PATRICIA 'Not just to…?'

TREVOR 'No. I don't find you in the least attractive. I come here to relax. I find your conversation so banal it never disturbs my thought.'

PATRICIA [*angrily*] 'That's the foulest thing any man ever said to me.' [*Looking at script*] They kiss? What an odd play.

TREVOR puts his script down

THEONA I warned you, I told you the play was modern. The whole scene has to be keyed to that embrace…It's not your style of thing.

PATRICIA Isn't it? You think I couldn't play that? [*She puts her script down*]

THEONA It's not meant to be played—passionately. You see they're so much in love they can take their emotion for granted. They can even treat it as a joke.

PATRICIA If they can do that, then it can't be love.

TREVOR [*quietly*] 'And desire becomes desperation.'

PATRICIA What did you say?

TREVOR I was just going over my lines. You know the bit: 'the plateau, as you call it, is only another mountain…'

THEONA Trevor…

PATRICIA Yes?

TREVOR '…And I was noticing how cold that mountain is.'

PATRICIA [*now taking the line correctly*] 'That's the foulest thing any man ever said to me.' [*She kisses him: passionately*] Well, aren't you going to pick me up? It's also in the script. [*He does so*] Theona, was that better?

THEONA Much better.

TREVOR [*still carrying* PATRICIA] That was the way to stand,

Theona. Your mother does it much better. It's easy to pick her up. [*He walks across the room*] And carry her.

Enter DAVID

DAVID Going anywhere?

TREVOR We were rehearsing.

DAVID That's what I thought. Splendid, but I should have thought it was too hot for that. And what are you doing, Patricia? Being a stand-in? [TREVOR *puts* PATRICIA *down firmly*] Ah, 'a return to the boards', as they say. A little precipitate, or is that part of the scene? But congratulations, it's good to see you enjoying yourself in spite of...

PATRICIA [*aggressively*]...Of what?

DAVID In spite of this unsufferable heat, my dear.

THEONA Mummy's been showing me how I should stand so that Trevor could pick me up easily.

PATRICIA [*angrily*] I've been wasting my time. Trevor will never make an actor. He might make a good auxiliary fireman.

THEONA Mummy, that's unkind.

TREVOR Perhaps a fireman is just what's needed in this house?

PATRICIA What do you mean by that?

TREVOR Nothing.

PATRICIA Coward. I thought we had agreed that you always say what you felt. What precisely did you mean by that? Why is a fireman needed in this house?

THEONA Mummy, Trevor didn't mean anything.

TREVOR Yes, I did.

PATRICIA [*pleased*] What? Go on, say it.

TREVOR [*with casual cruelty*] I was thinking of all these valuable portraits and these precious examples of still life.

DAVID Are you referring to me?

PATRICIA I can visualise your room, Trevor. Yesterday's supper things still stand unwashed on a trestle table, beside a chianti bottle which has been improvised into a lamp shade. A dirty shirt lies over the back of the only easy chair. The walls are decorated with passe-partouts, cut-outs from magazines, or are stuck on with cellotape?

THEONA Cellotape.

PATRICIA ...The floor is uncarpeted; the boards are stained, fluff lies in the cracks between them; last Sunday's paper, a milk bottle and a pair of shoes furnish one corner, while your divan bed...

TREVOR Go on.

PATRICIA ...Stands in another. It is unmade. It is narrow.

THEONA [*to herself*] Too narrow.

DAVID [*to himself*] Sounds like my old room in Golden Square.

PATRICIA The filthy rumpled pillow stained with your disgusting hair oil; the sheets soiled like a diary, utterly sordid...Isn't that the sort of hovel you inhabit? Isn't that the kind of room you prefer?

TREVOR Yes. At least they're lived in. Not just a museum like this.

THEONA I don't feel like an Egyptian mummy.

TREVOR [*to* PATRICIA] You can sneer at my background. But shabbiness is not poverty. It's this luxury that is utterly bankrupt. There are only two items in this morgue with any life to them: that cheap dressing-room mirror which represents your past, and that shoddy card table covered with feathers which stands for his flight from the present...symbols of failure floating in a swamp of vacuity.

THEONA Trevor...

DAVID Don't worry, I couldn't agree with him more. I often feel a little marooned.

PATRICIA You've never complained of it before.

DAVID I lack Trevor's disarming honesty—and courage...I suppose they're the same thing.

PATRICIA As rudeness. If you don't like this house, why do you come here? Why don't you answer?

DAVID Leave it, Patricia. Trevor didn't mean to upset you...

PATRICIA [*almost proudly*] Didn't he? And his remarks were aimed at me, not you. They were meant to hurt. They did hurt. [*To* TREVOR] Thank you.

THEONA You weren't very polite yourself, when you said what you thought Trevor's room was like.

PATRICIA Fortunately, I've never been there.

TREVOR Fortunately?

PATRICIA Fortunately.

DAVID Surely it's hot enough? You mustn't get upset. Trevor isn't rude, he's young. I was just as aggressive and outspoken in my day.

TREVOR Did you have only one?

DAVID Why turn on me? I was defending you.

TREVOR Were you? How very kind of you. I don't like being patronised. But just because you're so damned successful you don't have to be so bloody smug.

DAVID As for being successful, you mustn't judge by appearances, you know. It's true I am established; I suppose you might call me part of the Establishment—but although I am the Chairman of an established Publishing House, and though I sit on innumerable committees—all with artistic affiliations, and the most liberal views, I wouldn't say I had arrived anywhere or was particularly successful.

TREVOR What have you got to complain of? You're rich, aren't you?

DAVID Very—in things. The success which you see is the failure which you do not see. When I was your age, I wanted to be a poet, and I say that now almost apologetically. But I was a poet. People said that my poems were new, some found them shocking, others thought they were disgusting. I was delighted when I found that reading my poems disturbed people as much as the writing of them had disturbed me...in those days I felt with such intensity that I was like the flame of a bunsen burner, or the jet of a blow-lamp. There was nothing I could not penetrate so long as I held a pen in my hand. But of course—or do I bore you—I couldn't get my poems printed, so I started a small publishing firm that would print poetry when it could afford to...I've devoted the last twenty years to building that firm up. And now I could afford to print poetry I've forgotten what the poem was I wanted to write...My success is my failure...

THEONA [*going to him*] You're not a failure to me.

DAVID [*taking her hand for a second but not looking at her*] ...I suppose somewhere along the line I mislaid myself—just as I've now mislaid those bloody scissors.

TREVOR They're in your hand.

DAVID So they are: no wonder I couldn't find them.

TREVOR No wonder. You didn't want to—scissors are things which cut. A cut is an act of decision. Perhaps you're too divided to divide. Perhaps a part of you wants to free yourself from something or somebody, and the other part of you hasn't the guts to cut that somebody out?

PATRICIA You mean me?

TREVOR You hope so.

THEONA A week-end is an English institution consisting of polite, unconsequential conversation, tennis and cucumber sandwiches...

PATRICIA [*ignoring her, to* TREVOR] You're suggesting that his trouble is: he married me?

TREVOR I didn't say so.

PATRICIA I'm asking you a question.

TREVOR That doesn't mean I have to answer: when my answer might be considered impolite.

PATRICIA A little late to think of that.

TREVOR Too late. [*To* DAVID] You say you were a poet. What made you decide to turn yourself into...

DAVID A poodle?

TREVOR ...Into a curator of a museum, where none of the objects have any history. Why did you decide to abandon being a poet?

DAVID I've told you. I couldn't get my poems published, so...

TREVOR That didn't mean you had to stop writing them, did it? Tell me: I'm interested, and objectively. So many people have aspirations and ambitions when they're young, I often wonder what makes them...

DAVID As I am?

TREVOR Yes.

DAVID [*he goes and adjusts the clock*] Since you're interested—objectively—I'll tell you. We get frightened; we lack courage; we find living is dangerous, that it is safer to exist. People think writing poetry is a comfortable occupation: I suppose it is, if you're writing other people's poetry. But to write your own is like performing an operation on your own eye with your own hand, and without an anaesthetic. A poet has to be as ruthless as a surgeon; he has to have the strength of a boxer, he fights himself and punishes himself; he has to have the courage of an explorer who discovers a land of terrifying loneliness, and then has to find the endurance to settle down there. But I don't think any of us decides to abandon our ambitions. It's not that I made the wrong decisions, but that I never made any at all. My life has been made up of compromises, which I've made without knowing that I've made them. I've let events involve me, till I became the victim of circumstance.

PATRICIA What he's saying is he sacrificed himself for me? You didn't have to—did you? I said: did you?

TREVOR Sadist.

PATRICIA How am I being cruel?

TREVOR Your question doesn't even leave him the consolation of thinking his failure is your fault.

PATRICIA No, it doesn't.

TREVOR He could ask you the same question.

PATRICIA What right have you to interfere?

TREVOR What right have you to involve me?

PATRICIA You could go.

TREVOR I could go. Do you want me to go?

DAVID Now who's being a sadist?

THEONA Trevor...

PATRICIA You keep out of this, Theona.

TREVOR I said: do you want me to go?

PATRICIA There'd be no loss of charm or good manners if you did.

TREVOR Are good manners all you want?

PATRICIA What do you mean? Anyhow, it's not what I want, it's what Theona wants.

TREVOR [*cruelly*] We could both go. Is that what you want? [*Pause*] Well, what do you want? What do you want me to do? [*Pause*] I can go or I can stay. I will do whatever you wish me to do. All you have to do is to say what it is you want, not

Q

what she wants, not what he wants, not what society wants but what it is you want.

PATRICIA [*to herself as though in a trance*] What I want?

TREVOR It's as simple as that.

PATRICIA I don't know what I want. I don't care whether you go or whether you stay...

She runs from the room in tears

DAVID That was cruel. To ask somebody what it is they really want is like asking them who they really are. Don't you know, we don't know, we don't want to know.

THEONA He knew that. I think you'd better go.

DAVID No, Theona; that might make things worse; you know your mother. She soon gets out of her moods; she has to—so that she can go into one again. We've weathered worse than this; indeed, this is our weather. After all, Trevor came down here to get to know your family: that's what he's doing. He's the sort of man who likes his whisky neat: after this week-end he'll have a hangover. I'm not in the least upset by anything he's said. [*To* TREVOR] I see you disapprove of me, but I see your disapproval is not of what I am but because I am what you yourself fear that you'll become. It's natural to be intolerant when we see our faults and weakness in others, they make them so excessive and parody them to ourselves.

TREVOR So you don't want me to go?

DAVID No. But isn't it now your turn? What's wrong with your doing what you want to do?

TREVOR I'll stay for Theona's sake.

THEONA Don't sacrifice yourself.

DAVID Shilling a ticket: children half price!

THEONA What?

DAVID Tickets for the roundabout which goes round and round and round. [*To* TREVOR] You'll find my wife down by the boathouse; she'll be throwing stones into the river—no, dropping them...

TREVOR Shouldn't you go down?

THEONA No, you go, Trevor.

DAVID ...She'll be wanting a cigarette and a drink too. Yes, over there. Not too much gin, fill it up with tonic, there's a good fellow. And Trevor, don't apologise to her and what ever you do don't show you're sorry for her.

TREVOR Why?

DAVID She's a woman.

Exit TREVOR

THEONA No, don't say it. I know what you're thinking.

DAVID Do you? I wonder. Well, what am I thinking?

THEONA That you don't like Trevor; that he's rude, aggressive and unsympathetic; that of all my boy-friends I've brought down here, he's the least likeable. That's what you are thinking.

DAVID I didn't say so.

THEONA I'm disappointed in you, Daddy.

DAVID In me? Why? I was just congratulating myself on the restraint I'd shown...

THEONA That's precisely what I mean! I'm sick of seeing you bullied by Mummy. Now I've had to watch you being humiliated by Trevor. If you didn't like him, why didn't you chuck him out?

DAVID But you couldn't have wanted me to do that—could you?

THEONA Can't you see it doesn't matter what I wanted?

DAVID No, I don't see that.

THEONA Can't you see that I want you to be yourself. If you're not, what have I to love, to look up to? Trevor is still here. But where are you? Nowhere. I'm tired of watching you hide behind Mummy, behind me. Why do you do it?

DAVID I suppose I want to. I suppose that's why we all cling to one another: in order to hide ourselves...

THEONA [*going to him*] It's not why I cling to you.

DAVID ...Life's a sort of blind man's buff: bearable because of the bandages. None of us know who or what we are: perhaps that's what mercy is?

THEONA Darling Daddy, if only you weren't so kind...

DAVID Perhaps that's what weakness is?

THEONA [*breaking away*] So you're not going to do anything?

DAVID Yes.

THEONA Good. At last. What?

DAVID What I always do: inaction is a kind of action; indecision is an action too. I shall let things take their course. It's what they do anyhow.

THEONA And you won't tell Trevor to go? Why not? You can't like him.

DAVID I understand him. Isn't that what you want me to do?

THEONA Of course it is.

DAVID Is it?

THEONA Why should I want you not to like him?

DAVID I don't know. Perhaps because you're not sure that you like him yourself.

THEONA No, I don't like Trevor. The trouble is I think I love him...

DAVID Think? Things that we have to think to know are not worth knowing.

THEONA ...And to love somebody is a different thing from liking them, isn't it.

DAVID I should know.

THEONA You should know. I can't understand Mummy.

DAVID Do you have to understand her?

THEONA What else can I do?

DAVID Accept her.

THEONA Is that what you do?

DAVID Try to. We are children. The world is populated entirely with children. Children of forty, children of sixty, children of twenty-three. The pity is that all children are crippled children...

THEONA Yes. What hope have any of us?

DAVID Some; when we no longer hope. Your mother makes the mistake of thinking that happiness is something you buy at a store. She knows she wants it; she goes out shopping for it and every day comes back empty-handed. If only she wouldn't try so hard, if only she wouldn't try. The only chance we have of happiness is when we abandon its pursuit...

THEONA Nevertheless, I wish I could understand her attitude to Trevor. She always got on so well with my other boy-friends:

I used to get quite jealous. But she brings out the very worst in Trevor. She seems to hate him.

DAVID It's not as simple as that. Perhaps she resents him for being young.

THEONA Anthony was young too. She didn't resent him.

DAVID Maybe. But Trevor is confident. He's young in a way that makes other people realise they are young no longer. And it's easy to hate a person for that. For your mother it's particularly easy.

THEONA No, that's not her reason...

DAVID Is it that she senses you love Trevor...?

THEONA And?

DAVID ...And dislikes him because he might take you away from her?

THEONA She wouldn't mind if he did. It's I who make Mummy feel old. She's often said things...

DAVID You mustn't believe what people say...All I know is I want you to be happy.

THEONA Without pursuing it?

DAVID Yes...

THEONA I don't have to. I am happy. Darling, I'm happy now. [*Going to him*] We always get on so well together, don't we?

DAVID [*breaking away*] But you were thinking of Trevor, weren't you? Well, that ties everything up. [*He picks up his scissors and a long feather and unconsciously proceeds to shear it.*] That's that, and I'm glad for you.

> *He goes and kisses her. She turns away. A pause*

THEONA You didn't have to say that. You don't have to like Trevor.

DAVID But I do, Theona. I do like him. And I think there's a great deal of good in him too, once the edges have worn off. It's your mother we've got to bring round. That shouldn't be difficult. As you say, she usually gets on so well with your friends.

THEONA [*hearing* PATRICIA's *approach*] No, I haven't read it...

> *Enter* PATRICIA

I get so little time to read in London.

PATRICIA [*gaily*] And so little time to learn to act too, judging by that performance. Your voice was a semi-tone too high, and you over-played the casualness. Besides, you know we don't discuss novels in this house, we live them. Don't be embarrassed, I know people always talk about me behind my back. I give them the chance in order to bring them to life occasionally...

THEONA How very kind of you.

DAVID [*quickly and good humouredly, covering up* THEONA'*s edge*] What have you done with Trevor? Pushed him in the river?

PATRICIA [*genuinely unaware of her previous mood*] Why should I do that? [DAVID *and* THEONA *exchange a glance of incredulity*] But the poor boy nearly fell in a moment ago. He found that old speedboat of yours in the boathouse. Pushing it out, he nearly pushed himself in. Did you say good? No, of course you didn't speak. Oh, he's so thrilled with it, he's cleaning it up now and can't wait to go up the river. Do be an angel and run down and show him where the petrol is. Will you?

DAVID [*going to door*] Of course. I'd hate to think of him having to row.

Exit DAVID. PATRICIA *goes to the window upstage*

PATRICIA It's such a wonderful evening.

THEONA Is it?

PATRICIA I've never seen such colours...

THEONA We know we never have anything to say to each other. It doesn't help to talk about the weather.

PATRICIA ...You should have seen the sunset. It was as if the sun was thirsty and had slid down the sky to drink from the river. The reflection made the surface of the water look like enamel: the clouds moved like swans; the swans, like clouds... [*She turns*] Good God, I'm getting quite poetical...

THEONA That's not what poetry's about.

PATRICIA It's what life's about. I've never seen such an evening. It was as if it was the first evening...perhaps it was for me? I've never noticed it before.

THEONA I'm glad you enjoyed it.

PATRICIA You could have enjoyed it too. Why are you sitting in here? It's so stuffy in here. I know it's going to thunder.

THEONA I've been talking to Daddy—while you've been talking to Trevor.

PATRICIA He's such a child. You didn't tell me he was such a child. You should have seen his face when he found that speed-boat. I've never seen anybody so excited. You never told me he was a wet bob.

THEONA Trevor didn't go to the sort of school where you're a wet bob or a dry bob.

PATRICIA ...You never told me he loves rivers. You should have seen him yanking the boat out all by himself—though I did pretend to help. He must be incredibly strong...

THEONA I gather he's not going?

PATRICIA Yes, he is, as soon as he can get the engine to go...

THEONA I meant he's not leaving here—now he's found the river?

PATRICIA Didn't you want me to get to like him? Isn't that why you brought him here? [*Pause*] He's hoping to go up to the lock and back before dinner. He'll soon have that engine fixed; he's very practical—not like your father. [*Pause*] I like men who can do things with their hands, don't you?

THEONA *picks up one of* DAVID's *salmon flies*

THEONA Yes.

PATRICIA Trevor's are such strong hands. They're square, the fingers are stubby; nothing flabby, feminine or indecisive about them. Tinkering with that engine I noticed his thumb was as strong as a spanner. Yet when he touches a thing it's as if he caressed it. He likes things...

THEONA Sometimes I think he prefers things to people.

PATRICIA ...And he gets himself in such a mess. He's like a boy and paddles in whatever he does. He couldn't find a rag, so he used his handkerchief. Then when his hands were covered in grease he just wiped them on the seat of his trousers...he's the sort of boy who should always wear dungarees. You should buy him some.

THEONA I'm not his mother.

PATRICIA Then you are nothing to him.

THEONA What do you mean?

PATRICIA I mean it's impossible to love a man without being a mother to him...you mustn't be so shy, Theona. You must remember...

THEONA Remember what, Mother?

PATRICIA It's difficult for a man to show his feelings for a woman unless she reveals some of her own. If I were your age which I'm not...

THEONA Yes?

PATRICIA I wouldn't be so casual. Why don't you go with him up the river?

THEONA Because I don't want to. Why don't you go?

PATRICIA I'm too old for that sort of thing. But if I were your age, I wouldn't be so casual. At twenty-three, life runs towards us: we think it is always going to run towards us—we become careless, spendthrifts with opportunity.

THEONA Is that what you did?

PATRICIA That's what I did—so don't.

THEONA Don't what, Mother?

PATRICIA Don't deceive yourself or let diffidence be mistaken for indifference.

THEONA When John was down here last November, you accused me of being a flirt.

PATRICIA Because you were being frivolous with your feelings. I could see you didn't care for John.

THEONA You mean you didn't.

PATRICIA I'm talking of you and Trevor!

THEONA Whom you don't like—or didn't.

PATRICIA My feelings don't enter into it!

THEONA No? Then why are you angry?

PATRICIA Because I can't bear to see you frittering your life away, not having a complete relationship with anyone.

THEONA With Trevor?

PATRICIA Yes, with Trevor...He's a fine type of man. A splendid animal.

THEONA Don't be vulgar. You talk as if I were a mare at stud.

PATRICIA There's nothing vulgar about Trevor's physique. True, his manners are a bit uncouth. But any woman would be attracted to him. He has a beautiful body. Though he is clumsy, he is more graceful than a dancer because all his movements have purpose and meaning. He has the kind of body which should never have to bear the indignity of clothes. He should go naked.

THEONA Mother, why are you going on like this?

PATRICIA Because I am trying to make you realise you are a woman...[*Now desperate*] You and Trevor should grab at life and clear out, right out!

THEONA And get married?

    PATRICIA *goes to her mirror and stares into it*
And get married?

PATRICIA Yes.

THEONA Do what you did? Seeing you and Daddy doesn't exactly...

PATRICIA We all have to make our own mistakes. That's what life is: one's own mistakes. But Trevor is different. He's not like your father, he's a man: he knows what he wants and he'll get it.

THEONA Two thousand pounds a year, eighteen-horse-power car, one life assurance, two brats and a villa in Bromley. Oh I forgot; he'll need a wife, one wife.

PATRICIA And don't you want to be that woman?

THEONA Not particularly.

PATRICIA Then you don't love him.

THEONA Don't be silly, mother. You can love a man without wanting to do his laundry, just as you can marry a man without loving him at all. I've got my career.

PATRICIA I had mine. I was already a star...

THEONA And you've looked upon Daddy as your eclipse. I don't want to punish Trevor like that. I don't want to make your mistakes, I want to make my own.

PATRICIA A woman has only one mistake to make and if she doesn't make it, she's not a woman; I can't understand you, you're calculating—and you're cold.

THEONA How can you know that?

PATRICIA I've seen you with Trevor. You must get over your shyness. You mustn't be so casual.

THEONA Mother…I've known Trevor for six months.

PATRICIA [*refusing to accept the implication*] Yes, you told me: you met at the Opera Ball.

THEONA You observed his strong hands, I know those hands. You visualised his room. I don't have to imagine it: it's not his room any more, it's mine too. Some of my things are there.

PATRICIA I suppose you dump things there on your way to the theatre. I used to do that when your father had digs in Jermyn Street.

THEONA A long way from the Lyric Hammersmith. Mother, I can't stop you deceiving yourself about yourself. But I can stop you fooling yourself about me. You talk to me as if I'd just left the Convent. I'm telling you I sleep with Trevor. Though you're right, his bed is too narrow for sleep.

PATRICIA Trevor seduced you?

THEONA No Mother, I seduced him…we'd had a quarrel outside Covent Garden about a week after we'd met. I'd run into an old boy friend. Trevor was rude to him. I said I never wanted to see Trevor again. I got into a taxi to go to my digs. But I didn't go. When Trevor got home I was already in his bed. It was he who was shy…

PATRICIA I don't want to hear!

THEONA There's nothing like it to heal a squabble. Perhaps that's why Trevor and I squabble so much?

PATRICIA I tell you I don't want to hear these sordid details.

THEONA There's nothing sordid in making love. He may be clumsy, but not in bed. He's a wonderful lover.

PATRICIA I tell you I don't want to hear.

THEONA Strong yet gentle, impetuous yet patient. I once asked him how he managed to be so patient.

PATRICIA Have you no shame? No pity…

THEONA …Do you know what he said? He quoted an Arab epigram: 'A good lover…'

PATRICIA I don't want to hear it!

THEONA 'A good lover satisfies his wife by thinking of his grandmother.'

PATRICIA But you're not his wife.

THEONA That doesn't disprove the epigram.

PATRICIA You're his mistress!

THEONA As you were Daddy's when I was conceived. Why call love names? Maybe I'll be his wife.

PATRICIA That makes it worse.

THEONA Makes what worse for you? Ten minutes ago you were talking like a procuress, wanting me to become a woman. Now that you hear I am you're upset. Why?

PATRICIA Because...because...

THEONA Why?

PATRICIA It's a shock to me. That's all.

THEONA I see. I'm sorry. Perhaps it's better if we didn't try to talk...I'll go and find Trevor. [*She pauses at the window*] It's such a wonderful evening.

Exit THEONA

PATRICIA *returns to her mirror*

PATRICIA [*staring into it*] Gina did try, didn't she? She did try.

CURTAIN

Act II

The same room the next day. PATRICIA *and* DAVID *are in the positions they held at the opening of Act One; she, before her mirror; he, making flies at his card table. Nothing has changed but time and an increase in tension.*

PATRICIA I wish it would break. I wish it would break.

DAVID [*not looking up*] So do I sometimes...

PATRICIA [*turning from it*] I didn't mean this mirror.

DAVID [*continuing to bind the hook*] My thread? I'd be very annoyed if it did.

PATRICIA [*moving towards his card table*] Annoyed, but never angry. I wish you were angry sometimes, I wish I could make you angry. But emotions are so vulgar, aren't they? Emotions are things women over forty feel, isn't that it? Isn't that it?

DAVID I didn't say so.

PATRICIA Of course not, you never commit yourself to anything. Well, what is an emotion? Tell me. As a poet or a publisher...

DAVID A nice distinction.

PATRICIA ...You should be able to give me a definition. Stop fidgeting with those damn fish-hooks. You used to say a poet's job was to define things. Well, tell me what an emotion is...

DAVID An interesting question...

PATRICIA 'Interesting'? Be careful, don't become too involved.

DAVID ...I suppose emotion might be defined as an unfinished thought.

PATRICIA You mean we feel when we cannot think?

DAVID Or dare not.

PATRICIA A nice distinction. And perhaps we think only when we can no longer feel or dare not face our feelings? That makes thought an escape from feeling and feelings an escape from thought, doesn't it?

DAVID Something like that.

PATRICIA Why do you hate me so?

DAVID I beg your pardon?

PATRICIA You heard me.

DAVID My dear child…

PATRICIA And don't give me that! Don't humour me. I asked you why you hated me?

DAVID You've a talent for the *non sequitur*.

PATRICIA Have I?

DAVID We were talking objectively. Or at least I was.

PATRICIA Were you? 'Objectively'? [*She laughs*] Can the man of letters tell me what objectively is? [*She goes to the mirror*] Or how our eyes can see themselves?

DAVID You're doing that now.

PATRICIA Do you know why I waste half my precious time staring into this bloody mirror? It's not because I'm searching for the beautiful girl I was, nor looking for the old hag I'll soon become, I look into this mirror because I'm sick to death of seeing through you. At least there's reflection here, something given back to me.

DAVID Splendid.

PATRICIA What?

DAVID Your remark. That you look into the mirror because you're tired of looking through me. I like that. I must make a note of it.

PATRICIA Do. I'm so glad I provide you with copy. A pity you never use it. A pity you don't write anything any more. Do you remember those passionate poems you wrote to me? They were beautiful:

> She sleeps as a rose
>   upon the night
> And light as a lily that floats on a lake
> Her eyelids lie over her dreaming eyes
>   As they rake the shallows
> And drag the deep
>   for the sunken treasures of heavy sleep.

You must have been inspired when you wrote that.

DAVID I didn't.

PATRICIA I thought it was yours. Anyhow, I was beautiful wasn't I? Tell me how beautiful I was.

DAVID You weren't, you were pretty, insolently pretty, a prettiness that was promise of the beauty I now see.

PATRICIA You have to work very hard, don't you? My vanity's insatiable: it's like a disease. After that effort you deserve a drink. I think we both deserve a drink.

DAVID Why not the four of us? There are at least three of you: The woman I know; the woman you know and the woman neither of us know.

PATRICIA That goes for anybody.

DAVID Anybody.

PATRICIA Quite an arab aren't you? Poor lamb, twenty-four years married to the wrong woman, I mean, women, twenty-four years of intimacy.

DAVID And never introduced!

PATRICIA [*She approaches him warmly*] And what would happen if we were introduced?

DAVID That could be the beginning. [*He turns away*]

PATRICIA [*thrown back on herself*] You said beginning; you meant the end.

DAVID Are Trevor and Theona back from the rehearsal yet?

PATRICIA How the hell do I know whether they're back. They live their lives, we live ours.

DAVID Yes, we live ours. [*He goes and winds the clock then returns to his table; she goes to the window back stage.*]

PATRICIA I wish it would break. Why doesn't it break. I loathe this sultry weather, a thunderstorm is coming, why doesn't it come and get it over? The air's like a boil, lightning could lance it. I can't stand this oppressive heat.

DAVID Why don't you turn the fan on? [*He does so*]

PATRICIA [*still at window*] Always ready with a practical solution. Well I've got one too. I can't bear the sight of those hideous flowers. [*She goes out to the flower-bed just outside the window, pulls the flowers root and all and brings them inside.*]

Poppies are so obvious, so vulgar. [*She slashes the flowers against the wall*]

DAVID Better? [*He gets up and goes and picks up the stalks which he puts on a side table. He holds one petal in his hand.*] Crimson joy?

PATRICIA What?

DAVID Nothing. [*He lets the petal fall*] Blake. [*He returns to his table*]

Enter TREVOR, *he wears no shirt*

Hello, Trevor. How did the rehearsals go? Where's Theona?

TREVOR Upstairs changing.

DAVID You must have found it intolerably hot working all the afternoon in that dreadful little theatre. It's stuffy at the best of times. Going for a dip?

TREVOR No. I thought of taking that boat out again. I changed the plugs this morning and tuned her up a bit. She ought to zip along now. Perhaps you'd like to come Mrs Maugham?

PATRICIA Thank you, no.

DAVID But it'll be fresh out on the river; a spin would do you good.

PATRICIA I said no thank you—and do you mind not treading those petals into the carpet. [*Exit* TREVOR] Disgusting. Why didn't you say something? Have you no respect for me? Why didn't you tell him? Are you afraid of him?

DAVID Tell him what, darling?

PATRICIA That he's no right to walk in here like that. He's your guest isn't he, this is your house, isn't it? Then why hadn't you the guts to say something?

DAVID What about?

PATRICIA I suppose you didn't notice that he strode in here without a shirt on, that he stood there half naked flaunting his disgusting chest in my face, rippling his obscene muscles as though he were a strong man at a circus? It was disgusting, a nauseating piece of exhibitionism. But you didn't notice I suppose strip tease is now *de riguer* in Henley drawing-rooms on Sunday afternoons?

DAVID Don't be silly, darling. Trevor was going for a bathe.

You were lucky he's got his trousers on over his costume. I've often seen you go through this room with nothing but a towel on and that's often fallen off.

PATRICIA Don't say you noticed it? [*Pause*] Well I suggest we tear this bloody week-end up and get Trevor out of this house before any harm's done.

DAVID What harm?

PATRICIA Before he has to prove his filthy masculinity by seducing Theona under your own roof. Or has that possibility not occurred to you?

DAVID You're exaggerating. Anyhow Theona can look after herself.

PATRICIA Can she? I wonder. Anyhow you needn't worry. I'm not asking you to throw Trevor out. I see you're not man enough for that, I know you hate unpleasantness. I suggest you tell him that you've found you've an appointment early in the morning and consequently we've decided to go up to the flat this evening.

DAVID If we both went up where would Theona stay?

PATRICIA On the divan of course, like she has before. Well, will you do that?

DAVID No.

PATRICIA Why not?

DAVID Because I think it's unnecessary and because it would be intolerable in that flat in this weather. Trevor's all right, a bit raw perhaps, but he'll tone down. I quite like him. If we'd had a son...

PATRICIA God!

DAVID ...he'd be just like Trevor at that age. They're all the same; intolerant of us, the last generation, not because of what we are but because we're in their way; confident they could do better than we did; sure of the destination and despising us for losing the way.

PATRICIA Shut up. Can't you see I can't stand any more, listening to your endless self-deprecation, your confession of failure laid at my feet because I'm the cause of your failure.

DAVID I wasn't talking about myself. But about Trevor. I think you're exaggerating there.

PATRICIA Oh, you do? Then I've no alternative but to tell you. Then we'll see if you're man enough to act.

DAVID You mean Theona...?

PATRICIA No, I didn't mean that. Something that touches you even nearer. Trevor has tried to make love to me.

DAVID I don't believe it.

PATRICIA Don't be so damned insulting.

DAVID When? When did he try to seduce you...?

PATRICIA This morning.

DAVID Where?

PATRICIA Here, in this room.

DAVID I don't believe it.

PATRICIA I was sitting there in that chair reading—well, looking at a magazine. I didn't hear Trevor come in. He moves quietly like a panther. The first I knew was I felt his breath on the back of my neck. Before I could turn, he turned me and kissed me on the lips.

DAVID Well? Obviously he mistook you sitting there for Theona.

PATRICIA I'm too old for a young man to want to kiss me? But I can assure you there was no mistake. He kissed me.

DAVID Affectionately?

PATRICIA Passionately.

DAVID And then?

PATRICIA And then?

DAVID Yes, then.

PATRICIA Then I pushed him away of course, I got to my feet and tried to leave the room. I ran; he followed. I'd got as far as here, when he caught me. He didn't stop me by taking hold of my hand or my arm; he didn't stop me by clutching my clothes or by putting his hand on my shoulder. I'd made my move as far as here, I'd got as far as here, when his hands came from behind me. He stopped me by clutching and holding on to my breasts.

DAVID I don't believe it.

R

PATRICIA ...Then he leant against me, he didn't push me, he just let the weight of his body lean against mine till I collapsed here across the end of the sofa.

DAVID Why didn't you scream?

PATRICIA I knew there was nobody in the house. He knew that too. You and Theona were playing tennis.

DAVID Yes; but your stage scream would have carried as far as there. I've heard it further when you wanted me to hear it.

PATRICIA At first, I was too frightened, too surprised to scream. And besides, I couldn't...

DAVID ...because he'd got his hand over my mouth.

PATRICIA ...Couldn't because his mouth was against my mouth. He held my tongue with his teeth. Trevor knows how to kiss. He was like a man possessed, possessed by something stronger than himself. It was not he who moved, but desire which moved him. He was so out of control, I felt quite sorry for him when he said—

DAVID Yes, what did he say? Tell me exactly what he said.

PATRICIA He said he wanted me. He said that his violence needed my tenderness and his tenderness needed my violence, that the passionate man in him recognised the passionate woman in me, whereas Theona...

DAVID Ah, what did he say about Theona?

PATRICIA He said Theona was still only a girl. He said he loved me for my years, was grateful for my wrinkles. What d'you think of that?

DAVID I think you're making the whole damn thing up.

PATRICIA So, you don't believe me?

DAVID Not a word of it.

PATRICIA Why? Why don't you believe that Trevor's attracted to me? Have you never been attracted to a young girl?

DAVID Yes, that's different. But you're telling me Trevor desires you. That's different.

PATRICIA It's true.

DAVID Yes, darling. It's true that you're a good actress.

PATRICIA I tell you it's true. [DAVID *moves to go*] [*hopefully*] Where are you going? What are you going to do to him?

DAVID I promised Theona I'd give her a driving lesson. That's what I'm going to do; give Theona a driving lesson. [*She puts her head in her hands. He turns back from the door and puts his hand on her shoulder.*] Why don't you go and lie down for a bit? [*He kisses her head*] It will pass: I tell you it will pass. [*He goes*]

PATRICIA [*not looking up*] Can't you see it's your kindness that's so unkind?

> *She stands up; she is crying. She goes to her mirror. Recovers herself, attends to her make-up as though in a dressing-room preparing for another scene. Then she goes and sits in the chair, picks up a magazine. Enter* TREVOR. *He comes from the garden and is intending to go through the room.* PATRICIA *sees him come in and looks down at her magazine. She waits for him to approach her. Then looks up just as he is about to go off through the other door.*

PATRICIA Hello, Trevor. I didn't hear you come in. Did the engine start up all right?

TREVOR Yes, thank you.

PATRICIA Good. Clever boy. Then why aren't you out on the river?

TREVOR I thought I'd take Theona out. [*He turns to go*]

PATRICIA She's not in her room.

TREVOR Where is she?

PATRICIA Out. Her father's giving her a driving lesson.

TREVOR Is he?

PATRICIA Yes. [TREVOR *turns to go again*] So where are you going?

TREVOR To get my penknife out of my coat pocket. The spar isn't quite right. Probably carboned up. I may have put too much oil in with the petrol. These little two-stroke engines are very tricky, sensitive things. [*He turns again*]

PATRICIA Are they? There's a penknife, there, on David's table. That will do. [*He crosses to the table*] Won't it?

TREVOR No, the blade's not strong enough. Those points can get terribly caked up. This would break. [*He turns towards the door again*] I'll get my knife. A file is what I really need.

PATRICIA Would any sort of a file do?

TREVOR Yes.

PATRICIA A nail file? A steel nail file?

TREVOR That would be perf...

PATRICIA There's one by that mirror. You can use that. Wouldn't that do the job?

TREVOR [*picking it up*] Yes, but it would spoil it. You could never use it again.

PATRICIA Take it.

TREVOR No, I'll get my knife.

PATRICIA Take it. I've dozens...

TREVOR Thank you. [*He turns towards the garden*]

PATRICIA ...And come and sit down, Trevor. [*He goes to sit on the sofa*] No, don't sit down. Come here behind me. I've got a headache. Would you mind rubbing my neck a little. You've got such sensitive hands.

TREVOR There?

PATRICIA That's wonderful. You've no idea what a relief that is. Tell me, did you change your mind and decide to stay on in this morgue, as you call it, just because you found the boat; or had you some other reason? [*Pause*] More. That's wonderful. Now lower. There. Do your fingers hurt?

TREVOR No.

PATRICIA They should; they've taken the pain from me. It must be somewhere. No don't stop. I like it. Soon, I'll begin to purr. [*She now waits hoping that the fantasy she described to* DAVID *will now occur as she imagined it. She waits for his hands to turn her head and for him to bend down and kiss her. He makes no movement. So she begins to move round towards him just as though the pressure was being made.*] What are you doing now?

TREVOR Nothing.

PATRICIA You mustn't. [*She continues to turn her head round as though it were being turned.*] No, you mustn't. [*He takes his hands a few inches away from her neck. Her head continues to turn till she looks up at him.*] Silly boy. [*She closes her eyes, waiting for the kiss, she has already described. He makes no move. Yet she experiences the sensations of the kiss.*] Silly boy. You shouldn't have done that. [*She stands and turns away from him. Then moves quickly towards the sofa as though being pursued. He makes no move. Then she stops at the end of the sofa and with her back to him, takes her arms from her sides as though anticipating his taking hold of her breasts. She waits.*]

TREVOR Thanks for the nail file. With a good spark, the engine should start. [*He moves to go*]

PATRICIA [*without turning*] Come and sit down, Trevor. [*He moves back towards the chair*] No, not over there. Here, beside me on the sofa. I want to talk to you. But first let me get you an ash-tray.

TREVOR What about?

PATRICIA Us. [*She lights a cigarette—pause*]

TREVOR That's a pretty vase. I've never noticed it before. Italian, I suppose? Is it?

PATRICIA Yes, Italian.

TREVOR I want to go to Florence sometime. Have you ever been to Florence?

PATRICIA Yes.

TREVOR Did I tell you about those two pieces of Battersea pottery I picked up in the Portobello Road...

PATRICIA Yes.

TREVOR Theona says they're worth a lot.

PATRICIA Does she?

Pause

TREVOR Something rather amusing happened at rehearsals this morning.

PATRICIA [*without interest*] Did it?

TREVOR Perhaps Theona's told you?

PATRICIA Give me your hand.

He makes no move

TREVOR We'd just finished a run through of the first act...

PATRICIA [*taking his hand*] Your hands fascinate me.

TREVOR And Tony was giving us notes. You know the sort of thing?

PATRICIA Yes, I know the sort of thing.

TREVOR The whole company was there on the stage being very solemn and serious...

PATRICIA Each of your fingers is like a limb...

TREVOR ...When the Mayor's wife swept in once again to see how we were getting on. She's President of the club or something. I dare say you know her...?

PATRICIA ...Like a limb. Strange how strong things can be so gentle.

He withdraws his hand

TREVOR ...She patronises the Arts, indulges in cultural slumming. The most affected over-dressed woman I ever met. She likes to impress us with her Paris background. She talks of Jean and you're not sure whether she means Sartre or Anouilh. Anyhow, this morning she excelled herself. She was wearing a new hat, a sort of inverted birds nest festooned with figs and trailing scarlet feathers. It was so dotty even Tony dried up. The whole company just sat and stared. She enjoyed the effect. Then she went up to Theona 'Don't you adore it?' she asked, 'Dior. Quite *le derrier cri*, don't you think?' [PATRICIA *doesn't laugh*] I'm afraid we weren't as restrained as you are — we just hooted with laughter.

PATRICIA Yes, I can understand.

TREVOR [*giving her his hand to take*] Well, weren't you going to tell my fortune?

PATRICIA [*refusing it*] No, I was not. [*He moves to get up. She then takes his hand*] But I will if you like.

TREVOR [*He remains seated*] No. [*He withdraws his hand*] I wonder how long they're going to be?

PATRICIA Theona and David? Hour or so. Trevor...[*Pause*]

TREVOR I once had a friend who owned a driving school. An odd thing happened to him. I'll tell you about it, if you like?

PATRICIA Trevor...

TREVOR He lived out at Morden. In one of those new Estates, where every street is like the next street and every house is like the one next door. Each with its own garage, each with its own front door, garden in front, garden at back and a telly aerial on the chimney-pot. You know the sort of thing, or maybe you don't? Anyhow my friend lived at No. 85 Camden Road. There are one hundred and sixty-five semi-detached bastions of individuality and privacy in the road; but he lived at No. 85, you see?

PATRICIA No. 85.

TREVOR Yes. The odd numbers are on one side, the even on the other. Anyhow one evening last year my friend went home a bit later than usual. It was October and dark, about ten o'clock, he says. He got out of the Tube as usual, bought a packet of cigarettes as he always does and started to walk home up Camden Road, you see?

PATRICIA Yes. [*She puts her hands over her face*]

TREVOR He turned in the front gate, walked up the concrete path, opened the front door with his latch-key, hung his hat up, put his umbrella in the stand, straightened the Van Gogh reproduction which hung in the hall, and went into the sitting-room. He turned the telly on, watched it for a while then helped himself to a drink and finally decided to go up to bed. He saw that the light was off in his bedroom so he undressed in the bathroom in order not to disturb his wife. Thoughtful sort of chap. Anyhow he got into bed and then found he couldn't sleep. So after tossing and turning for a bit he started to make love to his wife...he hadn't got any sleeping pills I suppose. After doing this, he thought he'd have a cigarette, so he switched on the light. It was only then that he discovered he'd been making love to the woman next door. 'I'm awfully sorry,' he said, 'I see I'm in the wrong house.' 'That's not all' she replied and then added rather crossly 'Didn't you notice our chrysanthemums, they're much better than yours next door.' [*She removes her hands*] But you're not laughing, you're crying. Why?

PATRICIA Because you had nothing else to say but tell me a joke.

TREVOR I'm sorry.

PATRICIA Don't apologise, Trevor, stop making conversation. Why are you embarrassed? [*Pause*] Well, give me a cigarette— or is that asking too much?

TREVOR You're already smoking. Perhaps you'd prefer one of mine.

PATRICIA You're very polite suddenly.

TREVOR I'm sorry you think I'm usually rude.

PATRICIA For Christ's sake don't apologise. I like your rudeness, it's part of you. With me you can be yourself. That's a luxury few of us know. .[*She stands and almost dances across to the window*] Isn't the sun wonderful? It makes me feel grateful for being, for being alive. I feel so young. I feel just as I felt at seventeen. Is that silly?

TREVOR No, you're extraordinary for your—. You and Theona might easily be taken for sisters...

PATRICIA [*delighted*] Do you think so?...[*She moves across the room. Her mood now more calculating and controlled.*] But Theona and I are different, very different. And don't tell me you haven't noticed that difference. You're far too mature yourself not to have noticed some lack of maturity in her. Theona's pretty, very pretty; and quite talented too. She has great charm and is kind, very kind...But somehow or other Theona has never grown up, never developed as you might say.

TREVOR You mean she's young.

PATRICIA Very young. Of course, she's intelligent, much more intelligent than I am. But intelligence is not everything in a woman is it? I often worry whether she's not emotionally undeveloped—perhaps even cold. You know what I mean. Do you think Theona's cold?

TREVOR I don't know...

PATRICIA You should.

TREVOR People often mistake control for coldness.

PATRICIA Do they? You don't. I can see you know too much about women for that. Self-control is one thing, indifference is another. I shouldn't like to try to pull the wool over your eyes. You're far too intuitive, far too shrewd. No, Theona may have my looks but she takes after her father in temperament, they keep things bottled up and that's dangerous, isn't it?

TREVOR So they say. I suppose the danger of our not expressing our feelings is that in time we cease to feel them?

PATRICIA Yes, how clever of you. But I suspect that David and Theona don't feel as intensely as you and I do. They're made of different stuff...Trevor, how old are you? No, don't tell me, let me guess. I'd say you were thirty-two?

TREVOR Twenty-six.

PATRICIA I don't believe it. I'm older than you, yet we two are equals, equally selfish, equally cruel. And when we look into each other's eyes, we weigh one another and feel this equality, don't we? You're so extraordinarily mature. You're the sort of man who has no age. You were born wise. I only hope Theona's not too young for you.

TREVOR She'll grow up.

PATRICIA Growing old is not the same thing. [*Pause*] You are lucky.

TREVOR Why?

PATRICIA To have a skin like that. I never tan. I blush like a lobster, peel like an onion. Where did you manage to get it?

TREVOR The Lido...

PATRICIA I thought you'd never been to Italy?

TREVOR ...Lansbury's Lido; the banks of the Serpentine.

PATRICIA It's the same sun.

TREVOR Better company.

PATRICIA Probably fewer sandflies. What snobs you angry young men are: you divide the world into casts. You're Brahmins and the rich are untouchable. We're not really... Anyhow I wish David could walk around like you do. You look so relaxed.

TREVOR There's nothing to stop him.

PATRICIA No?...I had an uncle who used to amuse me as a child by pretending to blow down his thumb to make his muscles swell, let me see you do it. Go on—please.

TREVOR Like this?

PATRICIA [*clapping her hands gleefully, like a child*] Yes, that's it. Now let me feel. My uncle always used to let me. But Trevor, they're enormous. You must be as strong as nails. Do you do Swedish exercises every morning or something?

TREVOR Hardly.

PATRICIA Then you must do the Yogi Discipline?

TREVOR Never heard of it.

PATRICIA Haven't you?...I took a course once on Broadway.

TREVOR Hammersmith Broadway?

PATRICIA Ha, ha. Think you've got your own back, don't you?
Yes, I remember the first exercise was to sit on the floor,
[*She kicks off her shoes*] like this, your legs crossed, see—oh
damn this skirt. Then all you have to do is to stand up. But you
mustn't touch the floor with your hands. Sounds easier than it
is. God, I hope I can still do it. Damn, my suspenders are too
tight...Excuse me. [*She undoes them*] Now watch. There, you
see? Looks easy doesn't it? Now you do it. Come on. [*He
shakes his head*] Come on, don't be stuffy. That's right, sit
there and let's cross those legs. Don't cheat. [*She crosses his
legs*] Now, upsey daisey!

> *He tries but fails and goes to support himself with one hand*

PATRICIA That's not fair. No hands! I said no. Now, darling,
try again. [*He again tries*]

TREVOR Funny, it looks easy enough. Wait a minute.

PATRICIA Darling, don't use your strength. Just relax, it's all a
matter of balance. [*She sits beside him and does it again*] See like
that!

TREVOR [*trying again*] Confound it.

PATRICIA That's right, darling; lean forward. [*He gets half-way
up, she takes a feather from* DAVID's *table and tickles* TREVOR's
back.] I always wondered what these were for.

TREVOR [*collapsing*] You bitch!

> *He takes a cushion and flings it at her. She throws it back.
> He chases her. She flops down on the sofa in an abandoned
> position.*

PATRICIA Pax!

TREVOR That wasn't fair. [*He flops down beside her*]

PATRICIA [*miming him*] 'That wasn't fair'. Go and tell Mummy
then...What kids we are. But that was fun. [*She takes his hand*]
Wasn't it?

TREVOR Yes.

PATRICIA Yes it was. [*Pause*] Trevor...?

TREVOR Yes.

PATRICIA You remember yesterday telling me something...

TREVOR What?

PATRICIA That it was important that I should know what it was I wanted—you remember?

TREVOR I remember.

PATRICIA I do know now what I want.

TREVOR Do you? Good. [*He takes his hand away*] It's important that we should know what we want. But that doesn't mean we can have it.

PATRICIA I see. Your advice was a kind of tease, a way to increase the torture?

TREVOR It wasn't meant to be.

PATRICIA You know what it is I want.

TREVOR But I did not. [*He stands*]

PATRICIA Trevor, kiss me. [*He kisses her on her forehead*] That was a cruel thing to do. I said, kiss me. [*He turns to go*] Christ, it's not possible that I should feel this for you yet you...Am I nothing to you?

TREVOR No.

PATRICIA Then what? What? Tell me.

TREVOR Like a mother.

> *He goes. She stands. Her stockings are loose and wrinkled. In anguish, she puts her hands over her face, then slowly drags them down tearing her blouse as she does so. She has her back to the door. Enter* DAVID *and* THEONA.

THEONA Mummy, your stockings...[*She begins to giggle*] You don't 'arv look a slut...[PATRICIA *turns*]

PATRICIA That's what I am Theona: a slut, an old slut.

THEONA I am sorry...I didn't mean...

PATRICIA I don't want pity.

DAVID [*going to her*] Darling, what's happened?

PATRICIA Don't you touch me.

THEONA Who tore your blouse?

DAVID Trevor?

THEONA What? Don't be ridiculous...

PATRICIA Yes, Trevor. I warned you. You didn't believe me. Now perhaps you will.

DAVID You mean he...?

PATRICIA Yes, yes.

THEONA I don't believe it. [*To* DAVID] Do you believe it? [DAVID *turns from her, moves across the room and begins to tidy his card table*] Do you? Say something, Daddy. Stop tidying that table. What are you going to do?

PATRICIA Don't worry, Theona. He'll do nothing. [*She goes to him*] Well, why aren't you jealous? Why aren't you angry?

DAVID Do you want me to be? I didn't say I wasn't.

PATRICIA You're not. You don't look it, you don't feel it, of course you don't feel anything any more, do you? I killed all that. You just feel sorry for yourself and will retreat further into your little shell and make another fly for a rod you never use. Isn't that what you'll do?

DAVID No.

PATRICIA Then what? Tell me what?

DAVID I'm going to...

THEONA [*frightened*] Daddy...

DAVID ...make you tell me precisely what happened.

THEONA [*more fearful now at seeing her mother crumple*] Oh, no... Leave her alone. Leave the whole thing alone. Can't you see she can't stand any more. [*She moves to go*]

DAVID Where are you going?

THEONA To get Trevor.

DAVID Stay where you are. He's nothing to do with this. Now, darling, tell us exactly what happened. Go on, we're interested. Very.

PATRICIA You'd taken Theona out to give her a driving lesson.

DAVID We know that. We've just come back.

PATRICIA [*She sits on the sofa*] Almost as soon as you'd gone, Trevor came into the room. He said he was looking for a spanner or something to mend the engine. No, he wanted a penknife; I gave him a nail-file. I told him Theona was out, that you were both out...I was sitting here.

DAVID [*pointing to the chair*] You mean over there.

THEONA How do you know where she was sitting?

DAVID I do, Theona. And you were reading a magazine, weren't you? This magazine? [*He hands it to her*]

PATRICIA [*taking it and moving across to the chair*] Yes, I was sitting over here. I didn't hear him come in—you know how silently he walks...

> TREVOR *appears from the garden. He stands in the door unobserved by the others. He holds a rose in his hand.*

DAVID ...like a panther?

THEONA Daddy, stop interrupting.

DAVID I'm not interrupting. I'm prompting.

PATRICIA The first thing I knew was he was standing behind me. He started by caressing the back of my neck. I stood up. I tried to get away from him...

DAVID You moved slowly across towards the sofa. He followed. He stopped you. He stopped you by taking hold of your breasts.

PATRICIA No, David, that didn't happen. He never touched my breasts. He did not want me as a mother.

DAVID Then tell me what did happen.

PATRICIA We were on the floor.

THEONA Mummy!

PATRICIA We were doing exercises. I was showing Trevor how to do those Yogi exercises I learned in Hollywood.

THEONA I didn't know you'd been to Hollywood.

PATRICIA [*to* DAVID] You know what I mean.

DAVID No, I don't.

PATRICIA You sit crosslegged on the floor and have to stand up without using your hands. I can do it easily.

DAVID I've never seen you.

PATRICIA Well I can. There's a lot you never see. But although Trevor is incredibly strong and wiry he's no sense of balance. He tried several times but always cheated by using his hands. So I got tired of watching him. I took one of your silly feathers and tickled his back. That's how it started.

DAVID What?

PATRICIA Our pillow fight. Then I collapsed on the sofa. He

flopped down beside me. Then suddenly he gripped my hand. He didn't say anything. I knew he wanted me.

DAVID [*believing but complacently*] And you couldn't get away?

PATRICIA I couldn't get away.

THEONA Then what happened?

PATRICIA He held me as a man holds a woman. Then he kissed me on the lips...

> TREVOR *enters the room. He goes straight to* PATRICIA *and kisses her on the lips.*

TREVOR Like that.

DAVID I see.

PATRICIA No, it was not like that. It was like this. [*She pulls* TREVOR *down beside her*] I took his hand. It was I who wanted him. I made him kiss me. And he did, he kissed me on the brow like a son might kiss his mother. [DAVID *starts to whistle silently to himself*] Then he ran from the room. He fled from my passion. [*Through her tears*] What made you come back and...?

TREVOR Call it compassion.

PATRICIA Call it pity.

TREVOR I could not walk away, Patricia.

PATRICIA You used my name...Did your engine start. [*He shakes his head*] You used my name. Not just—her mother?

TREVOR Not just a mother. A woman; a rose that leans on the evening waiting to be picked. [*He gives her the flower*]

DAVID [*still whistling, now very angry*] I think you owe me some explanation.

TREVOR I don't owe you anything. But I'll give you an explanation so long as you don't take it for an apology.

DAVID Don't misunderstand me. I'm never intolerant.

TREVOR I wonder why you're not?

DAVID That's a silly question.

TREVOR I'm in the position to ask silly questions. I was asked down here to get to know the family. That's what I'm doing.

DAVID Well, now tell us what you find.

TREVOR That you and Patricia are both bigamists. Each married to the person they know, each married to the person they do not know. An awful lot of marriage.

DAVID Twenty-four years of it.

TREVOR You're both in flight, fleeing from yourself. Patricia from a capacity for tenderness she dare not yield to, and you from the poet whose vision was too uncomfortable for him to bear. You're both lonely, locked in hideous intimacy without a single point of contact. She was not pursuing me but her own youth. Perhaps she saw in me something of the son you refused to give her? Perhaps she wanted to live her own life again so put herself in Theona's place? It doesn't matter what the reason is, her misery's the same.

PATRICIA [*standing*] And I know what to do.

THEONA [*going to her*] What?

DAVID What are you going to do?

PATRICIA Murder Gina. Kill the girl I was, live the woman I am. Break it, now I am broken. Stop looking inwards, start looking outwards. I don't need a mirror any more. I want windows, open windows. [*She smashes her mirror. Then pulls her stockings up*]

DAVID I hate violence...

TREVOR Violence can sometimes heal.

> DAVID *continues to whistle. Suddenly* THEONA *gets up and almost runs from the room.*

DAVID Theona, don't let your mother upset you.

THEONA It's not mother, it's you.

DAVID Me? Why, what have I done?

THEONA I want to know why you're so angry?

DAVID Darling, I'm not angry.

THEONA You are. You're whistling. You've been doing that for the last three minutes. Only yesterday you told me you only did that when you were very angry.

DAVID But I'm not. [*His pipe breaks in his hand*]

THEONA No? But you weren't angry when you thought there was something in Mother's accusations about Trevor. You were complacent and tolerant at the idea that he might have raped her. But now that she's admitted there was nothing in it, you're almost beside yourself with fury. Why?

> DAVID *turns away*

TREVOR Don't ask him that, Theona.

PATRICIA Why not. It's true. Do you know the answer, Trevor?

TREVOR I don't know. But I can think of an explanation.

THEONA So can I.

DAVID [*burying his head in his hands*] Leave me alone.

THEONA Why? Is that what your tolerance to others has been— a demand for tolerance to yourself? You disgust me. [THEONA *moves towards* TREVOR. PATRICIA *goes across to* DAVID.] You'd rather have sacrificed your own wife than lose your daughter to him. [PATRICIA *puts her arm round* DAVID] Isn't that it?

DAVID [*standing*] That's it. That's it. [*He moves like an old man towards his card table and slowly pushes it over.*] [*He turns towards* PATRICIA] Now we're both broken.

    She goes and leads him to the sofa where they sit together

TREVOR That was very destructive of you, Theona.

THEONA It was true.

TREVOR It was still destructive.

THEONA I like the truth.

TREVOR Do you? Then tell me why you've brought half a dozen boy-friends down here—all as penniless as I am, all as uncouth as I am, all highly unsuitable. Was it that which made you select us so as to make it easy for your father to reject us? Because you didn't want to make your own home you wanted to stay in this upholstered womb? Or was it you brought us down here for your Mother, because you were guilty you were a girl and she had wanted a son?

THEONA Shut up! I'm sick of this amateur psychiatry. You tell me why you stayed on in this house, you were supposed to loathe, amongst this wealth you said you despised. Was it to be near me, or was it to be near her? You don't know: I shall never know.

DAVID [*to* PATRICIA] From the way these two are going on, it's obvious they should get married.

PATRICIA [*rising*] Yes, darling, let's go away and leave them to it.

THEONA You can't do that!

PATRICIA No? Children are such tyrants, aren't they? It's about time parents made a bid for freedom. Besides it's wrong for us to stay, trying to live our lives again through you.

DAVID What's more I want to go. I'm going fishing. I may catch a salmon. And I shall write again, perhaps it will be poetry now I no longer care whether I'm a poet or not. I feel grateful.

PATRICIA For what?

DAVID Your being.

PATRICIA I feel like a child...

DAVID We still are.

PATRICIA ...going for a holiday.

DAVID That's what life is. Our tenderness more precious than their passion.

PATRICIA *and* DAVID *leave*

THEONA Everything's broken. Even Mummy's mirror is smashed. [*She begins to pick up the broken glass*] A pity this weather doesn't break.

TREVOR It will.

He goes and picks up DAVID's *table, tidies it. Then almost unconsciously goes over and winds the clock as* DAVID *so often did.* THEONA *watches him. Now he returns to the card table. Then absent-mindedly she produces a mirror from her bag for a moment. They are self-absorbed, unaware that they are as her parents were at the beginning of the play. Suddenly* THEONA *becomes aware.*

THEONA What are you doing? For God's sake leave that table alone.

TREVOR [*turning*] And perhaps you could stop staring into that mirror.

They laugh and are suddenly serious again. They start

THEONA You see, we've no chance, have we?

TREVOR The last generation is like a hand in the glove of our minds.

THEONA This house wins. Here we'll sit. I wondering whether you prefer my mother...

TREVOR ...I suspecting you're homesick for your father.

THEONA Ridiculous, isn't it? [*It darkens, there is lightning, then thunder*] Good, now that's broken too. I hope the river floods and washes all the punts out to sea. [*He moves towards the window*] Don't stand there, Trevor. It's dangerous.

TREVOR I'd like to be struck by lightning. A quicker death than being struck by a house in Henley.

THEONA That was unkind.

TREVOR Don't worry, I mean what I don't say.

A pause, broken by a roll of thunder

THEONA Come back, Trevor. I feel frightened and lonely here. What are you thinking?

TREVOR About it.

THEONA About us?

TREVOR Yes, but we're such a small part of it. King Lear went mad on the desolate heath. Modern man will go beserk in a centrally heated flat. This lightning is our doubt, but it does not illumine, it shows the darkness where we are. We are utterly alone and consciousness makes us the only things which are alone.

THEONA [*not listening*] I dare say we'll hear from them from time to time.

TREVOR [*laughing*] I wasn't thinking of your bloody parents.

THEONA Come and sit down, Trevor. Here, put your head on my lap. I'm a woman. I don't see so much, therefore I don't fear so much. I'm just an ordinary woman. I promise to cherish you with my hands and in my mind. Use me, that's all I ask. [*Her mood lightens*] And I promise to be good tempered. Do you want any of this—of me.

TREVOR None of it. I want you as a woman, capricious and unpredictable as a woman. I want your good temper and your bad temper. I need you whole.

THEONA And what will you give to me?

TREVOR The man I am, rude, violent, uncouth and untidy. Who will love you at breakfast and hate you at supper and need you all the time. [*He gets up and goes towards the window*] It's getting lighter now after the storm. But there had to be the storm or there wouldn't be this peace after it. [*He looks out into the darkness, then turns to her*] Love is our only hope—perhaps that's why we've so little hope.

THEONA Ssh! Don't spoil it.

TREVOR You know, I don't say what I mean!

CURTAIN

The Seven Deadly Virtues

A CONTEMPORARY IMMORALITY PLAY

This play was first performed at
the Criterion Theatre, London, on 19 May 1968

CHARACTERS

DR SATAN	About 45
MISS ANGEL	A pretty blonde about 26
COLIN WOOD	An artist about 37
LAVINA	His wife, 30
HARCOURT WEBB	A famous art critic, 55
M. PUGET	An art dealer, 65
MELANIE	A pretty schoolteacher, 25
CHRISTOPHER GIBBS	A scientist, 28
GERARD	His friend, 30

Two Receptionists, one male, one female. The male receptionist doubles with M. Puget's assistant and the waiter.

The specific virtue or vice which is played is named on a board Stage Right, and changed with each scene.

Act I

SCENE ONE

Proscenium Right

DR SATAN *is seated at his desk in hell. He appears extremely bored. He doodles on his blotter and turns on the television, turns it off, yawns, goes to window, paces up and down and begins filing his nails. He rings a bell on his desk. His* RECEPTIONIST *appears. She wears a transparent knee length white coat, high-heeled red leather riding boots: little else.*

SATAN Not now, my pet. If there's anybody in the waiting-room don't keep them waiting. Show them straight in. [*The* RECEP-TIONIST *demurs*] What's the point of impressing them, making them sit there reading *Private Eye* while I have nothing else to do but look at *The Spectator?* I shall die of boredom. That would make the headlines, wouldn't it: 'Satan dies in Hell. Acute Ennui with spiritual complications.' This inactivity is more than any man can stand. It's weeks since I heard a really succulent sin. So if there's anybody waiting show them straight in—and let the unrepentant have precedence.

RECEPTIONIST I'm sorry, your Grace, but there's nobody there.

SATAN Not one?

RECEPTIONIST None.

SATAN Strange, I've been expecting General de Gaulle for weeks and I still wonder where that fellow Somerset Maugham got to—he can't have bribed his way into the other place...

RECEPTIONIST I brought you the evening papers, your Excellency.

SATAN [*picking one up*] Ah, things are looking up: earthquake in Sicily, 3,000 souls (I like that). And look: more riots in the States and another actor and a bishop passed over. We're going to be busy. Just run a duster over the chairs and don't forget: the unrepentant first.

RECEPTIONIST There's the lift coming down now, sir.

SATAN So it is. Show whoever it is straight in. I'm ready and waiting.

> *The* RECEPTIONIST *goes out.* SATAN *puts his glasses on, takes a new note book and sits.*

SCENE TWO

> *LIGHTS UP on Proscenium Left*
>
> MISS ANGEL's *boudoir. It is heavenly. A double bed, a telephone, a television set. She is in a negligée on a chaise-longue, enamelling her nails, eating chocolates. The floor is littered with glossy magazines. She is languid, petulant and vexed, like a pretty woman who can't find a mirror or a vain one deprived of flattery. She upsets her chocolates, flings a magazine across the room, and calls:*

ANGEL Gabriel, Gabriel, come here. [*Enter her* BUTLER *in a bath towel*] And why aren't you properly dressed?

GABRIEL I was taking a bath, madam.

ANGEL And how long are you going to keep me waiting before you bring me my coffee?

GABRIEL [*indicating tray on floor*] But, Madam, you've already had it.

ANGEL So I have. That's the worst of this place, time has no meaning; only waiting has any meaning. [GABRIEL *makes to go off. She lies on the chaise-longue.*] Where are you going? Come here. Look at me. Closer. [*He goes to kiss her*] How dare you! You don't have to take liberties just because I let you sleep with me occasionally out of duress. Now tell me, look closely, am I going cross-eyed?

GABRIEL No, madam.

ANGEL Is my skin clean?

GABRIEL Yes, madam.

ANGEL Is my breath sweet? Is my hair lank? Are my gums toothless?

GABRIEL No, madam.

ANGEL Then why have I no other company but yours? And I even have to pay for that. There was a time when every man aspired to reach me, and quite a number succeeded too. I could take Truth for a lover and find Truth was strong; or I could call on Charity and receive his generosity. But now Truth is always relative and Charity is a Trust.

GABRIEL Ssh! I think I hear the lift coming up now.

ANGEL Then quick, run and change. If they see you like that, they'll think they're in the other place.

> GABRIEL *goes out. She runs to dressing-table, puts on a dressing-gown of sack-cloth, dabs her face with ash and then she clips a couple of wings on to her shoulders and a halo on her head.*
>
> *LIGHTS UP on Proscenium Right*
>
> *The* RECEPTIONIST *shows* CHRISTOPHER *in*

RECEPTIONIST Mr Christopher Gibbs.

SATAN How d'you do? [SATAN *holds out his hand.* CHRISTOPHER *reciprocates with his iron hand*] That's a good idea! Wish I'd thought of that. Must have given you a considerable advantage. Do sit down. Now then. Tell me what brings you here. Don't be reticent. I'm not easily shocked.

CHRISTOPHER A life of moderation, I suppose.

SATAN I beg your pardon?

CHRISTOPHER And I've always tried to be tolerant...

SATAN Tolerant?

CHRISTOPHER Forgiven others. And practised what I preached.

SATAN Yes, so do I. I see you've quite a sense of humour. Now tell me, what's brought you here? In your own words...

CHRISTOPHER I was faithful.

SATAN So are we all. But to what?

CHRISTOPHER My wife, of course.

SATAN What d'you mean, of course? I suppose you know where you are?

CHRISTOPHER [*looking round him*] Heaven, I presume.

SATAN No, sir, this is hell! And I am Satan. Now perhaps you'll tell me what brings you here. And don't bore me with your petty excesses, or trivial omissions. I want to know your sins.

CHRISTOPHER I can't think of any.

SATAN Very promising start. Lack of conscience is always a good beginning. Well if you can't recall your sins yourself, let me prompt you. Whom did you betray?

CHRISTOPHER Nobody.

SATAN Come, you can't be all that absent-minded...Was it rape?

CHRISTOPHER Never.

SATAN Murder?

CHRISTOPHER No.

SATAN Robbery with violence?

CHRISTOPHER I believe in non-violence.

SATAN Even in Grosvenor Square? Good God...It's not often I call on him. But then it's not often I get a pacifist down here. Excuse me. This is interesting, you intrigue me. You didn't commit any of the seven deadly sins?

CHRISTOPHER Seven?

SATAN Seven! Yes—Let me enumerate them: Sloth, Envy, Pride, Avarice, Gluttony, Lust, Anger...Doesn't any of these prompt you to any admission?

CHRISTOPHER No—if I had a fault, it was diffidence. Money never interested me. As for my sensual appetites, they were most restrained.

SATAN That leaves anger.

CHRISTOPHER No, I seldom lost my temper with people. I could always see their point of view. Well enough to prevent me from expressing mine.

SATAN I see. This is not very encouraging, is it? After all, not everybody is eligible here. Certain basic qualifications are required—rather like getting into Whites, you know. Well, if you don't claim any of the obvious excesses perhaps it was something more subtle or insidious which brought you here?

CHRISTOPHER Such as?

SATAN Such as being generous to the point of undermining another person's will.

CHRISTOPHER I never had the means.

SATAN Or perhaps by being so damned tolerant and forgiving you drove another person to do the unforgivable?

CHRISTOPHER I don't think so.

SATAN [*standing*] Then what the devil brought you here? [*He rings bell.* RECEPTIONIST *enters*] Show Mr Gibbs to the basement. And I hope you'll find everything most uncomfortable—

CHRISTOPHER What will I have to do?

SATAN Nothing. Absolutely nothing. And don't try to reform any of my old members or undermine the traditional spirit here. Here's a book of the rules. You're not allowed to tip the staff, or sleep in your bed alone.

CHRISTOPHER Good heavens!

The RECEPTIONIST *shows him out*

SATAN What a man! This place is going downhill!

BLACKOUT

LIGHTS UP on Proscenium Left

GABRIEL *re-enters dressed in a Salvation Army uniform carrying a tambourine.*

ANGEL Is it any man I know?

GABRIEL No, madam, I'm afraid it isn't...

ANGEL Don't say it is— ?

GABRIEL Worse than that...

ANGEL Not another woman? [GABRIEL *nods and goes off*] Not a single man for a month. This is carrying equality too far!

GABRIEL *ushers* LAVINIA WOOD *in*

GABRIEL Mrs Lavinia Wood, madam.

ANGEL You'll take tea, of course?

LAVINIA I'd prefer a brandy. [GABRIEL *withdraws*]

ANGEL Shock.

LAVINIA No, just a thirst.

ANGEL Didn't the ascent upset you?

LAVINIA No, but I found the direction rather surprising.

ANGEL That's a new line. No, I don't mean your dress.

GABRIEL Will you take soda?

LAVINIA No, straight please, on the rocks. [GABRIEL *hands her the drink*]

LAVINIA Well, this is a surprise...

ANGEL Is it? Surely you expected some reward for a life of virtue? Most do. Which of the seven did you fall for?

LAVINIA None really. Oddly enough I only loved my husband. The rest were just men.

ANGEL But I was not referring to men, but virtues—the seven virtues—Diligence, purity of mind, humility, abstinence, charity, meekness—Dear, dear, I've missed out one...

LAVINIA Chastity?

ANGEL Yes. I must have felt unconsciously that it was hardly worth mentioning. Perhaps you were abstemious?

LAVINIA [*indicating her glass*] Hardly.

ANGEL You dedicated your life to charity?

LAVINIA No, I'd have got no money there. And I needed money —that's what turned me into a sort of...

ANGEL In other words you were a whore?

LAVINIA In a manner of speaking.

ANGEL In a manner of sleeping, I'm sure.

LAVINIA But I think you'll find my paper's in order. [*Hands* ANGEL *her passport*]

ANGEL I can't think what you're doing here; you drink, you— quite obviously you've been sent to the wrong place. [*She rings the bell*] But here you are and here you'll have to stay. [*Enter* GABRIEL] Show Miss, I beg your pardon, Mrs Wood to the West Wing. I think you'll be very comfortable there. The sexes are segregated; the beds, single. [*Exit* GABRIEL *with* LAVINIA WOOD. ANGEL *goes straight to the phone.*] Give me the hot line to hell. Hell O, double o, o—please.

LIGHT GOES UP Proscenium Right
The bell rings. SATAN *answers*

SATAN Hello! Oh, all right.

ANGEL Guess who?

SATAN Angel, of course. [*Pause*] Who else reverses the charges. I was just about to call you. What's up?

ANGEL Oh—they have made a mess of everything again. I've got a girl up here who obviously belongs to you. Otherwise business is very slow indeed.

SATAN Same here. I've got a fellow who was obviously meant for you—positively boasting of a life of tolerance. Quite good-looking. What's the girl like?

ANGEL Not bad-looking, but totally immoral.

SATAN Maybe we could swop?

ANGEL That'll take some doing. However, it's not merely a question of her sex. Something has gone drastically wrong somewhere. I think we ought to have a conference—soon.

SATAN Good idea. Something is seriously wrong with contemporary morality. The sorting has got out of hand. By all means, let's meet. But where?

ANGEL Maxim's?

SATAN I'm sick of Maxim's. Too many Americans. And don't suggest the Savoy Grill. Too cold for me.

ANGEL What about the Riviera?

SATAN All right.

ANGEL Monte Carlo?

SATAN No—please...too vulgar.

ANGEL The Reclamat—you know, just outside Cannes.

SATAN Of course I know it—I own it.

ANGEL When?

SATAN Now, of course. We've wasted enough time.

They both put the phones down. Their respective RECEP-
TIONISTS *enter.*

ANGEL We're going down to Earth for the week-end, Gabriel. Will you run a bath. Help me out of these damn wings, will you?

SATAN [*changing*] And while I'm away see that none of the members get up to any mischief—damn it, now I'm getting muddled. You know what I mean. I don't want to come back and find everybody holding prayer meetings in corners, do I?

RECEPTIONIST No, sir. Will you be wearing your...?

SATAN Don't be a fool. We are going incognito.

GABRIEL Madam will be wearing your Dior?

ANGEL Yes. Unzip this will you?

BLACKOUT

SCENE THREE

SATAN *saunters to* STAGE CENTRE *where there is
a cafe table and two chairs. He sits at one. He sings and
accompanies himself on his guitar.*
        SATAN'S RECEPTIONIST *appears*
SATAN Oh go and find me some candidates, and make sure they
    have correct qualifications.
        She withdraws. A WAITER *approaches—*GABRIEL *in
        disguise.*
    I'll order later. I'm waiting for somebody.
WAITER A lady, sir?
SATAN No. [*Enter* ANGEL, *très chic. She looks round her, admiring
    the view.*] An Angel. [*The* WAITER *withdraws*]
ANGEL Hello there, you old...
SATAN [*embracing her*] Angel...
ANGEL What a heavenly... [*She corrects herself...*] seductive
    place! But you always did know your way around, didn't you?
SATAN [*modest, but pleased, helping her to her chair*] The tempta-
    tions are particularly good round here—and the Lobster
    Mornay is always worth trying. [*They sit. The* WAITER
    hovers] A bloody mary—and a glass of milk. Well, darling, how
    have you been keeping—and how are all the commandments?
ANGEL On fairly chaste you know. Nothing to grumble at...
    much! And how are you—just as promiscuous as ever, I
    hope?
SATAN No.
ANGEL Getting past it?
SATAN That's one thing I do not have to fear.
ANGEL Then what's the difficulty?
SATAN My sex.
ANGEL You're not changing it?
SATAN Certainly not. My trouble was that I was always strictly
    masculine, as you know...
ANGEL It never troubled me much.

SATAN [*takes her hand*] Angel...Things wouldn't be so bad if we'd been blessed...[*He corrects himself...*] cursed with a touch of bi-sexuality. But I wasn't. I was, as you might say, condemned to women. I haven't had one for a month. A woman, that is. We only get men...down there.

ANGEL And I only get women. It's very queer.

SATAN Very. Mine are mostly old authors, politicians, schoolmasters and actors.

ANGEL My last girl has been as promiscuous...

SATAN As you used to be? Remember? Doesn't look as if we've got much of a future, does it?

ANGEL No! Some damn fool of a clerk in the sorting-office has got his orders muddled up. Instead of dividing good from evil, he is segregating the sexes as if heaven and hell were public urinals.

SATAN What I can't understand is I'm getting prigs: dusty with chastity, zipped with self-restraint, capable of nothing but an excess of tolerance or a bout of forgiveness.

ANGEL And I'm getting your kind...amateur-tarts, nothing less!

SATAN Morality must be in a hell of a mess up here!

ANGEL Don't you complain...

SATAN But I do. I invented seven Deadly Sins to assure a certain continuity of eligible membership...[*Reminiscently*] Gluttony, avarice, lust...

ANGEL Surely my virtues must shine as always? [*Enumerating on fingers*] Humility, charity, meekness...[*Pause*]

SATAN Chastity!

ANGEL Chastity.

SATAN Pride, Angel. They can't have run out of that!

ANGEL Perhaps my virtues have reformed your vices?

SATAN Nonsense! More likely the other way around.

ANGEL Well let's see...Why don't we find out how it all happened.

SATAN Good idea. We'll retrace the steps of those two misfits we've just received. We shan't have to go very far...[*As though reading stage instructions*] The Place, a villa outside

T

Cannes. Time, whenever it was. [*The LIGHTS DIM on the café*] We'll take yours first. I probably know more about her than you do. Married to a painter...

> *As the light instantly comes up on STAGE RIGHT where we have the suggestion of an artist's studio: various canvasses, easel, and a divan bed.* COLIN *is sprawled on it: he is wearing a dressing-gown. There is no luxury in the studio—it is used for other purposes too. But it is not La Bohème though there is a charcoal stove. The first sketch of a portrait of* LAVINIA, *wearing a blue shawl, stands on the easel.* COLIN *is smoking languidly. He is prone but not resting; he is bored. He decides to read, then gives the idea up when he finds he cannot reach the book without moving. So he continues to lie there, smoking.*

ANGEL ...on a couch—in his dressing-gown—on the easel beside him the first sketch of a portrait of Lavinia, his wife. Colin is smoking—languidly—

SATAN He is bored—

ANGEL He decides to read—

SATAN Gives up the idea when he finds he can't reach the book without moving—[SATAN *moves book further out of* COLIN's *reach*]

ANGEL So he continues—

SATAN To lie there...smoking.

SCENE FOUR

SLOTH

> LAVINIA, *a beautiful woman approaching thirty, comes in. She is dressed and carries a coffee-tray.*

COLIN Breakfast?

LAVINIA [*setting it down beside him*] No, darling. You had that two hours ago. Here's some more coffee. It might make you get up.

COLIN Pour it out, there's a love.

LAVINIA [*doing so*] Black or white?

COLIN Black. You've forgotten the sugar.

LAVINIA Shall I drink it for you? [*She hands him the coffee*] It's gone eleven.

COLIN What of it? What have I got to do?

LAVINIA Work.

COLIN [*indicating stack of canvasses*] And add to those? Two hundred of them.

LAVINIA [*looking at her portrait on easel*] I like that. What you going to call it? Please don't call it 'Portrait of my Wife', or 'Portrait of a Woman'.

> COLIN *moves enough to embrace her—then stands with her before the canvas.*

COLIN [*simply*] 'Mea Madonna'? [*He smiles*] Or simply, 'The Virgin'. [*He says with laughter*] That would be funny, wouldn't it—that would embarrass the critics. Religion is so *démodé*. They wouldn't know what to say.

LAVINIA Darling, why does it matter what they say?

COLIN [*looking at her*] I shall call it a 'Portrait of Chastity'—and to hell with fashion.

LAVINIA That's better.

COLIN [*picking up palette*] Let's get on with it. Get your shawl.

LAVINIA Not now.

COLIN Why not?

LAVINIA If I sit for you, who'll get the lunch? You'd better get on with earning it. [*She removes the portrait from the easel and replaces it by a half-finished advertisement poster which has the lettering but lacks the design.*] You'd better get on with this. It was supposed to be in a week ago, wasn't it?

COLIN Two weeks ago. [*He goes back to sit on the sofa*]

LAVINIA Then get it done. It won't take you ten minutes. Colin, it does earn the rent—and you don't have to sign it.

COLIN [*laughing bitterly*] Wouldn't matter if I did—nobody would recognize my name, would they?

LAVINIA They will. Darling, just do it and forget it. Now promise you'll dash it off while I do 'me chores'. Promise. [*She gets to the door*]

COLIN Darling, pass me an ashtray, will you?

>LAVINIA *crosses the room, then picks up an ashtray which is only about two yards from* COLIN *and places it beside him. She crosses the room again.*

And the coffee's cold. And there's skin on the milk.

LAVINIA [*turns*] But you were drinking it black. [*she picks up the tray*] All right, I'll heat it up for you. Now you knock that design off.

>*She goes off. He lies inert for a moment, drops his cigarette-stub into the coffee-cup then takes off his dressing-gown. He puts his shirt on; we see that the evening before he had taken his shirt and pullover off in one. They are still attached. He puts them on together, then picks up a tie which is already tied and puts it over his head. He runs his hand through his hair, lights another cigarette, stands in front of the easel, then goes over and lies prone on the divan again.*

>LAVINIA *enters with the coffee pot. She studies him silently, puts the tray down, then picks up some brushes and goes towards him menacingly.*

LAVINIA You promised. Why aren't you working?

COLIN I feel indifferent to detergents: suds don't inspire me.

LAVINIA If you don't get up and paint, I'll paint you! [*She does so; they brawl. In their struggle they knock into the poster on the easel, accidentally daubing it.*]

COLIN [*picking easel up, puts poster back*] Clot! Now look what you've done.

LAVINIA [*gaily*] Rather a nice design, isn't it? I'm a genius.

COLIN [*bitterly*] Yes. You ought to send that to the Leicester Galleries. They'd lap it up. That's what they think genius is today—a bloody accident after a stupid brawl. [*He flings himself on the divan again*]

>*BLACKOUT and LIGHT UP on café table*

ANGEL Well—and what was all that supposed to be about?

SATAN [*unenthusiastically*] Sloth. Accidia—the sin of indifference.

ANGEL You'll have to do better than that. I didn't find it particularly vicious.

SATAN Sloth can lead to spiritual torpor, it's a vice with considerable possibilities.

ANGEL I can't see that at all. It's a positive virtue *not* to do the wrong thing—and how do we know that Colin's laziness isn't a waiting for inspiration.

SATAN [*irritated*] Don't stand there criticising. Now—let's see what you can do with mine.

The LIGHT DIMS in café table, and slowly rises on:

SCENE FIVE

A Flat in London

The RECEPTIONIST *and* GABRIEL *are changing scenes.*

ANGEL All right! It is Spring. We are in Christopher and Melanie's flatlet in Bayswater. There are a few daffodils on the table. Melanie is in a dressing-gown...

SATAN How did I guess?

ANGEL They are having breakfast. Christopher, you've already met.

SATAN How a prig like him got sent to me I'm damned if I know.

ANGEL We shall soon find out. At this time Christopher is living a life of virtue [SATAN *yawns*] and diligently continuing his research...

SATAN In the purpose of virtue?

ANGEL In magnetism. He is a physicist with a brilliant future.

SATAN The only thing about him which intrigues me is where he got that iron hand. That's a gadget I could do with, especially when handling these modern idealists which all seem to end up with me.

ANGEL His iron hand is not an invention of his but the tragic result of a motor-cycle accident. The girl, Melanie, is a model—

SATAN How disappointing.

ANGEL Not of virtue, but of dresses. She works for a fashion house. Her father was a Bishop.

SATAN Then I'm bound to know him.

ANGEL They are a typical modern couple in a typical modern flat, at breakfast. Let's observe them.

CUT

HUMILITY

MELANIE *gets up, goes to* CHRISTOPHER *and slaps his face.*

ANGEL I should have told you: they are married.

SATAN So I see.

MELANIE I warned you: I told you I'd do that if you said you were sorry just once more.

CHRISTOPHER What else could I say? I asked you if you wanted some toast; and you said you'd no appetite because I was smoking. What else can I do but apologise, when you complain?

MELANIE And why d'you think I complain but to try to find something you won't apologise for?

CHRISTOPHER I don't understand. I don't understand you at all. We've been married a couple of years and in a way we've not even been introduced yet.

ANGEL 'A typical modern couple.'

SATAN Ssh.

CHRISTOPHER I don't understand you at all. [*He gets up and starts clearing the table*]

MELANIE Why bother? It's unimportant. Besides, it would be a pity to waste your brilliant scientific mind studying the quirks of human personality, especially female personality, wouldn't it? And, please, don't do that—I'll do the washing-up as soon as I'm dressed.

CHRISTOPHER I was only trying to help.

MELANIE Well, don't.

CHRISTOPHER I'm sorry.

MELANIE How did I guess.

CHRISTOPHER I suppose you think I'm clumsy? Frightened I'll break a cup or something?

MELANIE That's unfair of you. You know bloody well that I

never make you feel self-conscious about your hand. Never.
[*She goes to him and holds it tenderly but briefly*] That was mean
of you.

CHRISTOPHER Then why does my helping you upset you?

MELANIE Because it makes me feel guilty. And because I suspect
that you do that knowing it will have precisely that effect.

CHRISTOPHER Nonsense. I'm doing it because...

MELANIE Because?

CHRISTOPHER Because you have to rush off to work.

MELANIE I don't this morning.

CHRISTOPHER Usually. And I...

MELANIE [*finishing the sentence for him*] ...have no job to do or
lab to work in? This unholy sacrament of marriage certainly
put a weight round your neck, didn't it? You resent having
chucked up your research at the University and leaving
Sheffield because my job was here, don't you? [*Now dressed,
she starts to make-up her face, speaking into the mirror.*] They
make a big mistake. People who say that sex is all-important are
making a big mistake. Anyhow, that's what I brood about when
I'm modelling and look as if I haven't got a thought in my head.
And d'you know what's more important than sex? It's guilt.
It's guilt that keeps people together. It's guilt that keeps people
apart. [*She uses her lipstick*] And do you know what our crime
is that we all feel so guilty about?...

SATAN Isn't that your department?

ANGEL Shut up.

MELANIE I do. [*She runs a comb through her hair*] We feel guilty
for being, for being alive and wanting to stay alive. [*She has now
one shoe in her hand and is looking under things for another.*]
Having mislaid our purpose we feel we've no right to life
itself.

CHRISTOPHER Things don't have to have a purpose.

MELANIE No, any more than people have to be happy. We are
all right when we're in bed, at least, occasionally and briefly.
But for the rest it's war: your guilt against my guilt. We load
each other, never spare each other and wear ourselves away.
Why? It wasn't always like this, was it?

SATAN [*to* ANGEL] Well, was it? What went wrong?

ANGEL I'll show you. Let's suspend them there. [MELANIE *and*
CHRISTOPHER *freeze*] and have a flashback.

LIGHTS FADE

SCENE SIX

PURITY OF MIND

ANGEL Some students' digs in Sheffield four years ago.
Scene change. LIGHTS UP
CHRISTOPHER *sits at table. A book open before him.*
He pushed the book away, bangs his iron hand on the arm
of the chair, gets up and goes to the door and calls.

CHRISTOPHER Melanie. Melanie. [*He goes back to the table, opens*
the book and pretends to be working.]
MELANIE *comes in*

MELANIE Well? [*He doesn't answer. She picks up something from*
the floor.] Here I am. You were calling. What was it?

CHRISTOPHER Oh, nothing.

MELANIE I suppose you've lost something and just wanted me to
look for it for you. Your glasses? Your cigarette lighter?

CHRISTOPHER That's it. How did you guess? My cigarette
lighter.

MELANIE [*beginning to look for it*] You could have used a match.

CHRISTOPHER There aren't any.

MELANIE Are you sure?

CHRISTOPHER I can't find them. Anyhow you used to be good
at finding things. [*He takes lighter from his pocket and surrep-*
titiously slips it under the book.]

MELANIE Used?

CHRISTOPHER Well, I haven't seen much of you recently, have I?

MELANIE [*at table*] Don't tell me you've noticed it. [*She moves*
the book] Here it is, all the time.

CHRISTOPHER Good. Thank you. I'm longing for a cigarette.

MELANIE Let me light it for you. Now d'you mind telling me

what you really wanted? [*Pause*] [*Brightly and hopelessly*] I know, you're going out and you want me to tie your tie for you. [*She does so. He shakes his head.*] Or sew this button on for you. Threading a needle is about the only thing you can't do with that hand, isn't it?

CHRISTOPHER [*with self-pity*] Hardly. [*He puts his iron hand round her*] It has other disadvantages. [*He immediately takes his hand away and turns from her*]

MELANIE Don't. I can't bear to see you hurt. [*She goes to take his left hand, then deliberately stops herself and takes his iron hand.*]

CHRISTOPHER [*struggling to be articulate*] Do you want to know what I really wanted—I wanted you. I've hardly seen anything of you during the last two months: it has been two months of listening, of waiting. I have listened for your getting out of bed of a morning, heard your movements as you dressed, then waited to hear you running down the stairs, listening as you passed my door, hoping you'd look in. Then I have waited. Nobody has loved until they have waited. I haven't been able to work. I have waited all day to hear you coming up the street again in the evening. I have listened for your key, I have listened for the door, waiting for you to run straight up here as you used. But tonight I lost all hope. That's why I called—

MELANIE Perhaps the only hope we have is when we have no hope at all? I had given up hope that you would miss me. I used to come down the stairs from my room making more noise than I need, hoping you would hear me, hoping you would open the door to ask me for something, a cigarette, a match or a news-paper for I dared not hope that you would ever need me as I've needed you. But tonight you did call...

CHRISTOPHER Not for a match, not for a cigarette. But for you. [*They embrace passionately*] Forgive me.

MELANIE For what?

CHRISTOPHER The waste of you: the waste of time, the waste of a summer. You used to come in every day; I remember you used to sit by the window or curl up in that chair, and I would waste you while I worked. I suppose no man knows how much he loves till he loses what he loves: I need you.

MELANIE Why?

CHRISTOPHER I need you as the ivy needs the tree it climbs upon; I need you as a wave needs the beach. I need you as thirst needs water, as a man his sight, as a man needs hands.

MELANIE But do you love me?

CHRISTOPHER I've just told you I need you.

MELANIE ...Or do you love your need?

CHRISTOPHER Let's go away together, now: tonight.

MELANIE I'm frightened.

CHRISTOPHER Of what? Because we've no money, because I've no job, because we've no place, no home to go?

MELANIE No, those things are only things.

CHRISTOPHER Then what is it you are afraid of?

MELANIE That you don't love me.

CHRISTOPHER Then I'll tell you how I love. I love your loveliness.

MELANIE —That's not me.

CHRISTOPHER I love your gentleness.

MELANIE —That's not me. Sometimes I'm cruel. Sometimes I'm clumsy.

CHRISTOPHER I love your innocence.

MELANIE Christopher, I am not innocent.

CHRISTOPHER I am not jealous of those men you've loved before. I am grateful to them, for each has helped mould you. So you've no reason to be frightened, you see how much I love you.

MELANIE I see that but...

CHRISTOPHER But?

MELANIE But the person you love is not me. It is as if you had been talking about somebody I'd never met. I'm none of these things. I am selfish because I'm insecure; I'm insecure because I am vain, I'm vain because I am a woman. And because I'm a woman I can be cruel without reason.

CHRISTOPHER Do you love me?

MELANIE Yes, that's why I want you to love me in return and not put me on this pedestal. I want to be loved for my own sake, not as a projection from you.

CHRISTOPHER You don't know yourself. [*Pause*] Come, let's go. [*They go towards the door. She stops and turns back.*]

MELANIE Please, Christopher, tell me you love my selfishness, my meanness...

CHRISTOPHER I love your lips, your eyes.

MELANIE Please...

CHRISTOPHER ...and the mole on the back of your neck. [*Pause*] Well, let's go. Why are you looking so sad? This is our beginning. We'll start again. We won't take anything. We'll just go together now, so smile. [*She doesn't smile but embraces him. They go to the door again. She turns back and looks round the room.*] What are you looking for?

MELANIE Something you've lost...

CHRISTOPHER What?

MELANIE Me.

CHRISTOPHER [*taking her by the hand*] That's one thing I haven't lost. Come.

ANGEL There. You see? That's how it began.

SATAN I suppose that passes for mortal love. But it's all illusion. I think I'm the only person that can love a woman because I alone love them for what they are: I relish their frailty.

ANGEL It's why we all come back to you. But let them get on with it. Back to Scene 5. [*Enter* MELANIE *and* CHRISTOPHER *who take up their positions before the recap.*]

MELANIE Why don't you answer? I said it wasn't always like this, was it? [*She continues to look for her shoe*] Perhaps it was. In love, illusion is the only reality. Anyhow, we're strangers. You don't understand me. I don't understand you. Sex doesn't bring people together, it merely shows how far they are apart. Strangers. Our intimacy is indecent. [*She finds her shoe and stands watching him*] Why don't you say something? If I'm annoying you and that's what I'm trying to do, why don't you throw a cup at me or maybe a saucer? I'd be grateful for any gesture which proved I wasn't just talking to myself. Damn you. [*She bangs the heel of the shoe on the table*] The trouble with you is you're impotent, emotionally impotent. [*She examines her shoe and laughs at herself*] Blast it, I've bust the heel. Serves me right. I'll have to run and get it fixed. [*She goes to the door.*]

CHRISTOPHER [*turning*] And don't forget to bring some coffee and sugar. [MELANIE *turns back, crosses and embraces him.*]

MELANIE It's all my fault. Don't take any notice. I'm bad tempered this morning. I'm sorry. I said: I'm sorry.

CHRISTOPHER [*returning her embrace fondly*] Silly, you've nothing to apologise for.

MELANIE [*breaking away reverting to her anger*] I have! Yes, I have. Why should you have the right to be always sorry and never me? It's not fair. [*She turns to the door*] It's not fair!

> *She exits, slamming the door behind her.* CHRISTOPHER
> *registers no emotion, continues to wash up and clear away.*
> *There's a knock on the door.* CHRISTOPHER *goes to*
> *open it.*

SATAN That exit and this entrance are a bit confused. You'll never make a playwright.

ANGEL That's what life is, a bad play that runs for ever.

SATAN Who on earth is it?

ANGEL His 'best' friend.

SCENE SEVEN

DILIGENCE

Enter GERARD

CHRISTOPHER Gerard.

GERARD No wonder you sound surprised. It's taken me a week to find you. It seems Bayswater's full of couples trying to lose themselves. I discovered you've moved twice in the last three months. Restless?

CHRISTOPHER Melanie likes a change.

GERARD I see. How is she?

CHRISTOPHER All right. Didn't you meet her? She's just run out. She'll be back.

GERARD I hear she is a successful model. And you?

CHRISTOPHER I'm looking for a job. So far nothing's come to hand. Yes, that's the word...

GERARD And your research?

CHRISTOPHER [*looks round*] I'll get back to it one day.

GERARD That's what I've come to talk to you about. The University want you to accept a Fellowship. They wrote: they got no answer...not as if they don't know the answer.

CHRISTOPHER I'm not sure I do.

GERARD You can't mean it! You know how important your work is. This is what you always wanted. What makes you hesitate?

CHRISTOPHER Melanie won't want to go back to Sheffield...

GERARD Why not? There's no future in modelling—or anyhow, not a long one.

CHRISTOPHER No: she'd never live up there again, never.

GERARD Why not?

CHRISTOPHER Because people can't go backwards.

GERARD Then you must leave her. You must be realistic. You must put your work first.

CHRISTOPHER Don't be a bloody fool. I can't do that.

GERARD Why not? She'd leave you if she...

CHRISTOPHER ...got a better offer?

GERARD Any offer.

CHRISTOPHER As she once left you for me?

GERARD No, I don't mean that. Besides, it isn't true. She never left me for you. She was more ruthless than that—she left me to make herself more available, to be free to accept other offers when they came along, as you came along.

CHRISTOPHER You don't like Melanie, do you?

GERARD Let's say I know her. I know her better than you do. I know she is selfish, and ruthless.

CHRISTOPHER Nonsense. She doesn't want much out of life.

GERARD Not much. But fame, fortune, and men—

CHRISTOPHER She's insecure, that's all.

GERARD I believe you'd say that of a horse that kicked you in the face. Melanie's an attractive woman, but she's a bitch. She's been useful to you, you should be grateful to her for what she's given you, and even more grateful when she lets you go.

CHRISTOPHER Can't you understand I can't live without her?

GERARD You will. When they come, as they will, one day, to write your biography, they won't even find a line for her. It is not that I don't like Melanie, it's that I know her for what she is: an attractive, insincere little bitch. [*Enter* MELANIE]

MELANIE Darling, how lovely to hear your voice again. [*They embrace*] And what makes you call so early? You haven't even shaved.

GERARD Sorry about that. I've just come down from Sheffield overnight and I've got to catch the 2 o'clock plane to Munich.

CHRISTOPHER What are you doing there?

GERARD Annual Biochemists Conference.

MELANIE Sounds thrilling. And so you'd like some coffee? Damn... [*She turns to go*]

CHRISTOPHER No, I'll run and get it.

MELANIE Darling, I'm sorry. I forgot the sugar too. And you might pick up my shoes, love, they said half an hour.

CHRISTOPHER I'll go and get them. [*He goes to the door. He exits*]

SATAN Very contrived.

GERARD [*looking round room*] Chris must be lost without a lab or at least a kitchen table to work on.

MELANIE [*picking up a pair of stockings from table*] He has other things.

GERARD And how are you enjoying modelling?

MELANIE And how are you enjoying making conversation?

GERARD What d'you mean?

MELANIE You know what I mean. [*Pause. She kisses him*] You don't like me because I still attract you. Isn't that it? [*Pause*] I've often wondered when you would come. Pride wastes a lot of life. Were you playing at being a martyr or did you tell yourself you were giving Christopher and me a break?

GERARD You've got things wrong.

MELANIE You mean you prefer to make conversation? All right, tell me what films you've seen or not seen.

GERARD I haven't been in touch with you or Chris because I've been very busy at the University—and because I didn't know your address. I wrote once but the letter was returned.

MELANIE We'd moved. We often move.

GERARD Why?

MELANIE I suppose women change their clothes or where they live when they really want to change themselves or their husband. Or perhaps I insisted that we moved because I didn't want you to find me which is the same thing as saying that I hoped you would.

GERARD But I didn't come to see you, Melanie. I came to see Chris.

MELANIE Why?

GERARD The University have offered him a Fellowship.

MELANIE How wonderful. At last.

GERARD He says he'll refuse it.

MELANIE Nonsense. It's the one thing he wants.

GERARD He says he'll refuse it because you'd never go to live in Sheffield.

MELANIE Of course I would. Provincial university life can be hell. But the hell you want is the only heaven you can get.

GERARD Well, you must tell him that you'd go.

MELANIE [*angrily*] No. He told you he'd have to refuse because of me, then that's really what he wants. He wants the sacrifice of his career more than the success of it; he needs his virtuous martyrdom more than he needs me. Damn and blast his twisted deformed Christian soul. He makes me deny him with my frivolity, betray him with my vanity to the final Consummation, when Christopher the Genius is crucified on Melanie the Cross! But without nails of course—with hair-pins. [*She laughs hysterically and breaks down weeping*] It's not fair! It's not fair!...I loved Christopher; but he never loved me, he's never even met me. I could have borne it if he had loved another woman, I could have endured it if he'd loved another man, but I cannot bear to live with a man who doesn't love me at all, who is only in love with his own virtue. A wife who is married to a man who's in love with another woman gets some consolation; the

moments when his mistress is playing him up, is ill or unfaithful; there are moments of sympathy, contact and consolation, but Christopher is in love with himself, wholly faithful to
himself; there is nothing for me to console. He does not know
me; he does not need me. Take me away.

 Enter CHRISTOPHER, *catches them at it and goes out*

GERARD What! Now? Where do we go?

MELANIE Anywhere, I'll come with you. Oh I know you will
not want me for ever, a week is all I ask. I know we do not love
one another. Few people do. I need a holiday from love. I need
your disapproval, even your dislike: at least you see me as I am.

GERARD I'll take you. But are you sure you won't regret being
unfaithful?

MELANIE [*running to embrace him*] Oh Gerard, if you could give
me that, I'd have nothing to regret.

GERARD Then let's go before he returns. Scribble a note. Isn't
that the convention?

MELANIE No. I want to stay and tell him.

GERARD Why be so cruel?

MELANIE Cruel? Wait till you hear what he says when I tell him,
then you'll see which of us is cruel. [*She goes to the window*]
Here he comes now. Be firm. Don't let me down.

GERARD Do you think he'll start a brawl?

MELANIE No. Christopher is too strong to fight. He'll hurt you
with his understanding instead, torture you with his gentleness
and finally he breaks you with a kiss.

 Enter CHRISTOPHER

CHRISTOPHER [*handing her the shoes*] I had to wait for them,
love. And here's the coffee, sugar and a large bouquet. [*He
hands her a tiny bunch of violets*]

MELANIE Thank you, darling. What made you buy me these?

CHRISTOPHER Because. Just because.

MELANIE You couldn't bear to pass that old woman who sells
them outside the Tube, I suppose.

CHRISTOPHER Probably.

MELANIE Did you have to wait long in the shoe shop? These
heels are useless...

CHRISTOPHER I'll go and make the coffee. You sit and talk to Gerard. You've got to be at work in half an hour.

MELANIE Chris, I'm not going to work.

CHRISTOPHER Why?

MELANIE You made me leave one job—now I'm chucking another for Gerard... [*Long pause*]

CHRISTOPHER Can either of you tell me where I put that coffee?

MELANIE Chris, you don't understand. I'm telling you I'm leaving you and going away with Gerard.

CHRISTOPHER When?

MELANIE Does that matter?

CHRISTOPHER Yes. I should have thought it did matter.

MELANIE [*to* GERARD] You see?

CHRISTOPHER And where are you going?

MELANIE Nor is that the point either. Oh Chris, if only you would show your feelings...

CHRISTOPHER As you say, perhaps I've none to show?

GERARD Or daren't.

CHRISTOPHER Perhaps. You do take milk in your coffee, don't you?

MELANIE Chris, if only you would break in pieces, how I would love those pieces.

CHRISTOPHER You expect me to lose my temper? You want me to make a scene? I'm sorry...

MELANIE Oh no!

CHRISTOPHER But I don't believe anger or violence ever did anybody any good.

MELANIE Won't you miss me?

CHRISTOPHER [*picking up the violets and handing them to her again*] These can answer that. I can live without you but it won't be life without you.

MELANIE Don't you hate me—or Gerard?

CHRISTOPHER No. And the reason I don't lose my temper with people is that I find it so easy to stand in their shoes, it would be only losing my temper with myself.

MELANIE You see neither of us exists. As far as he's concerned we're both only projections of him.

CHRISTOPHER I do see what a strain it must have been for you living with only half a man, and that man with half his mind on his work. I know only too well how morose and melancholy I am. I'd have made you old before your time. I lack your sense of gaiety, of fun. I'm grateful for the amount of you I've had— I know that that was more than I deserved. Living with me must have been like reading a book, a dull book, over and over again, knowing what I would say and when I would say it, watching where I put this and knowing I would lose it...

MELANIE And hearing you apologise even now when I'm walking out on you.

CHRISTOPHER Yes, even that. [*Pause*]

MELANIE You see he only talks about himself. He doesn't mention me. Let's go, Gerard. Now. [*They go to the door.* GERARD *exits.* MELANIE *turns*]

CHRISTOPHER Take these with you. [*He hands her the flowers*] I'm sorry. [*She goes to strike him, runs from the room. They freeze.*]

BLACKOUT
LIGHTS UP in restaurant

SATAN Well?

ANGEL [*shrugging her shoulders*] I must say my sympathy was with her. This is very confusing.

SATAN Very. No wonder the sortings got out of hand. But I think I can still rely on envy.

ANGEL I wouldn't be so sure, if I were you. I'd like another drink. I need one after that.

SATAN [*beckons the* WAITER] Yes, so would I. [*Then turns to* AUDIENCE] Won't you join us?

BLACKOUT
CURTAIN

Act II

SCENE ONE

ENVY

ANGEL What's up with you? Feeling depressed?

SATAN Worse than that: alienated.

ANGEL Come on, don't sit there. We're committed.

SATAN Couldn't we have an orgy instead? I lose interest in evil unless it's done deliberately.

ANGEL I am waiting to see what you can do with envy.

SATAN I'm afraid the permissive society has played havoc with our categories, and universal mediocrity will cover all.

ANGEL That makes it even harder—I love you when you're being prophetic. But do get on with it. Act II, Scene One. The Woods' studio, late afternoon, the same day.

SATAN He is painting the portrait of the Virgin, using his wife Lavinia as a model. For this purpose she wears a pale blue scarf to cover her hair.

LAVINIA I'd give my soul for a sherry.

SATAN Did you hear? She said she'd give her soul for a sherry.

COLIN Only a minute more.

LAVINIA That's what you said half an hour ago. Well darling, may I have a cigarette.

COLIN The Virgin didn't smoke. No, don't move Lavinia. I'll light it for you.

He does so, then stands back to look at his work, makes a couple of touches and then begins to clean his brushes.

All right, you can relax now.

LAVINIA No, don't stop. I'm sorry, I only wanted a puff. Don't mind me.

COLIN I wasn't. The light's getting tricky. [LAVINIA *relaxes her pose*]

LAVINIA Is it, darling? I had no idea it was so late. What's the time?

COLIN Five. You've been watching me daub away for two hours. I'm sorry you've been so bored.

LAVINIA I haven't been bored.

COLIN Then why ask the time? It's not a thing that worries you except when you feel you're wasting it.

LAVINIA Colin, you know I don't think that. I asked because somebody is coming in for a drink this evening.

COLIN Who?

LAVINIA I'm not telling you. It's to be a surprise.

COLIN Not Tony Rutherford, your old boy-friend, is it?

LAVINIA No.

COLIN I suppose he's at his vulgar and expensive villa at Juan les Pins for the season?

LAVINIA I suppose so.

COLIN Don't pretend you don't know. I bet he's coining money painting the portrait of some film-star, or probably a Greek shipping magnate.

LAVINIA I shouldn't be surprised.

COLIN Well, I don't want him round here patronising me and leering at you.

LAVINIA I've already said I'm not expecting Tony.

COLIN Who is it then? Not that ghastly American woman who's taken the Château above the village?

LAVINIA No it isn't. But how do you know she's ghastly? You've hardly met her.

COLIN Haven't I? Long enough for her to tell me that she does a little painting herself too, in order to pass the time and keep out of mischief. I detest amateurs, who use art as if it were an aspirin.

LAVINIA It is not the American woman. Though it might not be a bad idea if I asked her—she's got plenty of money.

COLIN But no taste.

LAVINIA She might buy a picture.

COLIN Because she's got no taste?

LAVINIA No, dear, because she's got plenty of money.

COLIN Those kind of people don't buy paintings, they invest in names. And I haven't got a name.

LAVINIA You have.

COLIN Sure I have. This morning I was down in the village, and I ran into Bousac, the grocer. He was talking to the Prefect and introduced me: 'Meet Mr Wood,' he said, 'the most celebrated painter in the whole village.' I must say, he might have let me off with a district, or even a whole province. I simply crawled away.

LAVINIA It was meant kindly.

COLIN Said the monkey who'd just been run over by a tank. Anyhow, how do you think this is going?

LAVINIA Marvellous. A wonderful likeness.

COLIN I'm not a bloody camera. Yes, it's going all right. But it'll always lack something.

LAVINIA What, darling?

COLIN The right signature.

LAVINIA Oh don't be so bitter.

COLIN Why not? Do you know what that would be worth if Annigoni or Sutherland signed it? Thousands. And if only your boy-friend Rutherford signed it, the same portrait would fetch—God knows what it would fetch.

LAVINIA Twenty pounds.

COLIN Don't be silly.

LAVINIA Isn't that what you paid for that Rutherford in our bedroom?

COLIN That was before he became fashionable! It's true I only gave him twenty quid for it. We'd shared an exhibition in some God-forsaken Gallery in Litchfield Street. Remember? I'd sold six pictures, he'd sold none, so I bought one of his myself to cheer him up.

LAVINIA Precisely, darling. And doesn't that prove that every artist has to go through a period when nobody will look at their work. We've got to be patient till you get a break. It will come sooner than you think.

COLIN Patient! Haven't I been patient? Ten years! Do you know what the critics said when Rutherford and I had that exhibition together?

LAVINIA [*She has humoured him through this scene before*] Yes, they liked your work...

COLIN That's putting it mildly. Of course, I don't want to bore you, but I'll remind you what they did say—if I can find it. Yes, here it is: 'A critic often gets depressed viewing the work of the younger generation. That is why I shall go a second time to the Litchfield Galleries to indulge in the rare privilege of seeing work of such promise as Colin Wood's. This young accountant shares the exhibition with another young painter, Mr Antony Rutherford, who is not without a decorative talent. But it is Mr Wood who interests me...' Are you listening? Then it goes on to say some rude things about 'poor' Antony Rutherford... That, Lavinia ,was in *The Times*. And do you know who wrote it?

LAVINIA No, darling, who wrote it?

COLIN None other than the great man himself—Harcourt Webb. That was ten years ago. It was this bit of paper that made me throw up my job as an accountant and devote myself to this drudgery. You can't say I haven't been patient. And a fat lot of interest he has shown in me since then. [LAVINIA *laughs*] What the hell are you laughing at? I'm glad you find it funny. I suppose failure is very funny.

LAVINIA I wasn't laughing at you. I was laughing from pleasure, from sheer relief. I told you I'd got a surprise for you. He's the surprise.

COLIN Who?

LAVINIA Harcourt Webb. He's down here on a holiday. I've asked him along to see your work.

COLIN You've done what?

LAVINIA Oh I admit I was a bit nervous about it since I know how you detest critics.

COLIN You mean to say Harcourt Webb will be here in an hour?

LAVINIA No. Unless he's late he'll be here in ten minutes.

COLIN Then don't stand there, woman, help me get some of these canvases unrolled; tidy the studio up; and put on a show.

Where shall we hang this?

LAVINIA Over there. Let me.

Light on café table

SATAN [*with false satisfaction*] Doesn't it look as if envy is doing its work. Nothing like it for undermining a soul or reducing it to bitterness.

ANGEL [*laughing*] Don't be so smug. His envy drives him to work. The will to emulate others isn't a vice but a virtue—a really creative force.

SATAN [*petulantly*] The trouble with you is you see good in everything!

ANGEL Maybe. Later I'll give you a sample of real purity of mind...

SATAN Shut up. I am not through with you.

COLIN I've been waiting fifteen years for this and now I can't find any tacks or cord to hang a damn thing.

LAVINIA They're in front of you.

COLIN We'll put this one over here—no we won't, it's against the light. Over there. There, I say. And you might empty those ashtrays. No don't bother now. Just put these up around the wall. How d'you think that looks? Oh—what's the use? An artist has to believe in himself. That belief is the most precious part of his being: everything else is secondary.

LAVINIA Everything?

COLIN Everything. God help anybody who tampers with that or tries to take that from me. It's the one thing I have left: belief in myself.

LAVINIA [*protectively*] So why not let him come? Darling, to please me! After all Harcourt Webb might at least give you some contacts, help you sell something...Just to please me.

COLIN All right. We'll put this one over here—no we won't... How do you think that looks...? [*Holding a picture on wall*] Is that straight?

LAVINIA No, down more to the left. The left. That's better.

SCENE TWO

PRIDE

They step back and admire the row of pictures they've hung. Enter HARCOURT WEBB *unnoticed.*

COLIN I suppose you'd better get the old bastard some sherry. Critics can't see straight unless they've got a glass to focus with.

LAVINIA Shall I get the Bristol Milk or the South African?

HARCOURT WEBB The Bristol Milk of course. He'll know the difference. [COLIN *and* LAVINIA *turn*] Good evening, I'm sorry. I did ring, but as no one answered I thought I'd better walk right in. I hope I'm not too early, Lavinia? But as you know, I like to be punctual. It is nice to see you again. Aren't you going to introduce me to your husband?

COLIN We've met before...

                    LAVINIA *goes off to get sherry*

WEBB Have we? Then let's call it quits. I've forgotten your face, you've probably forgotten my name. Don't let it worry you. I find absent-mindedness a positive advantage. It makes every experience seem so fresh...

COLIN It was at the Litchfield Galleries...

WEBB Indeed? Yes, Lavinia tells me you paint.

COLIN Ten years ago...

                    LAVINIA *enters carrying a glass*

WEBB That's a long time. I can't recall what they were showing then—They often have interesting exhibitions in those out of the way galleries, don't you think?

COLIN Yes. I often wonder what becomes of the artists.

WEBB I suppose most of them succeed in sublimating their creative urge and settling down, as they say, to leading happy and useful lives; and some take to advertising and a few more enterprising take to crime...

COLIN I dare say some go on working away in some obscure studio in France and are never heard of again.

WEBB I dare say. But you shouldn't be so morbid... [COLIN *turns to pick up press cutting*]

LAVINIA [*hurriedly*] Colin darling, do pull back the curtains or put the lights on so Harcourt can see your work...

COLIN [*handing cutting to* WEBB] Perhaps this may remind you?

WEBB [*reading the cutting*] '...Here is an artist with something more than a sense of colour, appreciation of form and an instinctive knack for design. Here is a man with original vision and the ability to translate that vision into visual form. In the last analysis, it is, of course, vision that differentiates the man with talent from the artist of genius. I am impatient to see more of Mr Wood...' I don't see what you've got to complain of. Whoever wrote this seems to have been very impressed with your work.

COLIN You wrote it.

WEBB [*turning cutting over*] So I see. But you can't expect me to remember that. You may, but I have to write a hundred or so in the course of a single year. And I must say, I protest.

COLIN You! I like that. That's rich.

WEBB Certainly. After all the encouragement I gave you there— and in *The Times* too—I have every right to complain that you didn't let me see more of your work. Fortunately, dear Lavinia has rectified your omission. You should be grateful to her. I must say, there's nothing like one of my own good notices for whetting my appetite. Well, aren't you going to let me see your work?

COLIN [*doing so*] There you are. Ten years of it. Whatever they are, I am. Let him see the lot, Lavinia. I'm off down to the village. [*Exit* COLIN]

WEBB He certainly has all the attributes of genius. Not even Dali is as rude to me as that. I'm sorry I offended him. You should have briefed me dear—

LAVINIA He's not offended. He's gone off because he's so nervous he can't bear the suspense. Apparently you're the one critic he respects.

WEBB Then we've something in common. [*Before portrait on easel*] Ah, I see you are his model.

LAVINIA Sometimes.

WEBB And a very pretty one.

LAVINIA It's not finished.

WEBB So I see.

LAVINIA He's been working on it this evening.

WEBB Has he?

LAVINIA It's called 'A Portrait of Chastity'.

WEBB [*turning from portrait to her*] He doesn't do you justice. Don't be offended. I'm not implying that you're not faithful to him. I'm sure you are. But that that looks more like a Portrait of Frigidity, and Frigidity is not Chastity. Chastity is an achievement, frigidity merely an inhibition. It doesn't do you justice.

LAVINIA It is not finished.

WEBB Nothing ever is. He gets the likeness of his wife, but misses the portrait of the woman: a woman who is warm, whose wantonness plays hide and seek with modesty behind her eyes, and whose lips are eloquent when they are still. Don't be frightened, you needn't look away. Art interests me, life bores me. All I was saying is that this is not yet a portrait of chastity, for it fails to show that warmth which, though it yielded would still not betray your love. Let's look at something that is finished.

LAVINIA This Spanish landscape he did last year is one of my favourites.

WEBB And that?

LAVINIA Much earlier. Years ago.

WEBB So I guessed. Before you both went to Brignolle.

LAVINIA How do you know we did?

WEBB Picasso lived there. This picture shows his influence as plainly as a visa stamped in a passport. [*He looks round the studio*] Your husband certainly has worked. Ha! Le Pont Frigene—a charming place.

LAVINIA I adore that picture—so full of light you can almost feel the sun, can't you?

WEBB A charming place. Do you remember the Ristorante August there? Of course you do. I know of no better place for Sole Cardinale. You know, rolled round a puree of prawns and served with lobster sauce. Quite an experience, don't you think?

LAVINIA And this is a portrait of his mother.

WEBB And do you remember their Langouste à la Chef? I drank Champagne Nature with it—no, I believe I had white burgundy.

LAVINIA She's so proud of Colin. I adore the way he's painted her hands, don't you?

WEBB Yes, it must have been white burgundy. 1951 I think. Always a risk, of course. A trifle rough, but plenty of character to it.

LAVINIA Not only the position of the hands, but the way he's brought out both their usefulness and their tenderness. One feels that he's seen those hands doing the weekly wash, and that he remembers being caressed by them, too. Don't you get that impression?

WEBB Quite.

LAVINIA And this is a view of Cotignac.

WEBB Is it?

LAVINIA And that's of the harbour at Santa Ferrugia.

WEBB Ah, how interesting. [*He peers at the picture closely*]

LAVINIA [*hopefully*] Yes it is, isn't it?

WEBB For a moment I thought I recognised that yacht.

LAVINIA [*a little sadly*] And here's my favourite: it's called Le Sang d'une Poete. He painted it at Marrakesh. [*Pause while* WEBB *examines the painting*]

WEBB It seems to me that your husband...

LAVINIA [*very hopefully*] Yes?

WEBB ...travels a good deal. [*He sits down*]

LAVINIA Well?

WEBB What?

LAVINIA What do you think of Colin's work?

WEBB You want to know?

LAVINIA Of course. Colin's worked hard for this moment.

WEBB That I don't doubt.

LAVINIA He needs your encouragement. Well? Tell me. He'll be back in a moment.

WEBB Very well, I will. I think they're...

LAVINIA Yes?

WEBB Terrible. I've rarely seen such a display of unrelieved mediocrity. I'm terribly disappointed.

LAVINIA But you thought he showed such promise. It was because of your opinion that he gave up his job.

WEBB I really am terribly disappointed. But it happens to many painters; they show promise and then run into...

LAVINIA Marriage?

WEBB No, my dear, he was fortunate there. They show promise till they meet an influence which they cannot digest. Your husband ran into Picasso. There's none of your husband left, just an imitation of Picasso.

LAVINIA You mean, he'll never be a success?

WEBB Not at this. There are other things to do. TV want designers. I dare say films have openings too. Well, Lavinia, it's been splendid seeing you, after all these years. I must be going. I've promised to go to the Opera. Do give me a ring if you're in Cannes. I think I can give you a good dinner. Here's my address. [*He gives her a card*] No, please don't show me out. After all, I did find my way in.

WEBB *exits*—LAVINIA *sits dejected*

BLACKOUT
LIGHT UP *on Restaurant*

ANGEL And what are you looking so smug about now?

SATAN I'm just feeling proud of Colin's pride. You see my vices are just as vicious as ever.

ANGEL That wasn't a vice.

SATAN It was always accounted one.

ANGEL Nonsense. It's no vice to refuse to be patronised. That was an example of integrity, always a virtue.

SATAN I tell you it was pride. But now—let's get on with it— let's take a look at—*Avarice*.

SCENE THREE

AVARICE

LAVINIA *sits dejected, then hearing* COLIN *coming in, she instantly pulls herself together.*

COLIN Has the great man gone?

LAVINIA Yes.

COLIN He didn't stay long then. He might have waited to see me.

LAVINIA Darling, you might have stayed while he was here.

COLIN I'm sorry, but I couldn't. I couldn't bear the strain. I could never stand under a notice-board to wait till they'd pinned up the results of an examination. I had to send an office boy out to find out if I'd passed my finals. Well, what did he say? Do I have to go back to being an accountant again? For God's sake woman, have some pity—speak—or are you wondering how to soften the blow?

LAVINIA No, darling, I was wondering how to live up to being the wife of a genius.

COLIN He liked them?

LAVINIA Yes. He was terribly impressed.

COLIN Then why didn't he stay?

LAVINIA It was he who was frightened of you. I suppose he felt guilty too for having neglected you for so long.

COLIN But he was impressed?

LAVINIA Immensely. He said your drawings had a wonderful certainty of line, that you were a new Gaudier-Breszka.

COLIN He said that? [*He goes to his folio*] But this hasn't been opened? All my drawings are still here.

LAVINIA He had every one out on the floor. I've just put them back again.

COLIN Gaudier-Breszka! What else did he say? What did he say about these? Tell me everything he said. Darling this is wonderful. This is—what we've waited for.

LAVINIA He said that you'd absorbed the innovations of Picasso. And that your sense of design...

COLIN I knew it! I knew these savage bastards of mine were all legitimate children. I knew these geese were swans.

LAVINIA ...Your sense of design never failed you, and your use of colour...

COLIN Don't bore me. What do I care what he said. Critics should applaud or remain silent.

LAVINIA Is that all?

COLIN Their only use is to help the artist sell his work. They're middle-men. And this is where I cash in. [*He goes and takes a picture down*]

LAVINIA What are you going to do?

COLIN Nothing. It's what you're going to do. Take this straight away into Cannes. Go to the Puget Gallery. Tell them what Harcourt Webb said. They'll buy.

LAVINIA What, now?

COLIN Now.

LAVINIA I can't get there and back this evening.

COLIN Then stay the night. Ask 5,000 francs.

LAVINIA But that's absurd. That's more than ten times what you've asked for a picture before.

COLIN No. Ask 10,000 francs. They'll pay it now—on my signature alone. Well, what are you waiting for? There's a bus in half an hour into town. What are you looking for?

LAVINIA Harcourt Webb left his card somewhere. I thought I would call on him when I'm in town and thank him for all he's done.

COLIN Yes, do, and tell him I'm very busy but I'll look in myself one day when I can find the time.

LAVINIA All right, work hard darling. [LAVINIA *exits carrying the canvas. He continues to work on the portrait.*]

BLACK OUT STUDIO
LIGHTS UP on the café table, front stage centre. There is now another table. HARCOURT WEBB *in evening dress is seated at it, drinking.*

ANGEL I don't think that's a particularly good example of avarice. Besides, his picture might be worth it.

SATAN Then you buy it. You'll soon get the chance. And don't talk so loud.

Enter LAVINIA *immediately, carrying the canvas.*

WEBB Lavinia! This is a surprise. I didn't expect to see you here. You look as though you need a drink. I know I do. Nothing's so exhausting as *Tannhäuser*. It was a good performance. But nobody has the right to bore me, not even Wagner. I think this calls for some champagne. Waiter! [*He gives an order to the* WAITER]

SATAN Always a cue for me—[SATAN *plays the* WAITER]

LAVINIA Thank you.

WEBB Now tell me what it is you want me to sign.

LAVINIA How do you know I do?

WEBB That's easy. I have two things, myself and my reputation. You can't want me so it follows that you must need my name.

LAVINIA What makes you think I couldn't want you?

WEBB Darling, don't bother to let me down lightly. If you wanted me you wouldn't have come here, alone like this. You wouldn't be so brazen. You would allow me to have the impression that I was chasing you.

LAVINIA Beast!

WEBB Besides, you'd come armed with a black nylon nightie concealed in your handbag—not with one of your husband's paintings. You know they don't seduce me.

LAVINIA You win. How is it you know so much about women?

WEBB By not marrying one. Once a man's done that he dare not look at women as they are.

LAVINIA And what are they? [*She crosses her legs*]

WEBB Adorable but predatory. Every gesture calculated, even unconsciously. [*She uncrosses her legs*] Well, what is it you want me to sign?

LAVINIA A note to the Puget Gallery to help me sell this picture to them, that's all.

WEBB That's all.

LAVINIA Yes, will you?

WEBB Certainly not. If I did that I would jeopardise my reputation. Anybody can see that that painting has nothing but your husband's patience to commend it. Well, perhaps not everybody. Even some of the dealers might be taken in. Though I doubt if Puget would be. But I won't sign anything recommending your husband's work. It would be dishonest. And my integrity is all I have.

LAVINIA Like virtue to a woman?

WEBB What do you mean?

LAVINIA Didn't you once say that even whores could be chaste? And that chastity lay not in the act but in the spirit...? That love can make anything an act of love.

WEBB I did. But you forget, Lavinia. I do not love your husband. But I see you do. What a mystery it is. He looks just an ordinary man to me, yet for you he is unique. Why?

LAVINIA He needs me.

WEBB A good reason.

LAVINIA He's terribly vulnerable and weak, pretending he is strong. I try to protect him from the world and himself.

WEBB That's a better reason.

LAVINIA And I love him.

WEBB That's all of reason. Well, I don't know what sort of a mess you two are in but I'd like to help you. How much will it cost me?

LAVINIA I need two hundred pounds.

WEBB I'll give you fifty or lend you a hundred. Which would you prefer? Well?

LAVINIA I'd rather you gave me fifty and—we can cut the cards for another fifty.

WEBB Very well, my dear, but you may end with nothing. We need a pack of cards. [*He turns to call the* WAITER. SATAN *slips* LAVINIA *a pack.*]

ANGEL This isn't fair.

WEBB You to cut.

LAVINIA No, after you.

WEBB [*doing so*] Jack of Spades.

LAVINIA Ace of Hearts.

WEBB [*taking out cheque book*] One hundred pounds...

LAVINIA No. Guineas of course—

WEBB [*writing*] Just so. Much more professional. [*He hands her the cheque*] After that I hope you will keep me company for dinner.

LAVINIA Thank you. I must go to the Gallery with this.

WEBB So you shall. After we've dined. [*He beckons the* WAITER *again*] Tell the *Maître Hôtel* I'm ready to order dinner. [*He stands and puts a note down on the table*] Come, let's have a look at the bay.

> *He leads* LAVINIA *off. She turns back, picks up the note from the table and replaces it with a coin, then follows him off.*

ANGEL How disappointing. I didn't think that was very evil. I've often picked up a tip from a table myself—when I needed a coin in a hurry.

SATAN [*not very convincingly*] Her avarice went further than that.

ANGEL It was not for herself. Charity is nothing to do with money, nor is avarice. I'm beginning to suspect that you're not really evil—you're just medieval. Anyhow, you've been hogging it. It's my turn now—

SCENE FOUR

CHARITY

> *A summer evening a fortnight later.* CHRISTOPHER *stands looking out of the sash window which is open at the bottom. After a few moments he sees somebody on the street below. He hurries away from the window to the table now covered with his electrical equipment. He puts on a pair of rubber gloves, makes an adjustment, then, as he hears a door, off, he hurriedly crosses the room, tidies the mantelpiece and empties an ashtray. Then he rushes across to the table again and pretends to be absorbed in*

his work, and not to hear MELANIE *enter. She carries a*
suitcase.

MELANIE Damn those stairs!

CHRISTOPHER [*turning with mock surprise*] Hello, darling!

MELANIE That was heavy!

CHRISTOPHER [*going to her*] Sorry, love, I didn't hear you come
in or I'd have carried it up.

MELANIE Didn't you get my wire?

CHRISTOPHER Yes. But you didn't say which train. I discovered
there were three. Otherwise, of course, I'd have met you.

MELANIE Why are you wearing those rubber gloves? They
make you look awfully clinical.

CHRISTOPHER Just a precaution. I'm working with some high
voltages. I had a bad shock a week ago through my lightning
conductor.

MELANIE Good idea. But do take them off now. How's your
work going?

CHRISTOPHER Splendid. I'm on to something very exciting.

MELANIE I'm so glad. What is it?

CHRISTOPHER Well, I think I've stumbled on a connection
between gravitation and magnetism. I've always felt intuitively
that it was there. But now I've got something to go on a little
bit more scientific than intuition.

MELANIE Good. [*Pause*] How have you been?

CHRISTOPHER I'm very fit.

MELANIE Darling, I wasn't inquiring after your health. That
never varies. How have you been?

CHRISTOPHER Fine.

MELANIE Splendid. I'm so glad. Well, that disposes of that.

CHRISTOPHER And you?

MELANIE As you see: sunburnt.

CHRISTOPHER Yes, I see. [*Pause*]

MELANIE Well what have you been doing with yourself—Have
you been lonely?

CHRISTOPHER No. I've been alone. It's not the same thing.

MELANIE Have you been miserable.

CHRISTOPHER Did you want me to be?

MELANIE Have you missed me?

CHRISTOPHER What do you think?

MELANIE I see you're not going to say anything. You're just going to make some tea, aren't you?

CHRISTOPHER A good idea. What d'you want me to say?

MELANIE I don't know. Perhaps I went away with Gerard to find out what you'd say when I came back. Well, what do you say?

CHRISTOPHER [*embracing her*] I'm glad you've come back.

MELANIE [*breaking away*] That's not enough. Well, since you can't be honest, I must be honest for both of us. You've been lonely but not alone, because my absence has been more noticeable to you than my presence. Once or twice you've caught yourself carrying a cup of tea in to me as you always do in the morning. Then at breakfast you've read the paper twice. Then after tidying up meticulously you've tried to work only to find you couldn't because you were thinking about me. So you've gone for a walk to get away from me, then only to find you were hurrying back in case I was here. Christopher darling, isn't that how you've been?

CHRISTOPHER Things have been pretty quiet.

MELANIE [*almost in tears*] For Christ's sake tell me you've missed me as I...

CHRISTOPHER Yes?

MELANIE [*changing what she was going to say*] ...hoped you have. All right then, ask me what I've been doing.

CHRISTOPHER But I know.

MELANIE No you don't. As I said: I must be honest for us both. So I will tell you what I've been doing. I've been to Venice with Gerard for a whole fortnight...

CHRISTOPHER Yes. You sent me a card from there.

MELANIE It's the most fascinating city on earth. The one place that doesn't let you down.

CHRISTOPHER Yes. I thought the Doge's Palace easily the most beautiful building I've ever seen...

MELANIE I didn't notice it. We didn't do any sight-seeing. We bathed, sunbathed, danced and...why don't you ask me?

[*Pause*] We made love. I've been unfaithful to you: We made love. At first gently, almost casually, one afternoon. I've no regrets. I say I've no regrets. We were a fortnight alone together.

CHRISTOPHER Perhaps. But I don't believe you made love.

MELANIE You think I'm lying. That I'm incapable of being faithless to you? You still see me on this damn pedestal? Christopher. Well, what d'you say?

CHRISTOPHER It's happened before.

MELANIE Is that all? Aren't you going to hit me—now you see me for what I am? Well, say something.

CHRISTOPHER [*He goes to her and puts his iron hand on her shoulder with infinite gentleness*] You came back. That shows you love me.

MELANIE But I've been unfaithful to you!

CHRISTOPHER You came back to me. That proves that you love me.

MELANIE [*getting up slowly, and picking up her bag, defeated*] You mean you forgive me?

CHRISTOPHER Of course I do.

MELANIE That's unforgivable of you. [*She goes to the door*]

CHRISTOPHER Where are you going?

MELANIE Back to Gerard. Didn't you turn down that Fellowship because you said I wouldn't live in Sheffield?

CHRISTOPHER Yes.

MELANIE That's where I'm going—to Sheffield.

> *She goes out sadly. He watches from the window for a moment. Then opens her suitcase and starts putting her dresses on hangers.*

BLACKOUT

> *The LIGHT goes up on* SATAN *and* ANGEL's *table at the restaurant.* HARCOURT WEBB *and* LAVINIA *can be seen dining at another table.*

ANGEL Any comment?

SATAN That's not charity. That's indifference. And indifference is the sin which will eventually bring all the world to me.

SCENE FIVE

GLUTTONY

The LIGHT goes up on the table where HARCOURT
WEBB *and* LAVINIA *are just finishing dinner.*

WEBB Won't you have a chocolate soufflé?

SATAN Ah, food! Let's try what gluttony can do.

LAVINIA Thank you, no. I couldn't eat a thing!

WEBB A water ice?

LAVINIA Not even a lemon water ice.

WEBB Some coffee then and some vieux curé? I must say that's about as good a meal as I've ever eaten. The oysters were perfect: I was cross you only had a dozen. As for the Canard Presse, I think they do it here just as good as the Tour d'Argent don't you? A poem of a sauce...

LAVINIA [*faintly*] Please... [*She gets up*] I won't stay for coffee if you don't mind. That was a wonderful meal. But I must go to Puget's Gallery or I shan't catch him. I hope he'll buy the picture.

WEBB A good dinner like that even makes me optimistic—

LAVINIA And thank you for the cheque.

WEBB [*good-humouredly*] Yes, I knew it was only my signature you wanted.

LAVINIA I don't know how to thank you.

WEBB [*handing her the picture*] By not forgetting this—or your gloves. [*She goes off*]

BLACKOUT on Restaurant
LIGHT UP on the Puget Gallery as LAVINIA
enters carrying canvas. The door bell sounds behind her.
A bearded ASSISTANT *appears.*

ASSISTANT [*stuttering*] Bonjour, Mademoiselle. What can I have the pleasure of doing for you?

LAVINIA Could I see M. Puget, please?

ASSISTANT I'm afraid he is engaged. Is there nothing I can do?

LAVINIA No, thank you. I'll call later.

SATAN That's my cue! I insist on playing this one myself.

ANGEL You old ham! [*Enter* M. PUGET *from office*]

M. PUGET (SATAN) Ah! Madame Wood. How nice to see you. We haven't had the pleasure of seeing you in the Gallery for some time. A pity, some of the Exhibitions would have interested M. Wood and you too.

LAVINIA We seldom get into town. The bus services are so erratic.

M. PUGET And uncomfortable too. And those drivers, they are mad! Now, do let me get you some refreshment. A glass of cognac?

LAVINIA No, thank you.

PUGET Some Green Chartreuse?

LAVINIA No, thank you.

PUGET I insist. [*He pours it*] There, now tell me what I can do for you.

LAVINIA I have brought one of my husband's canvases in to show you.

PUGET Ah, he still paints.

LAVINIA Yes. It's a picture of Le Pont Frigene.

PUGET Did you have a good holiday there?

LAVINIA Do you like it?

PUGET Ah, what memories I have of Frigene.

LAVINIA Perhaps you would care to buy this.

PUGET I cannot. As you see, my Gallery is full. There's a Modigliani drawing there. Absolute bargain. Only 15,000 francs. It's been there a week, but nobody's picked it up.

LAVINIA I think my husband would take less than 15,000 francs.

PUGET Ah, I'm sure!

LAVINIA What would you give me for it?

PUGET What would you give me if I bought it? Your company for dinner for instance?

LAVINIA But...

PUGET We can discuss it over an entrecote—eh? Come.

    He leads her off. LIGHTS UP on Restaurant as
    PUGET *and* LAVINIA *sit at the table where she has just*

dined with HARCOURT WEBB. *The* WAITER *approaches with trolley.*

ANGEL Poor kid. This looks like an act of noble self-sacrifice.

PUGET Two entrecotes underdone—or would you prefer a T-bone? Yes, I think a T-bone. And what to start with?

LAVINIA Nothing, please nothing at all.

PUGET Come, something light, some smoked eel, for instance or some paté? [LAVINIA *is silenced*] Madame will have paté.

ANGEL [*to* WAITER] I think I'd like that lemon ice.

LAVINIA [*as the* WAITER *serves her the paté*] Now how much will you give me for this picture?

PUGET But Madame, I have no wish to buy! I'll tell you what I'll do for you. I'll find a place for it on the wall of my Gallery, and if somebody should take a fancy to it, well, I will take a small commission. You never know, somebody might like it.

LAVINIA Mr Harcourt Webb liked it!

PUGET Did he? Whom did you say?

LAVINIA Mr Harcourt Webb.

PUGET The great Art Critic?

LAVINIA Certainly. I've just din... He called at my husband's studio yesterday to see his work. He thinks very highly of it. He left his card in case my husband would let him buy a painting whilst he's in the district.

PUGET [*abandoning the meal to examine canvas*] Did he? Did he see this?

LAVINIA Yes, he wanted to buy that. But my husband thought he should offer it to you first as you've been so kind to him...

PUGET It's certainly interesting...[*The* WAITER *serves the steaks*]

LAVINIA Five thousand francs. In dollars, of course.

PUGET Of course. I tell you what I'll do. You leave the picture with me...

LAVINIA I can't do that.

PUGET And come back to the gallery tomorrow afternoon. I am lunching with Mr Webb tomorrow.

LAVINIA No.

PUGET And if he tells me he likes it, I will pay for it in dollars.

LAVINIA No.

PUGET But I thought you wanted dollars.

LAVINIA No. I've changed my mind. The picture's not for sale.

PUGET Oh come!

LAVINIA No. I've changed my mind. [*She rolls the canvas up*] And I'm terribly sorry but I must go. I must catch the last bus—

PUGET Well you can always change your mind again—good night.

LAVINIA Good night and thank you. [*She leaves the restaurant then pauses, repairs her lipstick and then deliberately undoes the top button of her dress and lights a cigarette.*]

SATAN [*getting up*] I think she needs my help.

ANGEL [*restraining him*] Believe me, no human does.—Let's jump ahead a month—my turn.

SCENE SIX

ABSTINENCE

ANGEL The same as before but a month later. The room is empty. MELANIE comes in wearing a raincoat and carrying a small case. She looks round the room, then calls—listens—

MELANIE Christopher…Chris, darling.

> *She puts her case down, takes off her raincoat. Examines the mantelpiece, picks up a letter there, reads it, then goes over to* CHRISTOPHER'*s working table and picks up an electric soldering iron and puts it against her face to see if it is still warm. She frowns, puts her finger on it to confirm that it is cold. Then she turns and noticing a kettle boiling, smiles and turns it off. She sits, lights a cigarette, stubs it out, and gets up and unconsciously starts tidying the room. Suddenly she stops in the middle of doing this and goes and looks out of the window. She frowns, fetches a dustpan and starts sweeping the hearth, into the pan. Half-way through this she suddenly stops dead, then deliberately pours the contents of the pan back on the floor. She now runs and puts her raincoat on again, picks up*

her case and lifting it high, drops it on the floor. Then runs
quickly to the chair, picks up the letter she's been reading
and places it carefully where she'd found it behind an
ornament on the mantelpiece. She returns and picks up her
case.

Enter CHRISTOPHER *hurriedly*

CHRISTOPHER Hello love. Well, what are you doing here?

MELANIE [*happily*] You mean you don't want me here? I've only
this second arrived. I can easily go.

CHRISTOPHER [*embracing her*] Silly goose...I was downstairs
with Angela.

MELANIE Who's she—or shouldn't I ask?

CHRISTOPHER You know her perfectly well.

MELANIE [*gaily*] Obviously not as well as you do!

CHRISTOPHER The girl who has the room beneath this. She's an
air hostess or something.

MELANIE Yes, I remember—very pretty. Well. This is a surprise. [*Hopefully*] Have you got to know her well?

CHRISTOPHER Hardly met her. She asked me to help her carry
up her coal. Then asked me in for a cup of tea.

MELANIE She knew you were all alone?

CHRISTOPHER I don't know. I suppose—anyhow she'd just
given it to me when we heard a noise up here—

MELANIE I had accidentally knocked my case off the table. I hope
I didn't disturb or interrupt.

CHRISTOPHER You interrupted nothing. I hardly know her.

MELANIE [*annoyed*] A pity!

CHRISTOPHER For heaven's sake why?

MELANIE I'll tell you why. If you were attracted to another
woman—I didn't say fall in love with her—it might make
you...

CHRISTOPHER Less dependent on you?

MELANIE No. You don't understand at all.

CHRISTOPHER But I thought my understanding, as you call it,
annoyed you?

MELANIE You've never met me. It's the blank cheque of your
forgiveness that drives me mad. Oh, if only you would

occasionally let me see you as a man, then you might be able to love me as a woman and not just as an idea. If only you'd been jealous occasionally, or been angry with me, everything would have been different. But I think I've put an end to this insulation you've wrapped round yourself. You're in for a shock. It will hurt and you'll be hurt and I welcome that hurt. That's what being together is, it's hurting together, being in pain together, forgiving together and being sorry together. I've come back because I believe we could start again now after what I've done...

CHRISTOPHER What have you done? You've come back again. What else have you done?

MELANIE [*pause*] Something unforgivable. Two months ago when I came back from Venice you forgave me for going away with Gerard. You were charitable, you forgave me, but you weren't charitable enough to give me your jealousy and that's what I wanted. That is the only true proof of love. And when you didn't give me that I was driven to lie to you and tell you I'd been unfaithful because I resented that I had been faithful. But you forgave even that, so I went back to Gerard, back to Sheffield...

CHRISTOPHER Yes, I know all that.

MELANIE And this time I really did live with him.

CHRISTOPHER But you have come back. So why should that be unforgivable?

MELANIE I've come back because I am pregnant.

CHRISTOPHER You mean...my child. [*He goes to embrace her fondly*]

MELANIE [*She withdraws*] No, his!

CHRISTOPHER Then why have you come back to me? Surely it would be natural...

MELANIE A woman doesn't want to stay with a man merely because he's given her a child.

CHRISTOPHER [*he goes behind her and gently removes her coat*] Forgive me for driving you to this.

MELANIE No. Say you hate me.

CHRISTOPHER But I cannot. Now you've come back. [MELA-

NIE *bursts into tears*] Darling, don't cry. Why are you crying, love?

MELANIE [*picking up her coat and putting it on*] Because you love your forgiveness more than you love me.

BLACKOUT

LIGHTS UP on Restaurant

SATAN And that?

ANGEL Abstinence.

SATAN You don't sound very convinced. I always thought abstinence was when you didn't do what you wanted to do—abstaining from drinking and smoking and that sort of thing?

ANGEL Did you? But Christopher abstained from recriminations, refused to indulge in jealousy. He exercised commendable self-restraint.

SATAN You don't sound very convinced of the virtue.

ANGEL Well, I am a woman too.

SATAN That reminds me—lust! Back to the studio—we are not doing too badly, are we? Ready?

SCENE SEVEN

LUST

SATAN Colin's Studio. The next morning. He is continuing the portrait.

COLIN Keep your head up, woman, blast you.

LAVINIA Sorry, maestro.

COLIN If you call me that again I'll fling a tube of Chinese white at you.

LAVINIA You're very gay this morning. It's years since I saw you like this.

COLIN Of course I'm gay. Now tell me what happened when you went into the Gallery.

LAVINIA But I've already told you.

COLIN I know. I want to hear it all again. You went in. The bell clanged behind you. The bearded assistant who stuttered gave

you a leer, and then M. Puget himself came out of his upholstered lair and gave you a glass of Benedictine.

LAVINIA No, Green Chartreuse. Then I showed him your
canvas of Le Pont Frigene.

COLIN And he asked you if it was for sale?

LAVINIA Yes.

COLIN Before asking who'd painted it.

LAVINIA Yes.

COLIN And before you'd mentioned Harcourt Webb's name.
How much did he offer?

LAVINIA Five thousand francs. Then I casually mentioned
Harcourt Webb had been to your studio, then I asked him for
fifteen hundred francs.

COLIN And he gave it to you?

LAVINIA Yes, in cash. Have you finished?

COLIN A moment. There's just something in your expression I
want to catch. There—It's odd how a reckless touch sometimes
achieves what a week's grind will miss. Now take that scarf off.
We'll raise the stakes. [*Goes to wall. She gets down*] Take this to
M. Puget, it's not as good as the first, but ask double for it. Not
a penny under two thousand pounds. No—make it the equivalent in dollars, they always hurt more.

LAVINIA Shouldn't we leave it a day or two? Won't he wonder
why you're so anxious to sell?

COLIN No. He'll merely think himself lucky, and be glad to get
in before the other dealers.

LAVINIA [*sadly*] All right.

> *Exit* LAVINIA *with second canvas.* COLIN *continues on
> portrait.*

FADE OUT STUDIO

> *LIGHTS UP on Restaurant.* ANGEL *and* SATAN *are
> still seated at their table.* LAVINIA *enters: Something
> about her appearance suggests her intentions, but some-
> thing about her manner reveals that her heart is not wholly
> in her work. She is carrying the second canvas and seats
> herself at the other table and surveys the restaurant as
> though selecting her prey.*

SATAN I thought she'd be back. Quite a metamorphosis.

ANGEL Skin deep. Women are all whores: some know it, some don't know it. Even when they give themselves to God, they do it for payment. So many dollars of redemption for so many prayers.

SATAN You shock me. That's not very charitable of you. You're getting contaminated down here—or maybe it's my company?

ANGEL Don't overestimate yourself...

SATAN Poor girl, she really does need my help.

ANGEL If you keep intruding, then I shall too...

SATAN [*about to get up*] Then let's say I do this as a 'sacrifice'—to do you a favour!

ANGEL You know how much she needs. You'll never be able to afford it.

SATAN I've always regarded an overdraft as a sign of credit.

ANGEL But you're going to find it impossible to depict lust here.

SATAN I don't think so.

ANGEL Well don't be long.

SATAN Lust never is.

ANGEL And what happens to me if I'm picked up sitting here alone.

SATAN Just bless him my dear. [*He goes over to* LAVINIA's *table and sits down* (*as himself*) May I order you a drink?]

LAVINIA Thank you.

SATAN And perhaps you will dine with me?

LAVINIA Wouldn't that be a waste of time?

SATAN I see what you mean. Well, just a snack. Some oysters perhaps?

LAVINIA No, thank you. I've already dined. I don't think you ought to have another drink. Besides, alcohol and...

SATAN ...sex don't go together. You're right. [*Calls* WAITER] Tell me what brings you here...I mean where you come from?

LAVINIA Guess.

SATAN Belgravia, I should say. Educated amongst the apples in a convent in Wiltshire, a mews cottage in Kensington, brought up and nurtured beneath the theology of Harrods. And married slightly beneath her.

LAVINIA [*taking off wedding ring and putting it on fourth finger of right hand*] You're very perspicacious...

SATAN I've been watching over you ever since you, as a child, put on your mother's silk nightdress, and fell hopelessly in love with your own figure...

LAVINIA Clairvoyant, aren't you?

SATAN Not at all. I know because you all do. Everybody's capable of love—for themselves. But what brings you here?

ANGEL [*beneath her breath*] Oh, get on with it.

LAVINIA I just flew down for the week-end. I'm going back tomorrow.

SATAN Air travel, certainly lends wings to our emotions, doesn't it? [*She gets up*]. It almost leaves them standing.

LAVINIA Aren't you coming too? My room's up there.

ANGEL Haven't you missed out a page or two?

LAVINIA I can see you find me attractive.

SATAN I would have preferred to tell you so.

LAVINIA We haven't time for that. [*She sits*] I need...I want 3,000 francs. You may do whatever you like with me for 500. I'm sorry, does that upset you? Is that vulgar?

SATAN [*taking out cheque book*] Nothing's vulgar if it's expensive enough.

LAVINIA [*taking cheque*] Thanks. Now then, let's go. [*Rising*]

SATAN There is no need.

LAVINIA But I can't take this...

SATAN Didn't you say I could do whatever I liked to you?

LAVINIA [*sitting*] Yes.

SATAN Then just give me your hand.

LAVINIA You can't be that perverse.

SATAN But I am! [*She gives him her hand across the table*] No, not that way. This way, all your fingers in between my fingers, the way you hold your husband's hand.

LAVINIA [*doing so*] How d'you know I do?

SATAN Because they all do. Now look into my eyes.

LAVINIA [*slightly disappointed*] Is that all you want?

SATAN Don't be offended. If I were an ordinary man you could satisfy me in an ordinary way: my eyes would be satisfied by your nakedness, my hands would rejoice in these fingers as they clutched the fruit of your breast and my sad soul would sing as I rode your thighs through the night, if I were an ordinary man. But I'm not: I love women so much that my senses cannot possibly satisfy my lust. My shadow is so dark, it needs their light entire: my soul is so thirsty for love it cannot be quenched unless it drains their soul too. That is what I wanted from you— that is what you gave me.

LAVINIA When? How?

SATAN When you took my hand, and though you may put that ring back on your other hand, make love to another man or a dozen men, you can only be faithful to me. Though other lips are on your lips, you will kiss mine; you may run from me only to run to me; you may bear their child, that child will be mine. You will hate me because you know I possess you whatever you do, you are for ever mine.

LAVINIA You're mad. How dare you threaten me like this. It's untrue.

SATAN If it were, you wouldn't need to shout. Now good-bye my dear. You have the rest to earn. [*He picks up the canvas*] This is mine. [*He tears it across*]

LAVINIA What did you do that for?

SATAN I get the same pleasure in destroying bad art as others do from admiring it.

She goes off L. SATAN *returns to his table*

ANGEL That was an expensive intervention, wasn't it?

SATAN Very. And though my cheque's good, I have a feeling her soul's going to bounce. Poor child, she's selling the only thing she has in order to give her husband the illusion that he's not a failure.

ANGEL A sacred prostitute. Nonsense: it's a sacrifice any woman might enjoy.

SATAN Though my vices turn out like virtues, it's no reason for you to plagiarise my cynicism. Where're you going?

ANGEL To prove that there is still such a virtue as chastity—I
fear.

SATAN Ah well, Lust and Chastity are very similar, almost
indistinguishable in the last refinement. [ANGEL *goes off R*]

SCENE EIGHT

CHASTITY

ANGEL An evening two weeks later. Christopher is working at
his table. [ANGELA *enters carrying a coffee tray*]

ANGELA [*played by* ANGEL] I've made some coffee. I guessed
you were still working as you didn't come down, so I brought
it up to you.

CHRISTOPHER Thanks. What time is it?

ANGELA Gone ten. [*She puts the tray on the floor and sits beside it*]
Come and sit down and have it while it's hot. You work too
hard.

CHRISTOPHER [*joining her*] No, it keeps me from thinking. I
really thought I might hear from her today. It's my birthday.

ANGELA So did I. [*Handing him a small parcel*] Anyhow, here's
a tiny consolation.

CHRISTOPHER Thank you.

ANGELA I bought it in Brussels this morning. That's just one of
the advantages of being an air hostess.

CHRISTOPHER There must be others.

ANGELA I don't know...the flights are so brief nowadays...

CHRISTOPHER What a splendid tie.

ANGELA I'm glad you like it. [*She jumps up and takes off his old
one*] I gave you this because I wanted you to realise that there is
no tie between us—whatever happens between us.

CHRISTOPHER It's beautiful. I've never had a tie as splendid as
this. [*She waits to be kissed*] What d'you think the reason is?

ANGELA The reason for what?

CHRISTOPHER She couldn't have forgotten it was my birthday,
could she?

ANGELA [*bored*] I suppose not.

CHRISTOPHER Therefore it follows she wanted to hurt me, doesn't it?

ANGELA It does.

CHRISTOPHER A card would have been enough. It would have made all the difference.

ANGELA [*making an effort*] Maybe you'll get one in the morning? Maybe she missed the post?

CHRISTOPHER No. This proves that she's gone back to Gerard and can't even send me a card for fear of making him jealous! What d'you think? Tell me...

ANGELA Every evening for the last month you've asked me what I thought her motive for doing this or that was. You've become obsessed with her. And it's not...

CHRISTOPHER Very flattering to you. I'm sorry...

ANGELA Don't apologise.

CHRISTOPHER Funny you said that...What d'you think I ought to do?

ANGELA Accept the fact that it's finished. And be glad—she's not good enough for you anyhow. Make up your mind it's over.

CHRISTOPHER I can't believe that.

ANGELA I'm not saying she won't always be fond of you. Perhaps she even loves you. But you must realise she's not in love with you any more.

CHRISTOPHER Nonsense—Oh I know people can't recapture the warmth of their first weeks together, but they find something deeper. There's only one kind of love...And different degrees of it.

ANGELA Which proves only that she doesn't love you at all or is in love with herself.

CHRISTOPHER Nothing of the sort! I think...

ANGELA [*interrupting*] Come and sit down and have some more coffee. And relax. No sit here on the floor beside me. [*Pause*] Christopher, don't you like me?

CHRISTOPHER Of course. Why d'you think I come down to your room every evening?

Y

ANGELA Someone to talk to. But you don't find me attractive, do you?

CHRISTOPHER There's only one way to answer that. [*He kisses her*]

ANGELA Are you being kind? Are you being polite—or just hospitable.

CHRISTOPHER Three questions require three answers.

ANGELA That's what I hoped. [*He kisses her passionately three times*]

SATAN You've had it, Angel.

CHRISTOPHER Now are you convinced?

ANGELA Yes. But I'd like to hear some more of your argument. [*She embraces him*] Don't you like my figure?

CHRISTOPHER Yes of course.

ANGELA [*about to undress*] But you've never seen it! Let me take this damned dress off. Clothes are just a bore with all their damned buttons, bras and zips. [*She turns for him to undo her zip*] Go on, I'm waiting.

CHRISTOPHER No.

ANGELA Darling don't tease me. It's almost indecent for us not to go to bed, isn't it?

CHRISTOPHER [*with shame*] No. And I do find you attractive.

ANGELA [*sadly*] Yes I know. You mean you want to be faithful.

CHRISTOPHER [*with shame*] Yes.

ANGELA [*triumphantly*] You want to be chaste.

CHRISTOPHER [*fearfully, and not understanding her tone*] Yes.

ANGELA Ah, my child. You don't know what you've given me tonight. You've reassured me in a way no man has done for years. [*She kisses him angelically on the brow.*] Bless you.

   Then she sweeps ecstatically from the room, leaving him bewildered.

BLACKOUT
LIGHT UP on Restaurant—enter ANGEL

ANGEL See! And don't say I didn't try.

SATAN Proving what?

ANGEL That at least one of my virtues is still functioning somewhere.

SATAN Nonsense. Chastity of that kind's a positive vice. He wanted you. But he wanted something more—the position of being able to punish Melanie with his self-restraint. Pity you didn't rape him.

BLACKOUT

SCENE NINE

ANGER

SATAN Now where have we got to—what's next—Ah, Anger—all right! Colin's studio, the next morning. He is working on the portrait. Knocking on the door. Colin ignores it. Repeat knocking louder.

COLIN You can wait. [*Knocking louder*] Damn and blast them whoever it is. [*He puts his brushes down*] All right. Don't knock my door down. [*He goes and opens the door*] I'm sorry, I didn't know it was you.

> WEBB, *furious, brushes past* COLIN. *He is carrying a painting.*

WEBB Where's Lavinia?

COLIN Lavinia?

WEBB Your wife. Where is she?

COLIN In Cannes. She must have missed the bus back last night. She went into town yesterday to sell one of my pictures.

WEBB Some hope.

COLIN Oh, I don't know. There's quite a good gallery there.

WEBB I repeat: Some hope!

COLIN On the contrary. M. Puget has quite an eye.

WEBB You're telling me.

COLIN And he's very interested in modern work. Mine particularly.

WEBB I think I'd better sit down.

COLIN As a matter of fact, only the day before yesterday he offered five hundred francs for my painting Le Pont Frigene. I'm sure you'd agree that wasn't enough, but I let him have it for fifteen.

WEBB [*showing the canvas of Pont Frigene*] Is this it?

COLIN Ah? You bought it from him then? You really shouldn't have given him the profit. I did sign it, didn't I?

WEBB I didn't buy this. What would I want with it? Lavinia tried to dump it on me only the day before yesterday.

COLIN There's some mistake.

WEBB Yes, and it's you who've made it.

COLIN Lavinia sold the picture to Puget. He paid 15,000 francs for it—when he knew how highly you thought of my work. I must say I'm grateful to you.

WEBB Don't mention it.

COLIN Even Johnson needed a Boswell. Lavinia told me you liked that picture particularly.

WEBB Did she tell you exactly what I said?

COLIN Yes.

WEBB I'm quite sure she didn't. Let me repeat it.

COLIN No, you praised too high. It's not all that good.

WEBB It certainly isn't. It's punk, a poor imitation of Picasso. Like the lot of it.

COLIN You mean...?

WEBB She lied. To save your pride she said I liked your work. I don't. I'm sorry.

COLIN But the money.

WEBB I gave her £100 as a present, thinking you were hard up.

COLIN She lied!

WEBB Only because you couldn't stand the truth. To thank me for the loan, she went straight to Puget's Gallery, armed with my card, and told Puget a pack of lies. But he didn't believe her. He thought he'd have a word with me today and he told your wife to come back later. She didn't.

COLIN How do you know?

WEBB After Puget had told me what your wife had been up to, I went back with him and waited in the Gallery for her. But she didn't return. She knew her bluff had been called.

COLIN And the picture?

WEBB She had taken that with her. Puget and I then went round to Maireton Gallery. We found she's sold the picture to him for

200 francs, also using my card. In the circumstances I couldn't do anything else but give him his money back, get my card back and give you your bloody picture back too.

COLIN But where did she get the rest of this money from?

WEBB Ask her. Here she is.

> WEBB *withdraws so that* LAVINIA *entering doesn't see him.* LAVINIA *runs in gaily.* COLIN *has his back turned to her.*

LAVINIA Darling, shut your eyes. I've got a surprise for you. [COLIN *remains silent*] Don't turn round, and shut your eyes.

COLIN I don't see anything with them open.

LAVINIA [*she opens her bag and produces a wad of money*] Now you can look. You're a success. Look!

COLIN And in dollars! Why not silver?

LAVINIA Aren't you going to kiss me?

COLIN Shouldn't you kiss me? [*she does so*] That's more appropriate. Now tell me how you got this.

LAVINIA From the Gallery. Puget bought your picture. [COLIN *indicates the first picture which rests against a chair.*]

COLIN Like Maireton bought that. [LAVINIA *turns and sees it, and at the same time notices* WEBB *for the first time, standing in the corner.* COLIN *goes to her bag and from it produces the second canvas which is folded up inside.*] Now tell me where you got all this money from, and what precisely did you sell to get it?

LAVINIA Nothing of any value.

COLIN What?

LAVINIA Nothing of any value.

WEBB It's obvious. She means herself of course.

COLIN I want the truth!

WEBB It's because you couldn't stand the truth that she had to give herself to protect you from it. [WEBB *goes off into garden*]

COLIN Where have you been? How did you get all this? Answer me.

LAVINIA Juan les Pins.

COLIN From Rutherford?

LAVINIA Yes.

COLIN You spent the night with him? [*She nods. He puts his hands around her throat.*] Out of gratitude? Or did you earn the money first and find it on the mantelpiece afterwards? Rutherford prices you too high. You bitch!

> *He strangles her. Her body falls. He stands and stares down at her face. Then he angrily snatches up his palette and brushes and goes to his easel. He paints furiously. He flings his palette down and laughs. Enter* HARCOURT WEBB.

WEBB [*looking at the portrait on the easel and entirely ignoring the body on the floor*] Good God, what have you done!

COLIN Strangled a woman...

WEBB [*studying the portrait*] This painting's transformed. Before it was cold. Now it is vibrant with love. Only a master could have painted these tender eyes, or those gentle lips. It has an expression of infinite purity, a real madonna...

COLIN [*unaware of* WEBB, *at body*] I did it in a moment of anger...

WEBB [*at portrait*] Anger often releases genius. That was her gift to you.

COLIN ...she betrayed everything I loved...

WEBB Perhaps that's what genius is: a man's vision of love or the anger when he's deprived of it?

COLIN ...a whore.

WEBB [*turning angrily*] Never one more chaste or wife more faithful.

COLIN She lied!

WEBB To protect you—knowing you valued your self-esteem more than you valued her. That's all you were angry about, when you found out how she'd got that money. You weren't angry because you'd lost anything of her but only something of yourself, your belief in your own talent. Women can sometimes love men, seldom love anything but themselves, their work which reflects themselves, their reputation which glorifies themselves. Isn't that what you think you've lost?

COLIN Yes. She took even my self-deception from me. Sometimes I thought I had talent. I believed her, I believed you. Now I have nothing.

WEBB She gave you back everything you ever had. Something

precious you lost fifteen years ago. A personal vision. The stamp of genius: the proof's on that canvas.

> COLIN *goes and stands in awe in front of the portrait.*
> WEBB *stays by the body. Their positions are now reversed.*
> COLIN *again does not hear* WEBB, *he's lost in admiring his own work.*

WEBB Grief is brief unless it is for ourselves. Yes, it's a masterpiece. I will buy it. I will give you three thousand francs for it. [*He writes cheque*]

COLIN You mean it.

WEBB And my signature will help you to sell the rest, as you know. No, give me a receipt first. [COLIN *scribbles it and hands it to him.* WEBB *goes to the portrait.*] A masterpiece. A Portrait of Chastity, you called it...it will hang somewhat inappropriately above my bed. And I'll see you hang too. [*He goes to the door*] And that will enhance the value of your one and only painting.

> The *LIGHT DIMS till only the portrait is lit*

ANGEL I don't see how you maintain that deadly sin was a virtue.

SATAN Anger produces a lot of good art.

ANGEL He wouldn't really have strangled her. That was melodramatic.

SATAN He would have—symbolically. That's what people do all the time. They strangle each other's spirit; and according to you, that's all the life there is. I admit that in real life a man usually takes twenty years to do this but that's because life is crueller than the theatre. Anyhow, let's see what will happen with your last remaining virtue.

SCENE TEN

MEEKNESS

ANGEL All right, if you insist. Back in CHRISTOPHER's room. An evening several weeks later. Christopher is working at his table. He is wearing rubber gloves, soldering connections. Melanie comes in; he doesn't turn round.

CHRISTOPHER [*hearing door*] I shan't be ten minutes, Angela. I'll just fix this condenser, then I'll take you out to dinner. [MELANIE *goes up behind him*] And I promise you tonight I won't talk about her—I won't mention Melanie once. [*She smiles; then as he puts the soldering iron down, she takes hold of his iron hand. He doesn't turn.*] You! You've come back!

MELANIE Yes.

CHRISTOPHER I knew you would, in time. It's been a long time; a waste of time.

MELANIE We'll see. [*He embraces her. Good-humouredly*] And are you going to give me dinner—or shall I sit here and bite my nails alone?

CHRISTOPHER Silly. I hate cooking and I don't like eating alone. So I asked her out for a meal.

MELANIE Good. Why not?

CHRISTOPHER But that's all there is to it.

MELANIE [*disappointed*] Really?

CHRISTOPHER Yes.

MELANIE A pity.

CHRISTOPHER I've had to have somebody to talk to.

MELANIE Of course. No good my asking if you've missed me then.

CHRISTOPHER No.

MELANIE Did you hate me for leaving you as I did? [*Pause. He says nothing.*] I want to know.

CHRISTOPHER I will tell you. At first I felt resentment...

MELANIE [*pleased*] Yes...

CHRISTOPHER And I decided to let this resentment grow...

MELANIE [*hopefully*] And did it?

CHRISTOPHER ...no man ever worked harder at his hate than I did. I let my memory plant it and my imagination nurture it. Evening after evening, I have sat here tearing the veils from my mind, daring myself to see you as you are. [*She takes his hand again fondly*] To help me in my hate. I needed that hate because I did not have you; I listed all your faults in my mind; I thought of your unfaithfulness, made myself visualise the moment. [*She strokes his head gently*] And I went for walks, talking to myself aloud, telling myself of your deceit, reminding myself of your selfishness. No man ever worked harder to hate than I did. But I failed. [*She drops his hand*] Even after this, I still saw you as I've always seen you—innocent, essentially kind and lovable.

MELANIE [*quietly*] No, that's not me at all...

CHRISTOPHER I love you. I always will.

MELANIE [*broken*] No. You love yourself. That's the love you project on to me. Whereas I really do love you. That's why I wanted even your hatred—it would have been for me. Perhaps I've earned it now. Perhaps now you will at least hate me.

CHRISTOPHER What do you mean?

MELANIE I have been in a nursing-home. I've had an abortion.

CHRISTOPHER Why? Didn't I tell you? Didn't I make it clear that I forgave you. [*He takes her hand*]

MELANIE Yes, pitifully. But I had lied to you. Even that failed to make you see. It was not Gerard's child. It was yours.

CHRISTOPHER Then for pity's sake what made you do it?

MELANIE You'd have loved that child, not me.

CHRISTOPHER I don't understand.

MELANIE I warned you that by always forgiving me you were driving me to do something unforgivable. Now I have.

CHRISTOPHER Help me to understand.

MELANIE Do you remember that day in Sheffield? You told me you loved me, or rather your ideal, for it had nothing to do with me. But I really did love you as a person. And I was determined to make you love me as I am and not just the false image you had of me. So I tried to emerge from your fantasy; when you thought I was serious, I became flippant; when you thought I was domestic and economical, I deliberately became lazy and extravagant. But it didn't help, it only brought you closer to your own image of yourself. Oh Christopher, I did so much want something of you and if I could not have had your *love*, I wanted your *hate*. That's why I've done what I have done.

CHRISTOPHER You mean you were driven to all this, because I really didn't love you...?

MELANIE But I don't blame you. None of us can love very much, most of us can't love at all. Love is as rare as genius. You did not dare love me because you couldn't have borne the jealousy.

CHRISTOPHER Jealousy? How could loving you make me jealous?

MELANIE The jealousy would have competed with...

CHRISTOPHER ...my love for myself? Is that what you mean [*Pause*] I see it is all my fault.

MELANIE No, fault doesn't enter into it. Darling, I don't want your guilty conscience. I want you.

CHRISTOPHER I see I am to blame. I'm sorry. [*He takes his gloves off*]

MELANIE What are you going to do?

CHRISTOPHER ...There's only one thing to do. If you stayed with Gerard, I could have borne my loneliness because it would have been for you. If you had died, I could have endured my grief for it would have been for you. But now I feel something which is intolerable: a sense of shame, of remorse. [*He goes to the table and puts a plug into the wall.*] You wanted my love and you did not get it. You wanted me to hate and I do—I hate myself so much that I cannot live with myself.

MELANIE No Christopher. For pity's sake don't punish me with your death. No, no. [*She runs to him. He turns, smiles, grips the wires. There is a flash. He falls dead.* MELANIE *stands over the body then kneels and slaps his face.*] No, I don't forgive you. You knew what you were doing. [*She picks up his iron hand and lets it fall.*] It's not fair. It's not fair.

BLACKOUT
LIGHTS UP on Restaurant

SATAN Now who's being falsely melodramatic?

ANGEL Not at all. Most men die in themselves to punish people for loving them.

SATAN True. Love is a burden.

ANGEL They generally indulge themselves and take several years to commit suicide; our patience would not permit naturalism.

SATAN Now I understand why that young prig came down to me, having committed all your seven deadly virtues. I'll see he suffers for them!

ANGEL And poor Lavinia. I'll make her comfortable. I'll even share Gabriel with her.

SATAN You see, it's not just a question of the sorting getting muddled. Our code was a hopeless over-simplification. We ought to scrap it.

ANGEL I agree: we may as well close both our places down.

SATAN Precisely. What will you do?

ANGEL I was wondering that myself. Couldn't you...?

SATAN Yes.

ANGEL ...tempt me?

SATAN If you'll redeem me! [*They embrace*]

ANGEL The marriage of heaven and hell.

SATAN Second marriage, you mean. We ought never to have been divorced in the first place; light needs dark, good needs evil.

ANGEL Don't talk any more. Just seduce me over and over again. [*They go off hand in hand*]

CURTAIN

$$O-B-A-F-G \underset{\underset{S}{\diagdown}}{\overset{\diagup K-M}{\diagdown R-N}}$$

A PLAY IN ONE ACT FOR
STEREOPHONIC SOUND

This play was commissioned by the Department
of Education of Devon County Council. It was
first produced by Exeter University and Dartington
Hall.

$$O-B-A-F-G\begin{smallmatrix} \diagup K-M \\ \mid \\ S \end{smallmatrix}\begin{smallmatrix} \\ R-N \end{smallmatrix}$$

No actors are required.

The stage remains bare throughout except for rostra piled to cast effective shadows.

At the beginning of the play, both the stage and the auditorium should be in absolute *darkness (exit signs should be switched off and measures taken to prevent* any *light penetrating the theatre).*

During the Absolute Darkness, Complete *Silence should be endured for as long as the audience can bear it.*

When they become restless, a metronome is heard ppp *to* forte. *Listening to it, the audience achieves silence again.*

The metronome recedes till the audience have to strain their ears for the comfort of its sound.

It is completely silent again and still absolutely dark.

LOUDSPEAKER NO. 1
  (girl's voice)
Mummy, why is it so dark?
  (woman's voice)
I don't know, dear.
LOUDSPEAKER NO. 2
  There is no light
  Unless there is something for it to shine upon.
                    A long pause

LOUDSPEAKER NO. 1
   (girl's voice)
Mummy, why is it so silent?
   (woman's voice)
I don't know, dear.
LOUDSPEAKER NO. 2
Nor can sound exist
Until there is an ear to hear it.
LOUDSPEAKER NO. 1
Mummy, I'm frightened.
LOUDSPEAKER NO. 1
So you should be, my dear.
Fear is a condition of being
Hold on to your fear, grip it as if it were
   the handlebars of your bicycle.
Be grateful for your fear;
Where there is no light,
Where there is no sound,
fear alone defines us,
and then, the sense of loneliness comes as a caress
when loneliness is our only company.
But there was a time—yes, that's the word...
Once upon a time, a million griefs ago,
before fear had found its scream
and loneliness its sorrow, before light
had its limbs of shape,
and when sound, unheard, was silent,
when there was nothing but energy,
before energy had run down
   to be lamed and maimed with matter,
then the skirt of darkness swept
over the lawns of space, unendingly
and fear waited to be felt
and loneliness watched for its prey.
      The sound of the metronome ppp to silence
then, then, then, then, then
    Instantaneous full light on stage and audience and

simultaneously the sound of explosions. The light is
immediately switched off except for red spots beamed on
to the ceiling.

LOUDSPEAKER NO. 3
The Sun. The Sun.
Atoms colliding caused the sun to be, to burn.
There are many ways to explain it
but all explanations are in words
and words can only explain one thing in terms of another
    thing—
Sufficient is that it is, that it is.
Intermittent red, white and blue lights switched on for a
split second. Sounds of explosion. Then silence and out of
the silence, the sound made by moist finger revolving
round the rim of a glass tumbler.

LOUDSPEAKER NO. 1
Mummy, I'm frightened.

LOUDSPEAKER NO. 1
'ssh, my child,
You are not yet, you cannot fear;
fear has yet to find you,
Loneliness to devour you—'ssh, my child
you cannot fear.

LOUDSPEAKER NO. 3
    (1st voice)
Like a porthole in the sky, the sun
steers across a boundless ocean.
    (2nd voice)
A one-eyed panther on the prowl, stalking
The prairies, bleeding its prey upon the thin horizon.
    (1st voice)
Is not night the sun's lair, and day its blue pavilion?
    (3rd voice)
It is a sphere: of substance, but no solids;
Where Himalayas of gas explode over oceans of vapours;
Where nothing has shape, where there is no matter, no liquid;
Where nothing boils, fire without ash

z

Increasing its heat as it contracts, an endless Hiroshima
Blinding nothing but the blind moon.
                    Sound of finger on glass
For an eternity sole lord of its own ellipsis
Till from the recesses of the universe, a great cloud of atomic
    dust
Spiralled out of oblivion
    and then the force of this fathomless magnetic tide
tore a lip from the sun's entrails;
    the earth was born to solidify in its own orbit.
            Light on stage to suggest volcanic eruption, flames

LOUDSPEAKER NO. 2

Once upon a grief, 2,500 million tears ago
The belly of the Earth belched granite mountains,
                Reflection of flames round auditorium
Seas of molten iron lapped a sulphur shore,
The atmosphere was ash,
Acrid smoke blanketed the light.
                    Complete Darkness
The Earth turned within the groin of night:
    Creation and chaos look like the same thing,
    Order and death are also identical.
                    Sounds of explosions

LOUDSPEAKER NO. 1

Mummy, I'm frightened
I want to go.

LOUDSPEAKER NO. 2

'ssh, my child,
You cannot go, till you have arrived.
You have not long to wait, not long—
We will not say how long.
        *The noises of thunder which settle into the sound of the
        metronome.*
then, then, then, then, then

LOUDSPEAKER NO. 3

As the thin surface of the Earth began to cool,
ribbed with iron and fleshed with rock,

Sounds of steam and a candle of light on stage
the first gentle fingers of Light groped through the fumes
and the first day was followed by a second day
the Earth turned and returned to that mercy which is light
Increase light on stage
till, till, till, till, till
the steam within the fumes condensed
Sound of rain
and the first hot rain fell upon the hot rocks
Light playing on the ropes in the hall
and the steam put out the light again.
Darkness and rain
It rained for ten thousand years
   not day and night but through the night
for light could not penetrate the cloud
that caused the rain, that caused the steam
which kept the earth dark for ten thousand years or tears or
   fears.

LOUDSPEAKER NO. 2
Where there had been tides of molten iron
One scalding ocean of water
   now enveloped the fractured earth.
The great waves swept beneath a starless sky
and never found a shore.
There was no life in the seas
   or secret beneath them;
Sound of wind and waves
There was no movement
   but the wind ceaselessly combing the waves' mane
   as these wild horses stampeded over the prairies of night
   where the blind tide was drawn by an invisible moon
Night, night, night, night
   lay like a strata of slate over the lifeless earth.

LOUDSPEAKER NO. 3
Then once upon a dream, a nightmare of nights ago
The seas cooled, the clouds of steam dispersed.
Strong spots on stage

The sun daggered the horizon
  and the light, the light, the light
  entered its inheritance and walked gently over the waters
Sowing its seed of life over the fields of spray
till the great belly of the earth was pregnant.

LOUDSPEAKER NO. 2
How, how, how did life begin?
It is a question to which there is an answer.

LOUDSPEAKER NO. 3
  (3rd voice)
The first part of that answer is to refute the fallacy
that the difference between organic and inorganic substances
  is one of kind and not degree, of complexity.
The chemical principles which endower life
are not different from the principles and forces
  which govern inanimate elements or compounds.
Life did not arise spontaneously, nor has it existed eternally;
it is a condition in the evolution of matter.

LOUDSPEAKER NO. 2
St John, not the apostle, but C. St John,
  the Director of Mount Wilson Observatory
analysing the sun's spectrum, revealed that carbon
exists 600 miles above the sun's visible surface.
The carbon there explains the carbon here.
There is a miracle but no mystery to Helen's hair.
'Dust falls through the air.
  I am sick, I must die...'
  Lord, as we have waited in vain for your mercy
  Let us now show mercy to one another.

LOUDSPEAKER NO. 3
It is not that God created us,
But we created Him.
Life is a condition in the evolution of matter.
Death: part of the same process.
It is not that soul is eternal,
But that matter is eternal.

LOUDSPEAKER NO. I
Complete heresy, utter profanity!
Can't someone switch this rubbish off?
   Sounds of a disturbance in auditorium. 'Hear hear', etc.
   Noises of chairs and protest.

LOUDSPEAKER NO. 3
Matter can neither be created nor destroyed.
The Law of Conservation...

LOUDSPEAKER NO. I
Balderdash, pernicious piffle!
Man was created in God's image.

LOUDSPEAKER NO. 3
Matter is a condition of energy,
a temporary stability, temporary.
Matter can neither be created nor destroyed.
It can change. That is another matter.
Even you, Sir, may change:
When your fierce flesh slides from the brittle bone...

LOUDSPEAKER NO. I
I for one am not going to stand here and be insulted
By a microphone.
                    Further protests

LOUDSPEAKER NO. 3
...To reveal your immaculate, anonymous skeleton.
                    Noise of door slam

LOUDSPEAKER NO. I
   (A different voice)
You confuse organic with inorganic matter.
Life is different from inanimate objects.
Don't tell us: that matter can reproduce itself or grow!
Answer that.
                    Sound of agreement

LOUDSPEAKER NO. 3
It was a man called Traube
   who demonstrated that matter can grow;
That an inorganic chemical can reproduce itself.
He placed a crystal of copper sulphate

In an aqueous solution of potassium ferrocyanide.
At the surface of contact
A membrane of copper ferrocyanide is formed.
Copper ferrocyanide is insoluble in water.
This membrane is semipermeable:
It permits molecules of water to pass through it
and excludes molecules of any other compound.
Now as the crystal of copper sulphate
dissolves further, the osmotic pressure
Within the membrane increases,
causing it to break,
causing the copper sulphate to come into contact again
with the solution of potassium ferrocyanide,
causing a slightly larger membrane
of copper ferrocyanide to be formed,
which, in its turn, breaks by osmotic pressure.
In other words the compound has grown.
Traube perceived that living cells grew in the same manner.
    (Another voice)
Butschi demonstrated
that on rubbing a drop of olive oil
with a potash solution,
the droplet sent out pseudopodia;
moved about and engulfed particles
precisely as amoebae devour algae
    (Another voice)
Then Rhumbler in 1906
constructed an analogous model
which reproduced the movement,
            the feeding,
                the division of cells.
    (Another voice)
From these experiments to the understanding
    of the development of the protein cell
was but a step
A step which probably took a thousand million years
on the feet of enzymes.

Life is the result of continuous interaction
between nucleus and cytoplasm
in the nature of symbiosis...

LOUDSPEAKER NO. 1
Mummy, this sounds like Chemistry,
    not poetry.

LOUDSPEAKER NO. 2
Chemistry is poetry.
The difference:
chemistry is more accurately written.
$O_6H_{12}O_6 = 2CH_3CH_2CH + 2CO_2$
Alcohol fermentation, releasing 28 calories;
Whereas when free oxygen became available in the earth's
    atmosphere
$O_6H_{12}O_6 = 6CO_2 + H_2O$
    Oxidisation by respiration:
releasing 674 calories.
In other words, in other worlds, when the first light
fell on the earth's warm envelope of water
the ultraviolet rays disassociated the ions $H+$, $CH-$
till the semiliquid colloidal gels
developed into protein
till the protein became plankton
and the plankton nourished the whale
and the cruel sea became busy with cruelty.
                Record of sounds from sea bed
Then as the ocean receded; vegetation grew
falling into the swamps
rotting into methane, suffocating
the creatures who could not emerge;
but some, on fins and flippers crawled upon the carcasses,
found the oxygen of the air, breathed
    and were weaned from the sea's cruelty
    into the jungle's ferocity.

LOUDSPEAKER NO. 3
Where sabre-tooth tigers took their toll
and snakes were plumed like birds

and birds had scales;
Where slothful reptiles trod their clumsy way,
the ant's antennae built within the lion's brain,
and bracelets of maggots were intimate with the bone.
Out of this blood blind world dumb man developed,
his impotent tongue tethered to his teeth;
As strong as his hunger, fleet as his thirst;
fear describes him, fear defines him:
man, the anatomy of fear.
   Inarticulate human sounds, vowels without consonants
o, o, ee, ee, o, ee, a, ee
e, ee, ee, ee, o, o, o, u [*ad lib.*]
LOUDSPEAKER NO. 2
   In the be...
   In the begin
   In the beginning
   In the beginning there was no word.

And there was no time for we had no word for time;
We waited: waited for light when it was dark;
Waited for darkness when it was light;
Waiting for pain to pass and hunger come again;
   and the leaves like hands unfolded and fell,
   and our hands like leaves trodden underfoot.

And through all this waiting, we watched
   while the river washed away a mountain
stone by stone, winter by winter.
   While the blind mouth of the sea
Swallowed the dumb tongue of the river,
   and the waves of the sea washed over the forest
while the mountain rose from the sea again.

This is how long we waited.
You have not suffered till you have waited;
Waited for the word
   with the limb of your mind,

   inarticulate and dumb;
Your tongue like a drunken hand on your throat:
           Vowel effects and cries ppp beneath
Impotent, unable, strangling the will;
   Unable to communicate the need, or the fear;
And we had needs, we had fears:
Terror, without the word to describe them.
              First red glow suggests fire

LOUDSPEAKER NO. 3

Through a millennium of griefs
   The child's cry, the old man's groan
       was our only poetry.
Limpet our lips clamped to rock of our mind;
The blind tongue in the dumb mouth,
   a headless worm burrowing into our teeth.
              Vowel effects p-forte
Pain merciful; sea gentle to this;
   No agony to the mind like the mind's impotency:
Grief without tears, love without lips,
The amputated dancer danced towards his feet;
A wingless bird clamped in a dream of flight;
A spider spinning no web coming;
Wombed in silence, born, but not to be.
           On the stage the fire effects increase

LOUDSPEAKER NO. 2

   ee, i, oo, f, fi, f, fi   FIRE   FIRE
       *The fire effects decrease. Behind them a statue of a man
       similar to the figure of Perseus is revealed.*

LOUDSPEAKER NO. 3

Fear our first feeling, fire our first word.
Human consciousness carved by the word.
The poet, a chisel on the marble of pain;
Man is a metaphor for pain,
   no longer inarticulate.
              The statue alone is lit

LOUDSPEAKER NO. 2

Oh earth, I am in love with thee:

As with a woman, I am in love with thee.
I press my face to your cliff-flanks and cry
Oceans, wide oceans of tears till skin chaffs dry.
> *Behind this last speech Schubert's Opus 103 is heard*

My abundant blood forces'
your rivers' courses.
My bone your mountains' marrow, mine.
Your joy my fountain's fun.
  Limp my sorrow fill
  Your valley and hill.
Oh Earth, I am in love with thee:
As with a woman, I am in love with thee.

LOUDSPEAKER NO. 1
  (Boy's voice)
Mummy, is it finished?

LOUDSPEAKER NO. 2
That depends on you, my child.
> *The music is completed to silence from the microphones*

NO CURTAIN FALLS

The Gift

CHARACTERS

PERCY WORSTHORNE   A Bank Clerk, 59
MADELAINE WORSTHORNE   His Wife, 50
ERNEST TREMLETT   Her Father, 73
TONY WORSTHORNE   Their Son, 25
GERALDINE WORSTHORNE   Their Daughter, 23

Time: Now
Place: Any place

The Gift

*What is known as a living-room. But there is no window:
just a door (B.S.), a few uncomfortable chairs, a radio
and a TV set which are set one each side of the proscenium in the style of a Greek chorus. No walls are
necessary for the set: a hung picture or two will define the
room's limits.*

*The only essential prop is an enormous parcel which
stands (S.L.) It measures 6 ft long by 3 ft high by 2 ft
wide. This is wrapped in brown paper.*

*A small birthday cake with one candle is also conspicuous
on a side table.*

*Throughout the action, the TV and radio pursue their
irrelevant and frivolous commentaries—or, at least, they
do so at times as counterpoint.*

When the curtain rises, MRS WORSTHORNE *is tying
a large blue ribbon round the parcel: the others watch her
from the other side of the room.*

TV SET

Leeds United	3	Chelsea	2
Manchester City	1	Bolton Wanderers	0
Bradford City	3	Liverpool	2
Charlton Athletic	4	Hull City	3
Fulham	2	Tottenham H'spur	2
Arsenal	1	Southampton	1

MADELAINE

Doesn't it look pretty?
I think it looks very pretty.
Percy will like this, blue's his favourite colour.
Did you know blue was his favourite colour?

Blackpool	1	York City	6
Aston Villa	5	Coventry	2

ad lib.

Well, there it is. Doesn't it look magnificent? Doesn't it?

TONY
  Yes.
GERALDINE
  It does.
MADELAINE
  Don't you think so, Daddy? [*The two women begin to set the tea*]
TREMLETT [*marking football pools*]
  What?
TONY
  Mother said: doesn't it look magnificent?
TV SET
                    Woolwich   2   Middlesboro   2
TREMLETT
  That's another draw. And on their home ground
  Yes. It does. It looks magnificent but...
MADELAINE
  But?...
TREMLETT
  But I think it is too big. I suppose there will be another week,
  Next week.
MADELAINE
  As it couldn't be any smaller
  It is not very helpful of you
  To remark that it is too big.
RADIO
  Today for our Programme Any Questions
  The Team consists of...[*ad lib.*]
GERALDINE [*to her mother*]
  You've got a point there.
TV SET
  Worthington makes you worthier and worthier [*ad lib.*]
TREMLETT
  No, only six this week. Twelve draws.
TONY
  Yes, Mother is right. It isn't meaningful
  To discuss the size of the thing

Without relating the size to the function.
Some people might say that the Pacific Ocean was big,
But it is not big when you consider
The amount of water it has to contain.

TREMLETT
I still say it is big, too big.

TONY
Yet it may prove too small.

GERALDINE
That would be a pity.

TONY
After the expense we've all been put to.

MADELAINE [*to* TONY]
Don't worry. Your mother may not be a Bachelor of Science
As we all know you are:
[*to* GERALDINE] nor is she about to take her Diploma
In Psychiatric Nursing. But your Mother is practical.
She took precautions: I used a tape measure.

GERALDINE
Must we go into details?

TREMLETT
Too big for this room, I mean.

MADELAINE
I am sure Percy will be pleased with it.
Eventually. I am sure no man has ever received
A more appropriate birthday present.
Or one to which his family has given so much thought.
Now what shall we put on the card?

GERALDINE [*impulsively*]
Many happy returns... [*They look shocked*] Sorry.

TONY
'For Percy. With our undying love.' Then all of us sign it.

MADELAINE
Splendid. That's it. [*She writes*] 'Undying love.' I'll underline
   that.
He'll like that.

AA

There now, sign it. [*They all do so then she ties the card on to the parcel*]
Percy will never guess what it is.
Last year I gave him an electric razor
Or was that the year before last? I forget.
Now Tony help me to put this screen round it
Your Father enjoys a surprise. [*They do so*]

TREMLETT

The year you'll remember.

MADELAINE

We'll all remember. We all subscribed to it.
As a family what else could we do:
Once we had realised what he really wanted or needed?

TREMLETT

I could have given him an ounce of tobacco.

MADELAINE

You could have given him an ounce of tobacco,
And I could have given him a handknitted tie.
They could have given him a book token
Or a long-playing gramophone record.
But those would have been frivolous gestures of affection
And what we have given him here is something more than a casual gift.
It is a real token of love, our undying love.

GERALDINE

Something he needed, but didn't know he wanted
What else could we do.

MADELAINE

Nothing.

GERALDINE

Nothing. He's certainly not certifiable.
You have my word for that.

TONY

But assuredly as mad as a hatter.

MADELAINE

Tony, don't speak of your Father like that.
Though I admit his behaviour is far from sane

Ever since he resigned from his job at the bank
[*bitterly*] Only four months before his pension!

TONY

I still can't believe it.

TREMLETT

After thirty years: four months before his pension!

MADELAINE

To be precise: three months and seventeen days. [*a pause*]
Ever since that day, when he marched in here one afternoon,
With his valise full of poems which he blandly admitted
That he had written in the bank's time and on the tills
And announced that he had resigned his job
Because he had suddenly realised that he's mis-spent his life
Counting bits of paper there,
And that he was now going to devote the rest of his days
To important things such as persuading people to read poetry
(which they will never do) and urging them to love one another
(which they can never do)
As I say ever since that dreadful day, we have all known
That he would soon need more than a handknitted tie
Or an ounce of tobacco.

TREMLETT

Two ounces. I always gave him two for his birthday.

GERALDINE

Yes. What else could we do? I didn't mind
His sudden enthusiasm for poetry.
A lot of people write poetry
Some people even read poetry.
And some people keep bees; others tropical fish in aerated
    tanks;
There's no accounting for tastes.
But what I thought indicated that he's gone over the top
—and I'm not without professional experience—
Was when his manic depressive moods,
Fluct ated between such irrational and irreconcilable extremi-
    ties.

TONY

Precisely.

GERALDINE

His moments of despair were reasonable enough

Few of us can see any hope.

To me it's his moods of joyful optimism

Which prove he's now completely ga-ga.

MADELAINE

Geraldine! A spade's a spade

You don't have to call it a bloody shovel

He is your father.

GERALDINE

That's why I'm so concerned for his future

And why I've contributed to that.

Do you know, Mother, I actually caught him at it yesterday.

MADELAINE

Where?

GERALDINE

In Chelsham Road. I had been to see Betty...

TONY

Does it matter whom you'd been to see?

Keep to the point. What was Father doing?

GERALDINE

Going from house to house like a self-employed postman

Without any letters. He was singing gaily

And skipping over the railings which divide the front gardens

You can guess what he was doing.

He was popping a copy of Keats' *Ode to a Nightingale* into

   every letter-box.

I asked him what good he thought that would do!

And d'you know what he said?

He said: 'I'm blowing their indifference up.

            Poetry is more powerful than an atom bomb.'

TONY

It's sad.

TREMLETT

Very.

GERALDINE
And clear that he is no longer in touch with reality.

MADELAINE
Very clear. Think of the cost of printing all those copies.

TREMLETT
What convinced me he was barmy was when he turned the
    greenhouse
Into a carpenter's shop
And started to make those boards he carried,
Better if they'd been used for a strait jacket.
                    Singing heard off

MADELAINE
Ssh. Here he comes
    Enter PERCY *still singing gaily. He is wearing a sand-*
    wich board which reads 'Love one another'.
Have you had a good day, dear?
    PERCY *nods, takes the sandwich board off and props it up,*
    we now see the other side; it reads 'Read Donne. Listen
    to Schubert'.

GERALDINE [*going to embrace him*]
Many happy…

TONY [*ditto*]
I hope you have a happy day, Father.

PERCY
Thank you, my boy, I have
I am having the happiest day of my life
D'you know what I've done today?

MADELAINE [*fearfully*]
No, Percy. What have you done?

PERCY
I stood all the afternoon in the High Street
Outside the bank, my bank.
And I sang. (Schubert of course)
And I gave a £5 note to everybody who stopped to give me a
    penny.
It was wonderful business. You should have seen their faces.
Two women kissed me from gratitude.

MADELAINE

Expensive kisses. How much did you give away?

PERCY

Two hundred pounds or so.

It made my colleagues in the bank look pretty foolish.

MADELAINE

So I can imagine, dear. Half our savings.

PERCY

Not quite. I've enough for tomorrow too.

People seemed most grateful. I dare say they'd overspent

On their summer holidays. Of course some thought my notes
were counterfeit

They took them into the bank and were soon disabused

Because I'd drawn them out from there this morning.

And there were one or two who paused before they folded the
note into their wallet.

These may in time realise that I was not merely giving away
fivers

But values.

TONY

New lamps for old.

PERCY

Exactly. I'm hoping one or two others will join me at it
tomorrow.

We must cast our bread upon the water,

And if we haven't any bread, then paper has to do.

There's no alternative, otherwise it turns to stone: we turn to
stone.

It's simple.

MADELAINE

Yes, dear.

PERCY [*looking at table*]

Well, where is it? I've been looking forward all day to my
present.

Let me guess what it is. Don't tell me.

Some tobacco from Dad?

MADELAINE
Not this year, dear.
This year we all clubbed together.
To give you something special
Something you needed.

PERCY
A screwdriver and a plane?

MADELAINE
No.

PERCY
A handknitted tie? Perhaps two?

GERALDINE
No.

PERCY
Clubbed together. That's a clue.
A Schubert Song Cycle?

GERALDINE
It's not fair, Mummy. He'll never guess. Remove the screen.
They do so

MADELAINE
There.

TREMLETT
Big. I say it's too big.
PERCY *walks round it then reads the card attached*

PERCY
I was right you see:
Generosity is more contagious than measles
But I can't think what it is.

GERALDINE
Try.

PERCY
Something I need...? A printing press?

TREMLETT
For fivers?

PERCY
For poetry.

MADELAINE
  Cold.
PERCY
  A loudspeaker outfit?
MADELAINE
  Still cold. [PERCY *walks round it again*]
PERCY
  A coffin?
MADELAINE
  No. But you're getting warm.
GERALDINE
  Mother, Daddy will never guess. [*She goes and undoes the ribbon
    then rips the paper*] It's a deep freeze.
MADELAINE
  The latest model. Made in Sweden.
PERCY [*peering into it*]
  It's magnificent. Thank you.
  But we have a refrigerator already.
  We bought it only last year. It was all right this morning.
TONY
  A deep freeze is not the same thing as a refrigerator.
PERCY
  Similar surely?
TONY
  A model like that will keep things indefinitely.
  I knew a man who put a whole salmon in one.
  After ten years, after ten years, it came out
  As the day he'd poached it.
PERCY
  A pity I don't fish or poach.
TONY
  Indefinitely. Or you can put peas, beans and raspberries in them.
  At fifty degrees below zero decomposition is arrested.
PERCY
  But I haven't a vegetable garden.
TONY
  Pheasants. Some people put pheasants in them.

PERCY
  So would I if I owned a shoot.
GERALDINE
  You don't understand, Daddy.
  Any meat will keep in them for ever.
PERCY
  A marvellous thing if I were a butcher or a farmer.
  As it is I hope you won't be offended
  If I exchange it for a printing press, or something.
  [*to* MADELAINE] I can't think what I could put in it, can you,
     dear?
MADELAINE
  Yes, Percy, I can.
PERCY
  What?
MADELAINE
  Yourself, dear.
PERCY
  Myself?
MADELAINE
  You've talked so much recently about permanent values
  And immortal life. This can give these to you.
TONY
  It certainly can. Suspended animation.
GERALDINE
  Indefinitely, Daddy.
PERCY
  I see you are joking. [*He laughs alone*]
  I see you are not joking.
MADELAINE
  No dear.
  Of course we thought of several things we could have given you.
  At first Geraldine suggested a carpentry set with an electric drill
  And Tony proposed a press for your trousers.
  But we discarded these ideas as frivolous
  Because we all realised that you were no longer interested
  In things or in appearance...

TONY

...either sartorially or philosophically
But only in the reality behind things.
And so, Mother suggested we should give you something you
    needed...

MADELAINE

Something you really wanted
And this can give you immortal life
In a way no religion can.
The manufacturers guarantee it.

PERCY

I must say I've never had such a big present before.
All the same I feel a little depressed by it.

GERALDINE

You shouldn't be, Daddy. Think of the mammoths.

PERCY

Why? I don't hunt mammoths either.

GERALDINE

Because a few years ago they unearthed an entire Mammoth in
    Siberia
I read about it in one of the Sunday papers.
Apparently the beast had been overtaken by the last Ice Age
And frozen to death while grazing on the steppes.
Its mouth was still full of grass. And d'you know
When it thawed out, it was still so fresh
That it bled when they cut steaks from it
Which they found succulent after ten thousand years?
Think of that, Daddy, ten thousand years
Of assured preservation.

PERCY

Which of you wants to eat me?

TREMLETT

It's big, but not that big.
You wouldn't get much of a mammoth in that one.

MADELAINE [*pacifying* TREMLETT]

It will be the time for the News soon, Dad.
Just you sit quiet and wait.

PERCY
  This must have cost you all a great deal
  I can't countenance such extravagance...

MADELAINE
  You should talk.

PERCY
  ...for myself. I'm sure the shop will exchange it
  For some modest necessity or indulgence.
  I really do need a set-square, and some screws.

TONY
  Nonsense Dad. Think of Cleopatra, or Helen of Troy.

PERCY
  Why Tony?

TONY
  Think how you would have liked to have made love
  To either or both of them.

MADELAINE
  Tony!

PERCY
  Since they are both dead and since I am both a moralist and a
    monogamist
  At least in practice. I have never considered such liaisons.

TONY
  No, but what I'm trying to tell you is:
  Suspended animation makes such unlikely unions possible
  At least theoretically. If Cleopatra had stepped into a model like
    that
  Instead of suckling an asp, she could have skipped 2000 years
  And woken to embrace you as another Antony
  In your strong toil of grace.

PERCY
  A somewhat unlikely hypothesis.

TONY
  Maybe. But they've proved that the male seed
  When frozen to 80° can remain potent indefinitely.

GERALDINE
  I can't see where this is getting us.

TONY

Can't you? This deep freeze assures physical immortality
Completely.
Theoretically, Dad could, if he takes this step
Father a child five centuries from now.
—By artificial insemination if need be—
Not of course from Cleopatra, but on some unborn film star.
You could say that a deep freeze like that
Is a sort of savings bank
For a man's generative potential...

MADELAINE

I don't think that description will appeal to your Father
But I believe I know what will persuade him.
Percy, you threw up your job
Because you became interested in real and permanent values in
    life,
Didn't you?

PERCY

Yes.

MADELAINE

Then surely it's reasonable for you to take steps
To preserve those values permanently.
You explained that your enthusiasm for poetry
Was because you saw it as the highest point of human con-
    sciousness,
And you said that we should love one another
It being the only way to express that consciousness, didn't
    you?
You were right. None of us could disagree with you there.
But Percy you are before your time, a thousand years
Before your time, maybe even more.
Today nobody will listen to you, even if you give them fivers.
The golden age of poetry is passed
And nowadays people don't love one another, but occasionally
Hate each other intimately and passionately in corners.
In spite of what they say, they are only interested in appearance
And in labels, not in realities.

So you see, if you value your values, Percy, you must wait
You must preserve yourself and them
Then wake to an Age that will listen to your message:
That poetry is the way to consciousness
As love is the way to joy.

GERALDINE

Mother, I've never known you so articulate before;
The occasion has inspired you.
She is right, Daddy. Logically, there is no alternative for you:
If you continue as you are, you will die, as we all die,
With your values tarnished and our hopes dead with you.
You will eventually become as hopeless as we are.
Can't you see we want you to do this, not for your good
But for ours?
It's true that today poets and priests look hopeless and ridi-
culous figures;
But for all that, they are our only points of hope.
We must preserve you somehow.

PERCY

Your logic closes in on me like a prison.

GERALDINE [*running to embrace him*]

Daddy, you know I love you, you know I shall miss you,
And miss the poem you write especially for me
Every Christmas...
I couldn't bear the thought of you dying
And what you stand for dying too.
That's why I want to preserve you
That's why I want you to step in there.

MADELAINE [*to* TONY]

If anybody can persuade him, she will
He'll do anything for her.

TONY [*bitterly*]

I know.

PERCY [*to* GERALDINE]

I've already started to write something for you for next
Christmas
But it's not finished.

TONY
  A poem never is finished
  A poem is a point of growth.
MADELAINE [*aside to* TONY]
  Clever.
  [*to* PERCY] Well, Percy? [*She gets a pillow*]
  Shall we make you comfortable?
PERCY
  It will be cold in there.
MADELAINE [*taking his hand*]
  Colder for us outside when you can no longer warm us.
PERCY [*looking at her hand*]
  That was your best argument.
  But I will not get in this thing to preserve myself
  Or anything which I stand for:
  Either the bad poem I am writing
  Or the good poem I hope one day to write.
GERALDINE [*petulantly*]
  Oh, Daddy. How disappointing.
MADELAINE [*angrily*]
  What a waste of money.
PERCY
  Nor will I get into it to escape from the loneliness
  Of growing old, or from the humiliation
  Of being old. Or to evade the paralytic stroke,
  The fatal motor accident or the cancer we nurture
  That takes us unaware: though these fears are real fears
  I will not get into it because I am dying
  Because that it is what we are all doing
  Dying as we wear a new handknitted tie.
TONY
  Most disappointing. We shall drop twenty per cent on it.
PERCY [*taking his coat off*]
  But I will get into it because it was a gift from your love.
  It is that love alone which is worth preserving.
  If I stand here, I reject that love. [*he steps in*]
  But in here, I accept it.

It's cold; but not so cold as I feared;
Perhaps it was only my fear that was cold?

MADELAINE [*handing a scarf to him*]
Put this on, dear.

GERALDINE
Don't be silly, Mother.

MADELAINE
And he never had a slice of his cake. [*She goes to cut a piece*]

PERCY [*almost to himself*]
I can't feel my hands: I cannot feel my feet
My closest friends are lost:
It is in our extremities that we are vulnerable
But what matters, if in our hearts we are secure?
                    They gather round

GERALDINE
Is the thermostat switched on?

TONY
Full.

TREMLETT
Not too big, I was wrong there.

GERALDINE
Oh, Daddy, first recite something to me
Like you used to do when you came to sit on my bed
When I was a girl. Please, Daddy.
Oh his lips are going blue.

PERCY [*sitting up*]
What, Darling—one of the odes?
The Ode to a Nightingale?

GERALDINE
No. Something of your own
The poem you were writing for me for Christmas.

PERCY
If love is made of words
    Who can love more than I
If love is all self-love
    Who's more beloved than I.

If love is made of faith
  Who can love less than I
If love is to submit
  Who's less beloved than I.

If love is made of tears
  Who could love more than she
If love is to betray
  Who...

> *His lips move completing the poem but no sound is
> emitted. They lie him down.*

TV SET

Bolton Wanderers 2   Sheffield United 3
Leeds United   4   Liverpool City 3
       ad lib. to end

> *The family now turn to face the audience as though
> looking through a window.*

TONY

Strange: I see they are playing tennis next door
And sitting out in deck chairs: but I feel cold: very.

TREMLETT

Me too. There the roses lean upon the evening;
But frost feathers my brain, icicles nail my heart.
Now I know what you meant by them mammoths.

MADELAINE

I see my Michaelmas Daisies need tying up:
That proves it is summer still
Though winter is within us.

GERALDINE

His greenhouse door needs mending.
[*to herself*]
'If love is to betray
  Who was more loved than he?'

TV SET

Blackpool   1 Exeter   2
         etc.